Contested Spaces

Contested Spaces
A Critical History of Canadian Public Libraries as Neutral Places, 1960–2020

Whitney Kemble

Library Juice Press
Sacramento, CA

Copyright 2024

Published in 2024 by Library Juice Press.

Litwin Books
PO Box 188784
Sacramento, CA 95818

http://litwinbooks.com/

This book is printed on acid-free paper.

Publisher's Cataloging in Publication

Names: Kemble, Whitney.
Title: Contested spaces : a critical history of Canadian public libraries as neutral places, 1960-2020 / Whitney Kemble.
Description: Sacramento, CA : Library Juice Press, 2024. | Includes bibliographical references and index.
Identifiers: LCCN 2024936421 | ISBN 9781634001588 (acid-free paper)
Subjects: LCSH: Public libraries – Canada – History. | Library science – Social aspects. | Library science – Political aspects. | Library science – Moral and ethical aspects.
Classification: LCC Z735.A1 K46 2024 | DDC 027.471--dc23
LC record available at https://lccn.loc.gov/2024936421

Contents

IX	Acknowledgments		
1	Part I		
6	Part II		
7	1960 London, Ontario	41	2009 Vancouver, British Columbia
9	1978 Mississauga, Ontario	44	2012 Belleville, Ontario
13	1978 Oakville, Ontario	47	2013 Ottawa, Ontario
14	1990 Ottawa, Ontario	49	2013 Guelph, Ontario
15	1996–1999 Greater Victoria Area, British Columbia	51	2013 Waterloo, Ontario
		53	2013 Vancouver, British Columbia
15	1996 Victoria, British Columbia	57	2017 Saskatoon, Saskatchewan
21	1997 Victoria, British Columbia	60	2017 Edmonton, Alberta
22	1998 Colwood, British Columbia	63	2017 Toronto, Ontario
26	1999 Saanich and Colwood, British Columbia	69	2017 Ottawa, Ontario
		73	2018 Ottawa, Ontario
30	1997 West Vancouver, British Columbia	75	2019 Vancouver, British Columbia
		82	2019 Halifax, Nova Scotia
31	1999 North Vancouver, British Columbia	86	2019 Kelowna, British Columbia
		89	2019 Toronto, Ontario
32	1999 Vancouver, British Columbia	109	2020 Grand Prairie and Medicine Hat, Alberta
34	2000 Regina, Saskatchewan		
36	2008 Vancouver, British Columbia	111	2020 Vancouver, British Columbia
117	Part III		
140	Afterword		
169	Index		

*You have to act as if it were possible to radically transform the world.
And you have to do it all the time.*

Angela Y. Davis

Acknowledgments

This project was inspired by the activists, community members, and library workers who spoke out, organized, and protested against transphobes taking up space at Toronto Public Library. That collective action, which I am proud to have participated in, led me to this research, to stitch together other stories of public resistance and develop a better understanding of that history. I am so grateful for incredible librarians like Jane and Sam, whose work and words in this arena have guided me. And I'm thankful to Library Juice Press for being an important supporter and disseminator of critical librarianship.

Thank you to my wonderful UTSC Library colleagues, and to my Research Assistant Dael for his patience and diligence in dealing with hundreds of citations! Thank you to my dear friends Terri, Zack, Ryan, and Adam for all of the meandering, thought-provoking, and heartening conversations over the years. I've learned so much from all of you, you've made me a better thinker, and a better person overall. Thank you to Kendra for thinking, reading, and scheming with me. And I wouldn't be a librarian, or know half the things I know without Rrbr. They've encouraged and inspired me at every turn of my academic journey and been an incredible friend.

But above all, Amy. You are my biggest champion in this and every aspect of my life. Thank you for everything and love you. FF!

Part I

Introduction

On the evening of Tuesday, October 29th, 2019, I participated in a protest outside of the Palmerston branch of the Toronto Public Library (TPL). The protest was the culmination of weeks of coordinated efforts to prevent an event from happening inside the library. The event that prompted the protest was not organized by TPL. Like most public libraries in Canada, TPL allows third-party room bookings so that the public can use its spaces for events, in compliance with library policy and Canadian laws. While the majority of such events occur without incident, this one sparked controversy due to the topic—gender identity—and the speaker—Meghan Murphy—who does not recognize transgender identities.[1] Despite significant outcry from Toronto's 2SLGBTQIA+ community, among others, the library used protection of intellectual freedom and a position of library neutrality to honour the room booking and allow the event to proceed. Since we were unable to stop the event, we showed up en masse to condemn it. In the crowd of hundreds I saw many faces that I recognized, including many of my library and archive colleagues from around the city, who disagreed with the library's stance.

I will discuss this event in much more detail later, but I open with it because it is what started me thinking about this topic. All of the public and professional debates surrounding the event got me wondering about what other events at public libraries in Canada had created controversies and prompted protests. Were they third-party bookings or organized by the libraries? What were the issues at stake? What kinds

---

1   Liam Casey, "Hundreds Protest Controversial Toronto Library Event Featuring Meghan Murphy," *Global News*, October 29, 2019, https://globalnews.ca/news/6098974/toronto-public-library-meghan-murphy-event/.

of outcry or protest occurred? Did politicians get involved? Did the events happen, or did they get cancelled, and why? What kinds of effects or outcomes resulted? I could remember hearing about a couple of other controversial library bookings in the recent past, but I wanted to investigate more and gain a better understanding of how these things have been handled by public libraries across Canada.[2]

I also open with this event to introduce myself. I am a librarian who is critical of the concept of library neutrality and I am not neutral in this history that I am writing.[3] I am an academic librarian in the Humanities, and although I have no experience working in a public library, I have some professional knowledge and understanding of some of the work and some of the issues of public librarianship. I also come from an academic background in history, so I am using that training to inform my historical approach. I believe and engage in a variety of efforts to promote and work toward social justice. As a white, cis-gender, queer, middle-class, able-bodied, settler woman in Toronto, there are many layers of privilege in my life. In this work I am trying to apply my professional privilege (permanent status, academic freedom, and research leave) to critically examine a sensitive and important topic that public librarians might not have license or opportunity to speak or write about publicly, one that is relevant to the entire library landscape and the communities we serve.

In this work I take an historical approach to explore occurrences of public outcry and controversy over primarily third-party booked events and examine the material, real-world impacts of neutrality approaches in Canadian public library space use over time. I bring this Canadian historical context into the ongoing conversations that are critiquing the concept of neutrality in libraries, and I look at how critical race, queer, trans, and feminist theories can inform library policies and practices that foster community, care, safety, and social justice.

---

2   Content warning: In this work I'll be discussing uncomfortable topics and offensive opinions in the areas of homophobia, antisemitism, Islamophobia, and transphobia. I have included them to give a fuller historical picture, but that inclusion does not mean that I support or agree with them. Please take care as you read.

3   Instances in which I agree with an individual or group about a library event do not necessarily mean that I agree with them outside of that specific context. To be clear, I do not agree with conflating critiques of Israel with antisemitism, which I do not think forms the basis of the historical examples of antisemitism in this book.

Research Methods and Limitations

Although the idea for this topic came to me in the fall of 2019, I did not begin the work until after the COVID-19 pandemic was in full swing. Thus, some of the methodological decisions I made in developing the topic and its execution were in reaction to the uncertain and oft-changing circumstances of widespread closures and restrictions, as some other methodological options were simply not viable at the time. All of my primary source research was limited to online materials and I was lucky to get most of the secondary sources I needed online or in print.

To identify occurrences of controversial events booked at public libraries in Canada that caused public outcry in favour and against, I conducted extensive newspaper database, library literature database, and internet searches using search terms such as library, protest, controversy, event, room, booking, hate speech, free speech. To focus on Canadian content, I used the search terms of Canada, province and territory names, and a variety of city names. I made the choice to focus on mainstream news media sources as I figured that coverage in the mainstream news was a logical threshold by which to define a public controversy. This especially made sense for the pre-internet historical periods I covered, and I chose to maintain it across time periods for consistency and to keep a manageable scope. I will note that news sources have their biases, so the information published in them, which I cite extensively, reflects those biases in their reporting, editorials, opinion pieces, and the letters to the editor they choose to publish. As you read, it will be interesting to think about how and to what extent these media are both forming and reflecting public opinion, and the power they have in shaping our understanding of the past and how we think about confronting these challenges in the future. Through my searches for news coverage I was able to find many examples from across many provinces, but I found none in the territories or in Quebec, and only three from before the 1990s. I will also note that although I searched for Quebec incidents in English sources,[4] my degraded French language skills prevented me from searching in specifically French sources. While I fully admit that I have likely missed some occurrences from across the country, I am confident that my searching

---

4 Montreal Gazette, Sherbrooke Record, The Reporter (Gananoque), Bibliothèque et Archives nationales du Québec, and the databases I used for the rest of the searches.

captured the majority and will give a thorough picture of the history of Canadian public library event controversies.

Having found the controversial events and news coverage to examine, I then looked at the libraries involved and the relevant regional library associations for any information about the specific events or pertinent statements, publications, policies, etc. I searched for library worker union statements and I looked at the organizations and community groups involved for their statements. However, given the transitory nature of the internet, I found more of these kinds of evidence for the more recent incidents, and of course, the bigger the controversy, the more sources there were to find. I also reviewed the public library board meeting minutes that I was able to find pertaining to the events or related policies. Finally, although I did come across and occasionally include references to some relevant tweets and blog posts, I did not focus on those kinds of sources in my research process because it felt overwhelming in scope and magnitude. So I make no claims to presenting the full scope of public opinion expressed in those social media formats, which could be a whole project of its own.

Although there is much to say about the concept of neutrality in relation to library collections,[5] catalogues, services, etc.,[6] my focus is on examining how neutrality is deployed by Canadian public libraries for event bookings, as well as what circumstances and logic have overridden this neutrality. I see this work as part of bigger discussions in critical librarianship about neutrality, social justice, equity, diversity, accessibility, anti-racism, a feminist ethic of care, workplace safety, and more. I think this research connects with current work and future

---

5   The issue of book challenges and bannings has been escalating, in some places more than others, and is a huge topic of its own.

6   Indeed, much has already and continues to be said in the following sources and others that I cite: Hope A. Olson, "The Power to Name: Representation in Library Catalogs," *Signs: Journal of Women in Culture and Society* 26, no. 3 (2001): pp. 639–68, https://doi.org/10.1086/495624; Stacy H Simpson, "Why Have a Comprehensive & Representative Collection?: GLBT Material Selection and Service in the Public Library," *Progressive Librarian*, no. 27 (2006): pp. 44–51, https://doi.org/http://www.progressivelibrariansguild.org/PL_Jnl/contents27.shtml; Alison M. Lewis, ed., *Questioning Library Neutrality: Essays from Progressive Librarian* (Duluth, MN: Library Juice Press, 2008); Emily Drabinski, "Queering the Catalog: Queer Theory and the Politics of Correction," *The Library Quarterly* 83, no. 2 (April 2013): pp. 94–111, https://doi.org/10.1086/669547; Josh Honn, "Never Neutral: Critical Approaches to Digital Tools & Culture in the Humanities," (paper presented at the University of Western Ontario's Digital Humanities Speaker Series, London, ON, October 16, 2013), https://doi.org/https://doi.org/10.21985/N2SV08; Chris Bourg and Bess Sadler, "Feminism and the Future of Library Discovery," *Code4Lib*, no. 28 (April 15, 2015), https://journal.code4lib.org/articles/10425.

explorations of such topics as library staff and/or library users' perspectives on events and policies; policy shifts; political pressures; the role of library boards; a deeper examination of library and association records and archives on this topic; social media discussions of the issues; organizing to push back against library decisions; the teaching of neutrality in library and information science programs; and controversial events and/or neutrality approaches at work in academic libraries.

Part II

History

To understand the history of controversial public library events in Canada, the most basic questions I ask are where and when the controversies occurred; what were the controversial event topics; who booked or hosted the events; whether the events were cancelled or happened as planned, and why; who supported the events; and who spoke out against them. I also want to explore some questions related to the political, professional, and social factors involved in these controversial events: did politicians get involved or apply pressure in the decisions that were made to proceed with or cancel controversial events; were there any subsequent library policy changes; what positions did library staff unions take; what positions did professional library associations take; and did the libraries face any kinds of consequences subsequent to proceeding with or cancelling controversial events.

Through this historical examination we will see that concerns about discrimination and hate were at the root of most public protests around controversial events, and that public library commitments to neutrality in protecting intellectual freedom and freedom of expression were determined to outweigh those community concerns in most cases. Thus, in this history I will demonstrate an ongoing conflict between competing library values and a de facto hierarchy of those values that most commonly situates intellectual freedom at the top. My analysis will then consider relevant librarian perspectives and critical theories to interrogate the myth of library neutrality and look for positive and productive ways for libraries to engage with and serve their communities that honour library values and work toward social justice.

1960 London, Ontario

In August of 1960, the London Public Library received calls from about 10–12 people complaining that the library was spreading Communist propaganda with the programming for a planned August 9 event.[1] This program had been prepared by the library, to be presented by the Public Utilities Commission as part of a series of events at the bandshell in Victoria Park, and that evening was to feature the American-made documentary film *Iron Curtain Lands*, as well as two song recordings by celebrated African-American singer with Communist sympathies, Paul Robeson: Water Boy and Shenandoah.[2] The library cancelled the event based on this small number of objections in order "to avoid a controversy," but then received twice as many calls complaining of censorship and that the library and potential audience were "being dictated to by a few narrow-minded citizens."[3] So the next day they quickly rescheduled the program for August 15, alongside other previously scheduled films and music,[4] thereby fending off accusations of censorship.

In addition to the phone calls that the library received objecting to and supporting the programming, there was a scattering of letters to the editor in the *London Free Press* and the *St. Thomas Times-Journal*, the majority of which were voicing more concern about local censorship than Communist propaganda.[5] One opinion suggested that people should wait until they have viewed a film to decide if its contents are offensive,[6] while two others recommended pairing this film with another to show more than one perspective.[7] A handful of letters voiced frustration with the Mayor of London, J. Allan Johnston,

---

1   "Protests Force London Showing of Soviet Film," *The Globe and Mail*, August 10, 1960, ProQuest.
2   "Controversial Russian Film On Show Monday Night," *The London Free Press*, August 13, 1960.
3   "Protests Force London Showing of Soviet Film."
4   "Film Protest Boomerangs in Ontario," *The Gazette,* August 10, 1960. ProQuest.
5   A. Robertson, letter to the editor, *The London Free Press*, August 11, 1960; S. J. Smith, letter to the editor, *The London Free Press*, August 11, 1960; Hazel Smith, letter to the editor, *The London Free Press*, August 12, 1960.
6   "Should Not Condemn Without Prior Knowledge," *The London Free Press*, August 12, 1960.
7   A. Baltic, letter to the editor, *The London Free Press*, August 15, 1960; J. J., letter to the editor, *The London Free Press*, August 22, 1960.

for his censorial approach to the issue,[8] as he had recommended that a citizens' committee be formed, including members of the Board of Education and the Council of Women, to act as censors of future bandshell programs.[9] He also implied a lack of confidence in the professional decision-making skills of librarians and staff when he noted that "sometimes officials are too close to it to appreciate the propaganda that might be hidden there."[10] The letter-writers countered that the public's intelligence should be trusted, and one also suggested trusting the competence of librarians.[11] Overall, the public outcry on either side was quite limited, but the majority were in favour of a hands-off approach that let librarians and their patrons make their own professional and personal choices, respectively, without political interference.

From the library's perspective, the controversy had become "a bit ridiculous," according to Chief Librarian Dr. Richard E. Crouch.[12] He did not support the mayor's idea for a censorship committee and said he had great faith in library staff.[13] Countering the claims of Communist propaganda, Assistant Librarian Dean Kent described the film as "innocuous" and offered to host a private screening for those opposed to the programming, but there is no record of them taking up that offer.[14] Kent said that the film was purchased by the library from the Canadian Film Institute, after being reviewed by librarians, in response to requests from schools and organizations that wanted access to films about Communist countries. He explained that it is an educational film suitable for audiences from grade six and up.[15]

---

8 William Vosdingh, letter to the editor, *The London Free Press*, August 13, 1960; Kenneth Harris, letter to the editor, *The London Free Press*, August 13, 1960; "Loud Minority," *St. Thomas Times-Journal*, August 19, 1960.

9 There is no evidence in the London City Council or the London Public Library Board minutes for 1960 that such a committee was ever formed.

10 "Protests Force London Showing of Soviet Film."

11 Earle Sanborn, letter to the editor, *The London Free Press*, August 15, 1960.

12 "Russian Film Controversy 'Ridiculous' Says Librarian," *The London Free Press*, August 10, 1960.

13 "Russian Film Controversy 'Ridiculous' Says Librarian."

14 "Protests Force London Showing of Soviet Film."

15 "Iron Curtain Film Brought on Request," *The London Free Press*, August 12, 1960.

The public discussion and media coverage of the controversial program generated a large audience of almost 1000 people for the event, with no mention of protestors, but the *London Free Press* reported there was "not a single handclap" from the crowd in response to the "unremarkable documentary."[16] The debate did not lead to any policy changes for the library, nor the formation of any review committees, and there is no evidence that the library suffered any political or social consequences for their decision to go through with the event.

This early example of a controversial library event introduces many common arguments that we will see throughout this historical exploration. Opposition to censorship, or support for intellectual freedom is central to all of the controversies, and concerns about political interference into library policy become heated in some of them, often in connection with questions around librarians' professional autonomy. The suggestion of hearing from both sides on an issue also comes up frequently, as does the argument for waiting until after an event or speech to judge its content. It will be interesting to see how these ideas change or stay the same in different contexts.

1978 Mississauga, Ontario

A community group called Gay Equality Mississauga (GEM) planned to host a screening of the film *The Naked Civil Servant* and discussion at the Mississauga Central Library branch on February 7, 1978 at 7:30pm. The film, which starred John Hurt and had previously aired on CBC television and the BBC, is about the life of gay English writer and actor Quentin Crisp, and was to be screened as part of the library's "controversial series" called Films for Thinkers.[17] GEM hoped that showing a film and having a discussion about gay oppression would generate a public dialogue as "an important first step in ending violent discrimination and alienation."[18] However, despite no record of public outcry or expressions of concern about the film screening, the event was cancelled by the library board, prompted by a city councillor's complaint.

---

16   "No Cheers, No Boos As Controversy Ends," *The London Free Press*, August 14, 1960.

17   "Mississauga Rejects Plea: Homosexuals Argue Film's Merit," *The Globe and Mail*, February 28, 1978, ProQuest.

18   "Mississauga Rejects Plea."

Mississauga city councillor Frank Leavers learned about the planned film screening in the library's *Link* magazine. He had concerns about the film, so he brought them to fellow Councillor Hazel McCallion, who was a member of the library board and was running for that fall's mayoral election.[19] She then brought up the issue at the next library board meeting on January 18. Several of the board members had not heard of the film, but after a long discussion of the matter, the board voted 5–3 in favour of cancelling the screening.[20] The reasons that board members gave for cancelling the event included caution about how they spend taxpayer money, concern that minors might attend, and reluctance to promote a topic that is not generally publicly acceptable.[21] However, in March, library board chair Don Tough would share that board members were most concerned that the film was being publicized in the board's own *Link* magazine, which they thought "gave the impression that the board was promoting the film."[22] *The Mississauga Times* reported quotations from board members that demonstrate their homophobic views at the time. For example, they reported that Councillor McCallion pointed out that there would not have been a heterosexual present to offer a different perspective, and she compared homosexuality with communism and prostitution.[23] Clearly the majority of the library board were making no attempts toward a position of neutrality, nor were they concerned about censorship or intellectual freedom. GEM Coordinator Elgin Blair questioned whether any library board members had even seen the film, but he received "no comment."[24] Ann Edeie, Head Librarian of the Central Branch, also told the press that she was unable to comment on the controversy.[25]

GEM was unsuccessful in attempting to have the library board reverse its cancellation decision at the February 22 board meeting, then the

---

19 Spoiler alert: she won. And she served as mayor of Mississauga for 36 years, retiring in 2014.

20 "Homosexual Film Dumped by Library," *Mississauga Times*, February 1, 1978, Image 203, https://pub.canadiana.ca/view/omcn.MississaugaTimes_18/203.

21 "Homosexual Film Dumped by Library."

22 "Second Film Ruling Sought," *Mississauga Times*, March 22, 1978, Image 517, https://pub.canadiana.ca/view/omcn.MississaugaTimes_18/517

23 "Homosexual Film Dumped by Library."

24 "Homosexual Film Dumped by Library."

25 "Homosexual Film Dumped by Library."

matter was brought to a City Council meeting on February 27.[26] After more than an hour of debate on the motion to ask the library board to reconsider its decision, council voted 6–3 against it, with Councillors Mary Spence, Terry Butt, and Larry Taylor as the three votes in favour.[27] At the meeting, councillor and library board member McCallion affirmed the board's independence and gave a warning that some library board members would likely resign if city council attempted to change their decision.[28] Councillor Spence, who voted for the motion, suggested that since all of the films in the series could be considered controversial, the board should have cancelled all of them rather than singling this one out. She said, "this whole thing is really frightening" and accused the library board of "gross censorship."[29] Among the councillors who voted against the motion, Fred Hooper addressed GEM Secretary John Bodis in the meeting to declare, "I don't happen to believe in your rights" and "I thoroughly subscribe to moral censorship."[30] Councillor Frank McKechnie echoed the board's reasoning of not promoting homosexuality with taxpayer funds, but he also asked Bodis if he had ever tried "to have [his] sickness cured" and claimed that homosexuals tend "to seek out victims and try to inflict their wishes on them."[31] It is difficult to imagine that even in 1978 it would have been appropriate for elected public officials to speak to citizens in this blatantly hateful and homophobic way at a city council meeting. Meanwhile, Bodis and GEM offered to host a private screening of the film and a discussion for city councillors, library board members, and the 50 GEM members "to open a dialogue."[32]

GEM did hold a screening and discussion on March 14 at a Unitarian Church, with councillors and board members invited.[33] Library Board Chair Don Tough, who had voted in favour of screening the film, along with fellow board members Hazel McCallion and Genevieve Miller

---

26 *GEM Journal*, March 1978, pg. 1. Archives of Sexuality and Gender, Gale Online.

27 *GEM Journal*, March 1978, pg. 1.

28 "Mississauga Rejects Plea."

29 "Council Puts Lid on Film on Gays," *Mississauga Times*, March 1, 1978, Image 370, https://pub.canadiana.ca/view/omcn.MississaugaTimes_18/370.

30 "Council Puts Lid on Film on Gays."

31 "Council Puts Lid on Film on Gays."

32 "Council Puts Lid on Film on Gays."

33 *GEM Journal*, March 1978, pg. 1.

attended the event and found the film to be inoffensive if uninteresting.[34] Tough then suggested that the board reconsider its decision to ban the film once the library staff developed a film selection policy, as requested by the board, arguing that "the library does provide intellectual freedom" and the film could be shown with a parental guidance warning like other films in the Films for Thinkers series.[35] McCallion disagreed, saying, "it's not important" and that she would not change her vote "[b]ecause she does not believe taxpayers want their money spent to show such films."[36] In the first reporting of a librarian's comment on the matter, Mississauga's Chief Librarian Noel Ryan said that the film should not have been cancelled, "it's a great film, dealing with a current event. It's consistent with the other films."[37] This was in line with the position of the Canadian Library Association (CLA), whose president, Ken Haycock, wrote a letter to the Mississauga library board to say that he regretted their decision to censor the film and reminded them of the CLA's Bill of Rights, which highlights intellectual freedom and access.[38] As for library policy, it was updated with an expanded section on film selection and use, including a point that "the library will endeavour to admit an audience appropriate to the subject matter under discussion" for screenings of films that might be considered controversial.[39]

While politicians and board members had been debating the issue for a couple of months, there was still no indication of general public outcry or protest over the film screening. In fact, in April the *Mississauga Times* published an editorial condemning the library board for acting against the library system's existing policy, which states that the library "does not interpret its function to be the supervisor of public morals," and that parents and guardians are responsible for their

---

34 "Second Film Ruling Sought."

35 "Second Film Ruling Sought."

36 "Second Film Ruling Sought."

37 "Second Film Ruling Sought."

38 Elgin Blair, "Crisp Controversy Spreads to Oakville," *The Body Politic* 43, May 1978, pg. 6, https://archive.org/details/bodypolitic43toro/page/6/mode/2up.

39 "Intellectual Freedom is Essential to Society's Health," *Mississauga Times*, April 5, 1978, Image 605, https://pub.canadiana.ca/view/omcn.MississaugaTimes_18/605; Alvin M. Schrader, "Community Pressures to Censor Gay and Lesbian Materials in Public Libraries of Canada," in *Liberating Minds: The Stories and Professional Lives of Gay, Lesbian, and Bisexual Librarians and Their Advocates*, ed. Norman G. Kester (Jefferson, N.C: McFarland, 1997), 150.

children's use of library materials. The editorial further argued that "it is a good film about an important issue" and it should be shown because "[t]he citizens of Mississauga deserve the information. The gay community deserves the understanding."[40] In the same issue, a letter to the editor, which was also sent to city council, written by a gay professor at Erindale College (now University of Toronto Mississauga) accused the board and council of "an appalling act of arbitrary censorship" and noted that it was ridiculous given that the film has been shown on public television in Canada and England, and the book was available in the Mississauga Public Library system.[41] Later in April, in a 'person on the street'-type of feature in the *Mississauga Times*, some citizens were asked about the board's ban of *The Naked Civil Servant*: three were opposed to the board's decision, one was undecided, and four agreed with the ban.[42] However, these people were just responding to a question while going about their days, they were not motivated to write letters or call to complain. *The Body Politic*, a prominent Canadian gay publication, was also covering the controversy, and reported in April that John Bodis of GEM had received two death threats by phone.[43]

1978 Oakville, Ontario

The public library in neighbouring Oakville had also planned a screening of *The Naked Civil Servant* around the same time. Oakville's Chief Librarian, Richard Moses, supported the screening and was critical of the decision to cancel in Mississauga: "I'm very disappointed that only the gay community is protesting the barring of this film in Mississauga. I think that's a disgrace. It's a matter of censorship that everyone should be concerned with."[44] He did, however, face some local opposition, as some members of the Oakville library board, including board chair John Beatty, were critical of his decision to show the film, which

---

40 "Library Sickness," *Mississauga Times*, April 5, 1978, Image 605, https://pub.canadiana.ca/view/omcn.MississaugaTimes_18/605.

41 "Mindless Ruling," *Mississauga Times*, April 5, 1978, Image 605, https://pub.canadiana.ca/view/omcn.MississaugaTimes_18/605.

42 "Times Telescope," *Mississauga Times*, April 26, 1978, Image 789, https://pub.canadiana.ca/view/omcn.MississaugaTimes_18/789.

43 Elgin Blair, "City Survives Showing of Gay Film," *The Body Politic* 42, April 1978, pg. 6, https://archive.org/details/bodypolitic42toro/page/6/mode/2up.

44 Blair, "City Survives Showing of Gay Film," 6.

they claimed promoted homosexuality.[45] The board held a special meeting on April 17 to discuss the film event, where they voted 4–3 in favour of the screening, upholding Moses' decision, which prompted Beatty to resign.[46] The film screening went ahead as scheduled on April 26, 1978 at the Central Library branch.

1990 Ottawa, Ontario

On the morning of Monday Nov 19, 1990, the Ottawa Public Library cancelled an event that was to take place that night. Organized by a group called Citizens for Foreign Aid Reform, a group of self-described "populists" seeking to stop foreign aid and curb immigration,[47] the event was to be a lecture by two right-wing speakers, Ron Gostick, Director of the Alberta-based Canadian League of Rights, and Eric Butler, Director of the Australian League of Rights, but the Canadian Jewish Congress (CJC) contacted the library the previous week to object to the event, arguing that the speakers are "promoters of racist and anti-Semitic views."[48] There was very little news coverage of this event cancellation and no evidence of a broad public outcry in support of or against it, but Bernie Farber, Ontario Research Director of the CJC, said that his organization urged the library to cancel the event on the basis that Butler is a "long-time Holocaust denier" and Gostick has published "tonnes of material that are offensive to Jews and visible minorities and Franco-Canadians."[49] Chief Librarian Gilles Frappier said that the information they received from the CJC about the speakers' views gave the library "second thoughts" about the event, prompting them to later cancel it, and library board chair Phyllis Colvin stated that "[t]he individuals that were being brought forward were inappropriate for

---

45   Blair, "Crisp Controversy Spreads to Oakville," 6.

46   Blair, "Crisp Controversy Spreads to Oakville," 6.

47   "What Is C-Far?," CFAR, n.d., https://wayback.archive-it.org/227/20100803161133/http://www.populist.org/what_is_cfar.html.

48   Peter Hum, "Library Cancels Right-Wing Lecture," *Ottawa Citizen*, November 21, 1990, ProQuest.

49   Hum, "Library Cancels Right-Wing Lecture."

the library."⁵⁰ Paul Fromm,⁵¹ Research Director of the group hosting the event, was critical of the library's decision, accusing them of ignorance and bigotry, and Alex Cullen, a Director of a group called the Canadian Rights and Civil Liberties Federation (not to be confused with the Canadian Civil Liberties Association), said the cancellation constituted a denial of freedom of speech.⁵²

The Ottawa Citizen noted that this library event cancellation came two weeks after a lecture at the Ottawa Congress Centre by British Holocaust revisionist David Irving⁵³ was met with calls to cancel from B'Nai Brith Canada and a protest of about 100 people outside of the event.⁵⁴ Given this context it is likely that the library wanted to avoid a similar protest, which they seem to have achieved based on how little coverage I was able to find around the cancellation, suggesting it was not a controversial decision and there were no repercussions.

1996–1999 Greater Victoria Area, British Columbia

In the mid- to late-90s, Greater Victoria Public Libraries (GVPL)⁵⁵ were involved in a series of controversial events held at a number of their branches that were organized by the Canadian Free Speech League (CFSL) & the BC Western Canada Concept party (BC WCC), both of which were led by Victoria lawyer Doug Christie, who was known for representing Holocaust denier Ernst Zundel, neo-Nazis, and other right-wing extremists. The debate about these events being held in public library spaces centered around the argument of providing a platform

---

50 Hum, "Library Cancels Right-Wing Lecture."

51 The Canadian Anti-racism Network, in their study called Libraries and Hate in Canada (https://stopracism.ca/content/libraries-and-hate-canada), noted that the Ottawa Public Library refused to rent space to Paul Fromm for a meeting in 1998, but I was unable to find any record of this refusal, nor could the staff at OPL, who I contacted for research assistance on the matter. Therefore, without evidence I was unable to confirm the information and it didn't meet my criteria for having created a public controversy.

52 Hum, "Library Cancels Right-Wing Lecture". I was unable to find any information about the Canadian Rights and Civil Liberties Federation that the Ottawa Citizen mentioned.

53 Interestingly, David Irving would be banned from Canada and some other countries in 1992 after being convicted of Holocaust denial in Germany: "David Irving: Propagandists' Poster Boy," Anti-Defamation League, 2005, https://web.archive.org/web/20070405134246/http://www.adl.org/holocaust/irving.asp.

54 Hum, "Library Cancels Right-Wing Lecture".

55 The Greater Victoria Public Library system has branches across 10 municipalities. This discussion will look at events in the municipalities of Victoria, Colwood, and Saanich.

for racism, discrimination, and hate speech vs protecting intellectual freedom.

1996 Victoria, British Columbia

The Canadian Free Speech League hosted a seminar at the main downtown Broughton Street branch of GVPL on Saturday Oct 26, 1996. The private event was invitation-only with no media allowed because, as event organizer Doug Christie said, "The meeting is about freedom of expression and we do it in private."[56] Tickets to the event at the library and the CFSL annual awards dinner,[57] to be held afterward at a different undisclosed location, were $30 each, and the invitations indicated that the seminar would be a lecture by an internet provider.[58] *The Times Colonist* reported that about 75 people attended the library event, including controversial figures such as white nationalist and teacher Paul Fromm, North Shore News columnist Doug Collins, who had several outstanding Human Rights Council complaints against him at the time, and Tony McAleer, whose Vancouver telephone line for carrying hate messages was shut down by a human rights tribunal.[59] CFSL member and Victoria resident Sydney Carroll defended the group's right to hold their meeting at the library as taxpayers making use of a public facility, and he said: "We just want to meet peacefully. To have freedom of assembly in jeopardy is a very sad commentary."[60]

Library manager Jim Scott admitted a mistake was made in giving the CFSL a 50% discount off the room booking fee because it represented itself as a non-profit group but then charged attendees for tickets. He also explained the library's position of neutrality in allowing the event to take place: "we can't ban people on the basis of what they might do. It's a public space. We can't say we don't like your point of

---

56 Bob Rowlands, "Anti-Race Foes Angry–by Susan Danard–Times Colonist Staff," *Times Colonist,* October 27, 1996, ProQuest.

57 At the CFSL annual awards dinner in 1992, Holocaust denier David Irving, who was mentioned above, attended to speak and accept an award, but the police raided the event to arrest him and he was subsequently deported for having lied to cross the border since he had previously been banned from entering the country: Rowlands, "Anti-Race Foes Angry."

58 Rowlands, "Anti-Race Foes Angry."

59 Rowlands, "Anti-Race Foes Angry."

60 "Library Under Fire for Free Speech Rally–Meeting Space Provided -," *Times Colonist,* October 30, 1996, ProQuest.

view."⁶¹ Chief Librarian Sandra Anderson said, "[l]ibraries find it very hard to put staff in a position of deciding who is good and who is bad. It's a very subjective area" and she referred to the library's policy for room bookings aligning with the CLA statement on intellectual freedom.⁶² And yet, library board chair Maurice Chazottes said that the board may try to devise a policy that would scrutinize groups booking their facilities.⁶³

Although there was no evidence of a protest at the event, a number of community and advocacy groups were vocally critical of the library for providing a space to the CFSL. The Canadian Anti-Racism Education and Research Society (CAERS) expressed frustration that taxpayer money would subsidize an event by such a group.⁶⁴ Michael Peters, former chairman of the Capital Region Race Relations Association (CRRRA), criticized the CFSL for using free speech "as a front to disseminate hate literature"⁶⁵ and took issue with the library's position: "So what you're saying is the library will allow themselves to contravene the Charter of Rights and Freedoms, which guarantees freedom from fear and intimidation and hatred? The library has a responsibility to the municipality and to the people who live in the municipality to be a tolerant and healthy place in the community for people to go to."⁶⁶ Nikki Basuk, of the League of Human Rights of B'nai Brith Canada, said: "This isn't about free speech, this is about racism. It's unfortunate that we are in a free speech debate with the wrong people."⁶⁷ Harry Abrams, also of B'Nai Brith Canada, warned that the CFSL's views are "very dangerous and potentially socially destructive" and said the meeting was "something that should concern not just the library, but

---

61   Rowlands, "Anti-Race Foes Angry."

62   "Library Under Fire for Free Speech Rally"; "Statement on Intellectual Freedom and Libraries," Canadian Federation of Library Associations, April 12, 2019, https://cfla-fcab.ca/en/guidelines-and-position-papers/statement-on-intellectual-freedom-and-libraries.

63   Rowlands, "Anti-Race Foes Angry."

64   Rowlands, "Anti-Race Foes Angry."

65   Rowlands, "Anti-Race Foes Angry."

66   "Library Under Fire for Free Speech Rally."

67   Bob Rowlands, "Municipal Elections–City Bars Likely Hatemongers from Publicity," *Times Colonist,* November 8, 1996, ProQuest.

everybody."[68] Both Peters and Abrams stated their intentions to lobby municipal officials to change the library's policy.[69]

On the other side of the debate, local newspaper the *Times Colonist* published an editorial as well as an opinion piece[70] supporting the library's decision and arguing against censorship: "Whether we like it or not, even racists are protected by the Charter of Rights. This means that they, just like the rest of us, can say or publish anything they want. Then and only then can they (or we) be sued for libel or defamation, or charged for disseminating hate propaganda."[71] In the letters to the editor I found one article for each side. Tom Gore of the Victoria Civil Liberties Society wrote in support of the library's obligation to protect free speech and argued: "Those who hold views that most people consider abhorrent must be allowed to speak their piece. Then, and only then, can rational argument be used to rebut such ideas. Forcing repellent views underground will not make them go away but will make them much harder to refute."[72] Whereas, another citizen countered that: "As a society, we do not have the obligation to provide space for known racist groups to meet" and "[w]aiting to charge these groups with disseminating hate propaganda until after the fact is like chastising Pandora after she has released the demons from her box."[73] In this public debate over the event we see marginalized groups and individuals arguing that free speech is not sufficient justification for allowing people who are known for their racist views to express them in public spaces because of the harm those views cause to those marginalized peoples and to society as a whole. While others are arguing that free speech should be protected above other Charter rights to enable dialogue, and that those who break hate speech laws would be punished. For the former, they are talking about views that threaten and attack them based on their identities, whereas for the latter, it is a theoretical threat to speech and the ideas behind it.

---

68 "Library Under Fire for Free Speech Rally."

69 "Library Under Fire for Free Speech Rally."

70 Paul Minvielle, "Opinion–Truth and Falsehood Should be Allowed to Grapple Freely," *Times Colonist,* November 1, 1996, ProQuest.

71 Paul Minvielle, "Editorial–Free Speech Isn't just for the Politically Correct -," *Times Colonist,* October 30, 1996, ProQuest.

72 "Letters–More Parks? What About Housing?" *Times Colonist,* November 9, 1996, ProQuest.

73 "Letters–More Parks?"

In the political arena the controversy continued and raised tensions between city council and the library board. With a municipal election looming on November 16, Victoria Mayor Bob Cross said the city would consider the issue and raise the topic with the library board at its next meeting in November.[74] But before that could happen, City Councillor Bob Friedland brought a motion to Victoria's Committee of the Whole that would deny the use of public space to any group whose views "are likely to promote discrimination."[75] The motion passed with only one opposing vote on November 7, allowing it to be considered by city council the following week.[76] Friedland explained that he proposed the motion after speaking to the library board chair about public use of library space. He said that he got an unsatisfactory answer to his question of whether the Ku Klux Klan, the Nazi Party, or a "man-boy sex group" could rent library space, and he "thought these were people in need of a great deal of policy direction in this area."[77] Councillor Geoff Young, the lone opposition vote, said the motion was too broadly worded and, "[he didn't] agree with making laws to suit particular political events."[78]

In response to the committee passing this motion, Doug Christie booked a room for 3pm on Nov 9 at the Broughton Street branch of the library and challenged all of the councillors on the committee who voted in favour to meet with him and "explain how they will decide who is likely to promote hatred."[79] He also said they were "making fools of themselves" and accused them of censorship.[80] Fifty people attended this meeting representing both sides of the issues, but only one city councillor was present, Jane Lunt, who had been absent from the committee meeting, wanted to learn more about the CFSL, and said she was unlikely to support the motion.[81] A man named Jack Gardner, who lost 52 members of his family in the Holocaust, spoke up at

---

74 "Library Under Fire for Free Speech Rally."
75 Rowlands, "Municipal Elections."
76 Rowlands, "Municipal Elections."
77 "Letters–More Parks?"
78 Rowlands, "Municipal Elections."
79 "Letters–More Parks?"
80 "Letters–More Parks?"
81 "A Look Back in Anger–A Debate on Free Speech Evokes Painful," *Times Colonist*, November 10, 1996, ProQuest.

the meeting about how Christie's work has affected him, "[u]nder the guise of free speech, you have defended people who denied the death of my people," but then he was ironically told by CFSL supporters to sit down out of respect for the Canadians who died fighting the Nazis in WWII, while others in attendance defended Christie against accusations of hate.[82]

Chief Librarian Sandra Anderson responded to the motion by asserting that the library board is responsible for its own policy and noted that provincial laws shield public libraries from the interference of municipal politicians in order to preserve libraries as havens of intellectual freedom.[83] She said, "[i]f the public library doesn't support freedom of expression, what institution does? It's hard not to be cynical about the timing of all this – a week before an election."[84]

At the Victoria city council meeting on Nov 14, two days before the municipal election, the motion to ban the use of public facilities by groups that promote discrimination passed 6–3. Mayor Bob Cross voted against it, saying that he supports it in theory but that it would be too difficult to implement, while his election opponent, Councillor Laura Acton, voted for it.[85] However, the library was not beholden to that motion, and the library board held its own policy vote on Nov 26, voting in favour of continuing to allow controversial groups to use their space, but also passing a motion to add an amendment that groups using library facilities will not knowingly contravene the Criminal Code of Canada, which includes a section on hate propaganda.[86] The meeting room was filled to capacity at 26, and 14 people spoke to the motion, all in favour of the library's policy and arguing to protect freedom of speech and the Charter of Rights and Freedoms. Commenting on the strong feelings around this debate, library board chair Chazottes said, "[w]hat's at stake here is not the question of freedom to hold meetings in the library, it's the implication that it will spill over into an attempt to censor books and librarians are very sensitive

---

82 "A Look Back in Anger."

83 "Letters–More Parks?"

84 "A Look Back in Anger."

85 "Victoria Bans Hate," *Star Phoenix*, November 16, 1996, ProQuest.

86 Denise Helm, "Library Open to all Groups–Board Votes to," *Times Colonist*, November 29, 1996, ProQuest.

about that."[87] This comment reiterates the idea that it is more important to protect against theoretical attacks on library values than to protect marginalized groups from discrimination.

1997 Victoria, British Columbia

The CFSL met again a few months later on March 1, 1997 at GVPL.[88] At that meeting, which was open to the public, Paul Fromm, who had recently been fired from his teaching job by the Peel Board of Education for ongoing association with white supremacist groups,[89] spoke to about 50 attendees and there was no protest or evidence of public debate.[90]

The following month, the GVPL was given the British Columbia Library Association's (BCLA) Intellectual Freedom award for having upheld that principle in the 1996 policy debate that ensued from the CFSL event controversy.[91] Doug Christie and Paul Fromm offered their congratulations for the award, whereas Harry Abrams of B'Nai Brith said the award was "a slap in the face for every minority group in this city" and Joseph Ravick, CRRRA chairperson, said that the BCLA failed to consider that competing rights were at stake in the library policy.[92] Alan Dutton, Executive Director of CAERS, warned that the award "sets a very dangerous trend that ignores the rights of minorities and others to use public facilities."[93] The library board chair was pleased to

---

87 Helm, "Library Open to all Groups".

88 Susan Danard, "No Dissenting Voices Greet Christie Group," *Times Colonist,* March 2, 1997, ProQuest.

89 Frank Calleja, "Teacher Fired for Alleged Link to Racists Board Warned Paul Fromm in '92 about His Activities," *Toronto Star*, February 27, 1997, ProQuest. Fromm, represented by lawyer Doug Christie, and his union appealed his dismissal, but in 2002 the Ontario Labour Relations Board upheld the decision; Heather Sokoloff, "Board Upholds Teacher's Firing for Racist Views: Peel Educator 'Consorted with Known Racists'," *National Post*, March 13, 2002, ProQuest.

90 Danard, "No Dissenting Voices Greet Christie Group." This report notes that Fromm gave a speech in Vancouver the night before where police were called to break up a protest, but I was unable to find any new coverage of that event.

91 Susan Danard, "Library Honored for Allowing Controversial Christie Meeting," *Times Colonist,* April 25, 1997, ProQuest.

92 Paul Fromm, letter to the editor, *Times Colonist*, May 12, 1997, ProQuest; Danard, "Library Honored for Allowing Controversial Christie Meeting."

93 Douglass Todd, "Use of Library for Collins' Rally Sparks Outcry," *Vancouver Sun*, May 10, 1997, A6, ProQuest.

have the provincial library association endorse the library's stand for intellectual freedom, and Chief Librarian Anderson observed that "[o]ther libraries will look to this for the leadership it provided."[94] Indeed, the recognition and approval that such an award from the provincial professional association signals is empowering to a local library system, strengthening its policy position against future critiques. And we will continue to see library associations offering this support.

1998 Colwood, British Columbia

The lack of protest at the CFSL's March 1997 meeting was not a sign that the people of the Greater Victoria area had lost interest in the debate over hate speech vs free speech at the library. In fact, the controversy grew more heated in 1998. In February, B'nai Brith Canada released its annual audit of antisemitic incidents across the country, and it found that although there was a decrease in reported incidents in Canada and BC, there was an increase in the number of hate groups actively recruiting, and Ken McVay, who scans the Internet for hate sites, identified a growing trend of antisemitism spreading across the internet.[95] Against that backdrop, Harry Abrams of B'nai Brith Canada published a report called "Use of Public Facilities by Hate Groups," outlining what he identified as a trend of hate groups hiding behind the argument of free speech to use library spaces.[96] Commenting on his report, Abrams argued that by using library spaces for their events, hate groups are attempting to gain legitimacy in the public eye, and he echoed earlier calls to ban them from booking library rooms.[97] But Neil Williams, the new GVPL board chair, and John Westwood, Executive Director of the BC Civil Liberties Association, both contended that the library cannot ban anyone until they have done something illegal.[98] Sybil Harrison, of the BC Library Association, asserted a position of neutrality, saying, "[j]ust because the group is there doesn't mean the library supports

---

94   Danard, "Library Honored for Allowing Controversial Christie Meeting."

95   Judy Lavoie, "Anti-Racism Fighters Braced for Onslaught as Easterners Move," *Times Colonist,* February 6, 1998, ProQuest.

96   Marina Jimenez, "Libraries used to Push Hate, Group Says: 'Hate Groups' Masquerading as Free-Speech Advocates are Renting Library Facilities for Racist Propaganda Purposes, B'Nai Brith Says," *Vancouver Sun,* February 05, 1998, ProQuest.

97   Jimenez, "Libraries used to Push Hate."

98   Jimenez.

their point of view."[99] However, Abrams argued that the library should use community standards to determine appropriate room bookings and he suggested there is inconsistency in library policy around censorship, noting that the library has limits on what people can access over the internet using their computers.[100] With the annual Canadian Library Association (CLA) Conference set for Victoria on June 17–21, the issue of censorship would certainly be a hot topic.

The CFSL strategically booked meetings for June 19 and 20 at the Juan de Fuca branch of GVPL in the municipality of Colwood, overlapping with the timing of the CLA conference in downtown Victoria. Planned speakers included CFSL regulars Paul Fromm and Doug Collins, as well as Bernard Klatt, who ran an internet service out of his home in Oliver, BC, providing access to over 20 websites that appeared to violate Canadian hate laws.[101] The local B'nai Brith branch requested that Colwood mayor and council deny these bookings, and while council voted to publicly condemn activities that promote racism, they declared their confidence in the library board to manage the issue appropriately.[102] The Jewish Federation of Victoria and Vancouver Island, which represents 2000 Jewish people on Vancouver Island, then sought to have the library board adopt a policy similar to what Victoria City Council had adopted and the library board rejected in 1996, which involved denying the use of library space to groups promoting hatred on the basis of race, religion, sexual orientation, and other factors.[103] But the board voted 18-2 on May 25 to maintain its existing room booking policy[104]–which it had last voted on and amended in November 1996 to add a section requiring groups not to contravene the Criminal Code of Canada[105]–and the staff union, Canadian Union of Public Employees (CUPE) Local 410, held a special vote in support of the

---

99 Jimenez.

100 Jimenez.

101 Malcolm Curtis, "Libraries Uphold Policy of Open Access to Meeting Rooms," *Times Colonist,* May 27, 1998, ProQuest.

102 Lee King, "Controversial Group to Meet in Colwood," *Times Colonist,* May 9, 1998, ProQuest.

103 Curtis, "Libraries Uphold Policy of Open Access to Meeting Rooms."

104 Curtis.

105 Helm, "Library Open to all Groups".

board's decision.[106] Although several board members said they found CFSL views "repugnant," they felt more confidence in their existing policy than in their capacity to determine what groups would or would not be allowed under the proposed guidelines.[107] Library board chair Williams affirmed that the board considers themselves "guardians of freedom of speech" and said he did not "want to see the issue hijacked by fringe groups on the far right," which was a confusing and ironic statement given that such a group, with free speech in its name, had been at the centre of the issue for 3 years.[108] Robert Goldschmid, of the Jewish Federation, said: "We recognize the values behind freedom of speech. There are, however, the competing values of combating bigotry and hatred." However, Chief Librarian Sandra Anderson noted that the CFSL had no record of promoting hate according to the RCMP's and Attorney General's tracking of such crimes.[109]

Following the library board's vote, the *Times Colonist* published two long opinion pieces written by people on both sides of the issue. First, on June 9, Robert Goldschmid, lawyer and representative of the Jewish Federation, argued that "speech is only free when it does not infringe on the rights of others and does not pose a danger to anyone."[110] He also refuted the common claim that allowing hateful views to be expressed in public fora is beneficial to society because it brings them above ground and exposes them to common sense and rational debate:[111] "Underground hate speech is not the real problem. Hate speech becomes an issue when it gains an air of legitimacy."[112] Finally, he criticized the library board for their unwillingness to take on the work of determining if groups booking library rooms were promoting hatred or not, as he noted that the CFSL has been the only subject of

---

106 Norman Horrocks, "CLA Ponders Library's Role," *Library Journal* 123, no. 13 (August 1998): 24, https://link.gale.com/apps/doc/A21071926/CIC?u=utoronto_main&sid=bookmark-CIC&xid=b44980b5.

107 Curtis, "Libraries Uphold Policy of Open Access to Meeting Rooms."

108 Curtis.

109 Curtis.

110 Robert M. Goldschmid, "Library Cop-Out Provides Room to Grow for Message of Hate," *Times Colonist,* June 9, 1998, ProQuest.

111 An argument we just saw from Tom Gore of the Victoria Civil Liberties Society in "Letters– More Parks? What About Housing?" and will see in many more examples to come.

112 Goldschmid, "Library Cop-Out Provides Room to Grow for Message of Hate." He mentioned that studies have shown this to be true, but did not provide references.

such a complaint, so there is no evidence to suggest that this would become a significant workload burden.[113] CLA president Paul Whitney and CLA Councillor Alvin M. Schrader responded to that piece on June 16, stating their belief that "exposing racist ideas to public criticism is all that it takes to discredit them for the vast majority."[114] They also referred heavily to the CLA's Statement on Intellectual Freedom and repeated the neutrality argument that libraries do not endorse the groups that they allow to book their spaces, while affirming that the issue of hate speech is a responsibility of the proper legal authorities and not public libraries.[115]

On June 18, Esquimalt-Metchosin Member of the Legislative Assembly (MLA) Moe Sihota, CRRRA representative Carolina Choy, and Victoria Labour Council secretary Bill Fowler spoke outside of the CLA Conference to express their concern about the library allowing the CFSL to meet at the Juan de Fuca branch the following evening. Sihota, who was BC's first Indo-Canadian MLA, noted that such decisions are usually made "by people who are not of colour, who don't feel the potential for victimization" in the same ways that marginalized people might; he continued: "I am the potential victim, I am the person that they believe ought not to be involved in mainstream Canadian society. I am the person that they hate."[116] The trio also spoke about the peaceful protest planned for 6pm on June 19, outside of the library involving 50 organizations, including the Jewish Federation of Victoria and Vancouver Island and trade unions such as the BC Government and Service Employees Union and the Victoria Labour Council.[117]

At the Juan de Fuca branch on June 19, about 25 people attended the private CFSL meeting and about 350 protestors rallied outside chanting:

---

113 Goldschmid, "Library Cop-Out Provides Room to Grow for Message of Hate."

114 "Free Expression Doesn't Condone Discrimination," *Times Colonist,* June 16, 1998, ProQuest.

115 "Free Expression Doesn't Condone Discrimination"; "Statement on Intellectual Freedom and Libraries."

116 Roger Stonebanks, "Racism Foes Out in Force Tonight," *Times Colonist,* June 19, 1998, ProQuest. I will note here that Moe Sihota also made a comment on a radio show suggesting that the CFSL might be involved in the Jan 4 1998 murder of Nirmal Singh Gill in Surrey, BC by neo-Nazis. He soon apologized and admitted no evidence of connection, but he was sued by the CFSL for defamation; Kim Westad, "Free Speech Group Sues Sihota," *Times Colonist,* August 7, 1998, ProQuest.

117 Stonebanks, "Racism Foes Out in Force Tonight."

"Immigrants in, Nazis out!"[118] Meanwhile, at the library conference, the CLA passed a unanimous resolution commending the GVPL board and CUPE 410, which represents library employees, for supporting intellectual freedom.[119] The conference program included a session called "Intellectual Freedom and Library Space: Who's Allowed In" which was reportedly crashed by some B'nai Brith members and GVPL employees who criticized the CFSL and the library board policy, but the session remained civil if tense.[120] The debate continued in the public sphere for a few more weeks with an opinion piece in the *Times Colonist* contending that "democracy is not convenient" and controversial views must be tolerated, while recommending, as we have heard from others before, that driving these ideas underground is a mistake and it is better to "keep all views up front for public scrutiny no matter how repulsive or odious those views might be for some people."[121] What that argument is missing is the important point that Moe Sihota spoke out to clarify: it is not just that some views are repulsive to some people, it is that these views express hate against some people; they are not just words, they include threats of harm. Another opinion in the Globe and Mail critiqued "free-speech opponents" and commended the library board for its commitment to free speech.[122] A letter to the editor responded to that opinion, arguing that "[f]reedom of speech does not mean that everybody has the right to the use of public institutions," just as "[l]ibraries do not have to make space on their shelves available to every book published."[123] And then things quieted down until the following summer and fall.

1999 Saanich and Colwood, British Columbia

On June 5, 1999, the CFSL held a meeting at the Nellie McClung branch of GVPL in the municipality of Saanich. The meeting, which was

---

118 Malcolm Curtis, "Free Speech Supporters Jeered," *Times Colonist,* June 20, 1998, ProQuest.

119 Martin Dowding, "Canadian Library Association Checks Reality in Victoria," *American Libraries* 29, no. 7 (August 1998): 28, https://link.gale.com/apps/doc/A21043829/CIC?u=utoronto_main&sid=bookmark-CIC&xid=f76c558f.

120 Dowding, "Canadian Library Association Checks Reality in Victoria."

121 Jody Paterson, "The New Islander–Joe Easingwood," *Times Colonist,* June 28, 1998, ProQuest.

122 Paul Willcocks, "Their Views are Vile, but Rent them a Room the Victoria Library has Taken a Commendable Stand for Free Speech," *The Globe and Mail,* July 13, 1998, ProQuest.

123 Lionel Kenner, "Limits of Free Speech," *The Globe and Mail,* July 17, 1998, ProQuest.

attended by about 50 people, was a fundraiser for retired columnist Doug Collins in his court challenge of a BC Human Rights tribunal ruling that the cumulative effect of some of his writing for the North Shore News exposed Jewish people to hatred.[124] About 50 anti-racism protesters were outside the library, representing a coalition of front-line service providers, students, unions, and others, and there was pushing and shoving from both sides at various points, as attendees made their way through the crowd and a handful of protesters temporarily blocked the entrance door.[125] The police did not arrive until after the violence had started,[126] then they remained on the scene, and there were no reports of injury or arrest.[127] Protester Ben Isitt, of International Socialists and the University of Victoria Students Society, accused the CFSL of "propagat[ing] hate which infringes on the rights of others," while the latest chair of the GVPL board, Val Ethier, defended the rights of those on both sides to free speech: "these demonstrators have that right and those meeting have that right. The library is neutral. What we cannot tolerate as a society is violence."[128]

Another event at the Juan de Fuca branch in Colwood on September 10 was met with about 100 protestors, as Doug Christie's Western Canada Concept party (WCC) met to discuss immigration issues.[129] This time police planned ahead with six RCMP officers on site and things remained loud but peaceful.[130] Protestors hung a banner that read: "Racists Enter Here" above the library entrance and chanted outside for the duration of the meeting, then chanted at Christie as he left.[131] Ben Isitt deemed the protest a success, noting that although it gave

---

[124] Cindy E. Harnett, "Tempers Fly at Library: Anti-Racists, Free Speech Supporters Clash at Collins Fund-Raiser," *Times Colonist,* June 6, 1999, ProQuest.

[125] Harnett, "Tempers Fly at Library."

[126] An internal review found that the Saanich police failed to plan properly for the protest. Louise Dickson, "Police Failed in Library Clash: Internal Review Criticizes Lack of Planning for Collins Dinner in Saanich," *Times Colonist,* July 24, 1999, ProQuest.

[127] Harnett, "Tempers Fly at Library."

[128] Harnett.

[129] Malcolm Curtis, "100 Protest Christie's WCC Immigration Meeting: RCMP Officers Kept Busy but no Arrests made," *Times Colonist,* September 11, 1999, ProQuest.

[130] Curtis, "100 Protest Christie's WCC Immigration Meeting."

[131] Curtis.

publicity to Christie, it also led to more than 20 people turning away from the meeting.[132]

October brought a decision from the BC Human Rights Commission dismissing a complaint submitted the previous year by Victoria City Councillor Bob Friedland, the Green Party of Canada, the Victoria Labour Council, and the Status of Women Action Group.[133] The complaint argued that the library's meeting room policy allowed for discrimination and created a poisoned environment because it only refers to Canada's Criminal Code and does not include the Human Rights Code, but the commission found there was insufficient evidence "to establish that this neutral policy created a discriminatory atmosphere."[134] The complainants planned to appeal and Friedland commented that the decision was "wrong in fact and in law," while Doug Christie responded that the decision was right: "In order to maintain the right to freedom of expression, all groups have to be given equal opportunity."[135] Chief Librarian Anderson was also pleased with the decision: "I think they recognized we have perhaps a very unique responsibility and role to facilitate as wide an expression of opinion as possible."[136] She also noted that "[i]t's very difficult to see [the library] on the other side of people who oppose racism and hatred. We are hoping this provides closure."[137]

Anderson's hope for closure was not to be met, as Christie and the WCC party met back at the Juan de Fuca branch again on October 16 with about a dozen people in attendance and 80 protestors gathered outside.[138] This time there were 10 Royal Canadian Mounted Police (RCMP) on the scene who quickly broke up some shoving that occurred near the entrance.[139] Protesters expressed frustration about the Human

---

132 Curtis.

133 "Library Hails Rights Ruling on Speeches," *Times Colonist*, October 14, 1999, ProQuest.

134 "Library Hails Rights Ruling on Speeches"; Barbara McLintock, "Library Backed on Room-Rental Policy," *The Province*, October 14, 1999, ProQuest.

135 "Library Hails Rights Ruling on Speeches."

136 "Library Hails Rights Ruling on Speeches."

137 "Library Hails Rights Ruling on Speeches."

138 Louise Dickson, "Activists Rally to Protest Christie Meeting," *Times Colonist*, October 17, 1999, ProQuest.

139 Dickson, "Activists Rally to Protest Christie Meeting."

Rights Commission decision and the library meeting room policy, and the chief librarian was frustrated that protests were continuing despite the commission's decision and the library's neutral position.[140] However, since nothing had changed to address the concerns of those who opposed these kinds of meetings at the library, their presence should not have come as a surprise.

Although I found no records of protests at library events for a few years, the issue came up for debate again in March 2003 when the provincial ombudsperson released a report following an investigation into a complaint made by the Jewish Federation of Victoria and Vancouver Island in 1998 about the library board's refusal to amend its meeting room policy to exclude groups that "are likely to promote discrimination, contempt or hatred."[141] Ombudsperson Howard Kushner stated that it was not appropriate for his office to determine that policy, but it was appropriate to review how that policy operates from a fairness perspective, so his investigation focused on the aspect of fairness that "individuals know the conditions and restrictions under which permission to use public meetings will be granted."[142] He reported confusion in the communications he received from the library board around their expectations of the rules and laws to be followed by those using their facilities and concluded that the board's lack of consistent expectations and refusal to clearly state their expectations in writing resulted in an unfair policy: "I found the Board's policy to be deficient because it did not spell out what the Board said the public would be expected to adhere to. In that sense, the policy is incomplete, and the Board's expectation that the public adhere to a policy that is not known, is unreasonable."[143] In detailing his discussions with the library board throughout the investigation, Kushner notes that in May 2000, his office had recommended adding to the policy that people not contravene the BC Human Rights Code, along with the already stated Criminal Code, as Vancouver Public Library had made such an amendment that year. But the board chair responded in October that

---

140 Dickson.

141 Howard Kushner, *The Right to Know: A Complaint about the Greater Victoria Public Library Meeting Room Policy* (Victoria, BC: Office of the Ombudsman, 2003), 1, 4, https://bcombudsperson.ca/assets/media/Special-Report-No-23-Greater-Victoria-Public-Library-Meeting-Room-Policy.pdf.

142 Kushner, *The Right to Know*, 1.

143 Kushner, 2.

"Libraries cherish freedom of expression," and that adding a reference to the BC Human Rights Code in the policy "would create an expectation on the part of some that the Library will ban groups that are perceived as holding unpopular beliefs."[144] Kushner goes on to discuss further the library's reluctance to add clarity to their meeting room policy expectations as well as the justifications they offer for such vagueness–including the library staff's inability to determine if laws have been breached–in contrast with the thoroughly stated expectations of their users in the library's Internet Policy.[145] The report ends with the recommendation: "That the Library's stated expectation that persons using its meeting rooms comply with all federal, provincial, and municipal legislation and regulations be put in written form and be part of its leasing policy."[146] Currently, the GVPL's policy on Responsibilities and Conduct of Library Users, last amended by the board in 2010 and 2016, refers to the Canadian Human Rights Act,[147] whereas the Meeting Rooms policy, last amended in 2008, has the statement that, "[t]his policy is carried out in compliance and due regard to all relevant and appropriate legislation," but then it goes on to still only reference the Criminal Code by name.[148]

1997 West Vancouver, British Columbia

Across the Georgia Strait on the mainland of BC, the CFSL and Vancouver area public libraries were also embroiled in the controversy over free speech and hate speech in the late 1990s.[149] The CFSL held a meeting on May 11, 1997 at the West Vancouver Memorial public library to rally in support of Doug Collins as he faced a complaint before the BC Human Rights tribunal.[150] The library had received some

---

144 Kushner, 7, 9.

145 Kushner, 6–11.

146 Kushner, 13.

147 "Policy 1.8, Responsibilities and Conduct of Library Users," Greater Victoria Public Library, January 2016, https://gvpl.ent.sirsidynix.net/client/en_US/default/?rm=POLICY+1.8+-+R0%7C%7C%7C1%7C%7C%7C0%7C%7C%7Ctrue&dt=list.

148 "Policy O.7, Meeting Rooms," Greater Victoria Public Library, June 24, 2008, https://gvpl.ent.sirsidynix.net/client/en_US/default/?rm=POLICY+O.7+-+M0%7C%7C%7C1%7C%7C%7C0%7C%7C%7Ctrue&dt=list.

149 This discussion will look at events in the municipalities of West Vancouver, North Vancouver, and Vancouver, each with separate library boards.

150 Todd, "Use of Library for Collins' Rally Sparks Outcry."

complaints before the meeting for allowing the group to use their space, including opposition from CAERS, but there were no protests outside the library, and about 60 people attended the meeting.[151] In response to the complaints, Chief Librarian Jack Mounce said, "I find the group distasteful, but we don't impose censorship on our books or on those who use our facilities."[152] By equating books with groups of people, however, Mounce overlooks the material differences between the two and the uneven threats they pose. A person can easily avoid a book whose contents might harm them, but it is more difficult to avoid a group of people speaking about views that might harm them. And whether or not a group of people gathered in a library intends to harm others, their presence can be significantly more threatening than that of a book on a shelf to people who have been historically or currently marginalized and targeted by hate and violence. His statement also glosses over the reality that librarians select books according to collection policies and criteria, rather than haphazardly purchasing any and every publication.

I found two letters to the editor in the *Vancouver Sun* about this minor library hubbub, one criticizing Mounce for calling the CFSL "distasteful," and one applauding the library's support for free speech, echoing the familiar argument of exposing controversial ideas to "the full light of public opinion." I also found a couple of other letters not about the library, but supporting Collins' free speech rights in the tribunal.[153]

1999 North Vancouver, British Columbia

On May 14, 1999, the CFSL held another meeting in support of Doug Collins, this time a fundraiser for his court challenge against the Human Rights tribunal decision, at a public library in the municipality of North Vancouver.[154] I was unable to find any direct coverage of the event, but in July, the *Vancouver Sun* reported that library staff felt intimidated

---

151 Todd, "Use of Library for Collins' Rally Sparks Outcry"; Rick Ouston, "Controversial Columnist Launches Free-Speech 'Battle,'" *Vancouver Sun*, May 12, 1997, B1, ProQuest.

152 Todd, "Use of Library for Collins' Rally Sparks Outcry."

153 "Heralding Free Speech," *Vancouver Sun*, May 14, 1997, A14, ProQuest.

154 "Regional Roundup: North Vancouver: Neo-Nazis Spark Move to Ban Hate Groups from Public Space: Councillor Darrell Mussatto Raises the Alarm After City Library Staff Complained of Feeling 'intimidated and Uncomfortable' Amid 100 Skinheads Attending Seminars at the Public Library," *Vancouver Sun*, July 28, 1999, B5, ProQuest; Doug Collins, "Neither Skinheads nor Marilyn Manson," *Vancouver Sun*, July 30, 1999, ProQuest.

by a group of "neo-Nazis" among the 100 people in attendance at the event and that RCMP were called to the scene.[155] Doug Collins countered in a letter to the editor that they heard no complaints from the library and the RCMP were not called.[156] North Vancouver City Councillor Darrell Mussatto, however, did receive complaints from library staff, which prompted him to present a motion to develop a policy to deny the use of public space to groups promoting hatred, as we saw in Victoria city council in 1996.[157] The motion carried unanimously, was sent to the City Solicitor for a legal opinion,[158] and was then incorporated into city policy.[159] Councillor Mussatto said: "We pride ourselves on providing people with a racism-and-discrimination-free environment, but if we're going to talk the talk, we've got to walk the walk."[160]

1999 Vancouver, British Columbia

Later that year, at the main downtown public library branch in the city of Vancouver things grew more tense at a CFSL fundraiser for Doug Collins.[161] Leading up to the September 30th meeting, the Canadian Jewish Congress and the Vancouver Association of Chinese Canadians planned to protest at the event and they spoke out against the library for allowing the group to use its meeting rooms, arguing that "it's inappropriate for the library, a publicly funded place, to allow this type of hatred to happen."[162] Nisson Goldman from the CJC insisted that they are not opposed to the CFSL's right to free speech, but that does not mean they should be allowed to do so in public institutions, giving

---

155 "Regional Roundup." The article includes a correction notice after a previous version had erroneously reported that 100 skinheads attended the event and made staff feel uncomfortable.

156 Collins, "Neither Skinheads nor Marilyn Manson."

157 "Regional Roundup."

158 Minutes of the Regular Meeting of Council Held in the Council Chamber, July 26, 1999, City of North Vancouver, https://cnvapps.cnv.org/Minutes/1999_07_26_Council_Minutes.pdf.

159 *Policy for Community Events in Parks and Public Open Spaces*, Public Policy C57C, City of North Vancouver (2014), https://www.cnv.org/-/media/city-of-north-vancouver/documents/parks-and-environment/regulations/policy-for-community-events-in-parks-and-public-open-spaces.ashx?la=en, 5–6.

160 "Regional Roundup."

161 This is now Vancouver Public Library (VPL), which is distinct from the previously mentioned public libraries of West Vancouver and North Vancouver.

162 Petti Fong, "Library Won't Ban Collins Speech: It Remains Resolute Against Critics Who Want the Controversial Writer's Talk Cancelled," *Vancouver Sun*, September 30, 1999, B4, ProQuest.

them "a cloak of respectability."[163] Vancouver Public Library's Acting Director Eric Smith affirmed the library board's policy of neutrality and intellectual freedom, but also noted that some board members had concerns about the policy and wanted it to be reviewed.[164]

At the meeting there were about 100 protestors, including the aforementioned anti-racist organizations and a variety of other groups, such as International Socialists and Democracy Street, as well as about two dozen police officers and extra security guards hired by the library.[165] Once the meeting attendees were inside, the officers barricaded the library's doors, but at least 60 protestors got inside, and when another barricade was set up inside, a handful of protestors broke through that one and proceeded to bang on the doors of the meeting room while the rest chanted loudly to disrupt the meeting. One protestor was arrested, then the protest ended peacefully when the library closed at 8pm.[166] A long opinion piece by Paula Brook of the *Vancouver Sun*, written after the event, called out the CFSL for using library meeting rooms to gain attention and criticized the library for being irresponsible with public safety and money. However, she fell short of calling for a ban on such groups using the library, noting it is a "no-win" situation "and the best the library can do is reframe the question in terms of the broadest public good."[167]

What the library did next generated more criticism. According to another Paula Brook opinion piece in the *Vancouver Sun*, in January of 2000, a poster was put up across all VPL branches announcing a public forum to be held on February 9 at the main branch to discuss the topic of "Public Meetings in Public Spaces."[168] The poster featured an image of a group of faces with all of their mouths taped shut except for

---

163 Shane McCune, "Collins-Christie Session Draws Protesters, Cops to Vancouver Library," *The Province*, October 1, 1999, A3, ProQuest.

164 McCune, "Collins-Christie Session Draws Protesters."

165 "Protesters Try to Disrupt 'Free Speech' Meeting," *Canadian Press NewsWire*, October 1, 1999, ProQuest.

166 "Protesters Try to Disrupt 'Free Speech' Meeting"; McCune, "Collins-Christie Session Draws Protesters."

167 Paula Brook, "Limits on Free Speech a Double-Edged Sword: Impediments to Free Speech Aimed at the Political Far Right Cast our Society in the Uneasy Role of Censor," *Vancouver Sun*, October 6, 1999, A19, ProQuest.

168 Paula Brook, "Pass the Milquetoast: Library Puts Tepid Spin on a Stark Issue: Instead of a Colourful Poster Dealing with Censorship and Freedom, the VPL Employs the 'a' Word (Appropriate)," *Vancouver Sun*, February 9, 2000, A17, ProQuest.

one, and a caption that read: "Is it ever appropriate for the Library to censor free speech?"[169] The public responded swiftly with calls to the library complaining that the image of gagged people was inflammatory, so the library leadership quickly ordered the poster to be taken down.[170] They tried again a few days later with a new poster that had the same caption, but not the gagged image, and were met with the same response, so they took the new poster down and postponed the forum to later that spring.[171] I inquired with VPL to find out if the postponed public forum did take place, and they were unable to find evidence to confirm whether or not it happened. The VPL board did update its policy in 2000, adding that groups using their spaces must not contravene the BC Human Rights Act or the Criminal Code of Canada.[172] The BC Civil Liberties Association (BCCLA) was critical of that addition, stating that "[t]his requirement seems to be targeted at speech, and could place a 'chill' on expression since it is not at all clear ahead of time what speech might run afoul of these laws."[173] However, those laws apply within the library space whether or not they are mentioned specifically in the policy. Including reference to them in the policy at least makes that expectation clear and communicated to all users, not just singling out those who might be deemed controversial, which the BC Ombudsperson found appropriate.[174]

2000 Regina, Saskatchewan

The Queer City Cinema third bi-annual film festival was planned for May 2000, with most programming booked for a cultural venue, but it was a program booked at the main downtown branch of Regina Public Library–a panel discussion about what constitutes pornography along with the screening of some sexually explicit films–that caused a stir. The debate over the festival began in the provincial Parliament on April 28 when opposition education critic, MLA June Draude of the

---

169   Brook, "Pass the Milquetoast."

170   Brook, "Pass the Milquetoast."

171   Brook.

172   Kushner, *The Right to Know*, 7, 9.

173   "Banning controversial groups from public spaces," *The Democratic Commitment*, June, 2000, 7, https://bccla.org/wp-content/uploads/2012/08/2000_Summer_Newsletter_Democratic_Commitment.pdf.

174   Kushner, *The Right to Know*, 7.

Saskatchewan Party, accused the government of promoting pornography by supporting the film festival with public funds. Her fellow party member, MLA Arlene Jule, called on the government to withdraw that funding.[175] The issue of taxpayer money funding a festival that included programming that some people thought to be pornographic was the main concern,[176] with the opposition pressing the issue in parliamentary question period for two weeks despite the small sums at stake.[177] That persistence, when coupled with the reminder that one of the vocally opposed Saskatchewan Party MLAs, Ben Heppner, had also questioned funding for the festival in 1996 when pornography was not involved, led Municipal Affairs Minister Clay Serby to imply that homophobia was the reason and pornography the excuse to oppose funding the festival, which the Saskatchewan Party denied.[178]

With that focus on money, the library mostly avoided criticism, as library policy was never called into question in Parliament or the press, and the library staff and board did not get involved or make statements. But I included this controversy in this history because the library was mentioned a few times and it is interesting to see this case of the library flying under the radar of the controversy for the most part. The Film Theatre in the library, where the festival's pornography panel was held, is in the basement next to the children's area of the library,[179] to which MLA Draude objected, "[t]hey're going to have porno information, and they're going to be holding a screening right in the library, right beside the children's part of the library. Why would you have people there actively talking about pornography in a library

---

175 "Porn Panel at Regina Film Festival Comes Under Fire: Queer City Festival Director Defends Nature of Gay and Lesbian Pornography," *Star Phoenix*, April 29, 2000, ProQuest.

176 "Porn Panel at Regina Film Festival Comes Under Fire." The festival was funded through arts grants from various levels of government, including the Canada Council, and was sponsored by SaskTel and SaskFilm, which are Crown corporations.

177 Kevin O'Connor, "Controversy Continues: Panelists Say They're Proud of Gay Film Festival," *Leader Post*, May 15, 2000, ProQuest; James Parker, "Experts Said Festival has Merit: Official," *Leader Post*, May 3, 2000, ProQuest; Jonathan Petrychyn, "Networks of Feelings: Affective Economies of Queer and Feminist Film Festivals on the Canadian Prairies" (PhD diss., York University 2019), 117, https://yorkspace.library.yorku.ca/xmlui/bitstream/handle/10315/36773/Petrychyn_Jonathan_R_2019_PhD.pdf?sequence=2&isAllowed=y.

178 James Parker, "Sask. Party Keeps Up Heat on Graphic Films," *Leader Post*, May 4, 2000, ProQuest.

179 Petrychyn, "Networks of Feeling," 123.

beside children?"[180] Of course, the doors to the theatre would have been closed during the program, which was limited to an audience of 18 years of age and over.[181]

When the festival opened on May 8, 2000, there was a protest of about a dozen people outside the library.[182] Bill Whatcott, founder of a group called Christian Truth Activists, was there to protest "the very existence of this festival," taking issue with homosexuality rather than funding or location, while Bob Hughes, of the Saskatchewan Coalition Against Racism, was there in support of the festival and handed out leaflets condemning the "web of hate" of which homophobia is a part.[183] There was a slightly larger protest of about 20 people at the library on May 13 when the pornography program, attended by 120 people, was happening; one protester held a sign that read: "Shame on the Regina Public Library for hosting gay porn."[184] But soon after the festival, the controversy died down, aside from a few letters to the editor in the *Leader-Post*, two of which were from Whatcott,[185] and the following year the Canada Council significantly increased its funding for the festival.[186]

2008 Vancouver, British Columbia

In February of 2008 the Vancouver Public Library decided to host an event for Freedom To Read Week for the first time in years.[187] Controversial local author and former *Vancouver Courier* columnist Greg

---

180 "Porn Panel at Regina Film Festival Comes Under Fire"; Petrychyn, "Networks of Feeling," 123–25. Jonathan Petrychyn makes the connection between this concern and the homophobic stereotype of homosexuals as pedophiles.

181 James Parker, "Films Approved for Queer City Cinema," *Leader Post,* May 10, 2000, ProQuest; Barb Pacholik, "Films Appal Sask. Party MLAs," *Leader Post,* May 12, 2000, ProQuest.

182 "Queer City Fest Opens to More Controversy," *CBC,* May 9, 2000, https://www.cbc.ca/news/canada/queer-city-fest-opens-to-more-controversy-1.197824.

183 Barb Pacholik, "Protesters Greet First Day of Gay Film Festival," *Leader Post,* May 9, 2000, ProQuest.

184 Petrychyn, "Networks of Feeling," 101.

185 Bill Whatcott, "Statements Challenged," *Leader Post,* May 17, 2000, ProQuest; Carin Bergen, "Article Stirred Memories," *Leader Post,* May 18, 2000, ProQuest; Bill Whatcott, "Misinformation Claim Disputed," *Leader Post,* June 16, 2000, ProQuest.

186 Petrychyn, "Networks of Feeling," 177.

187 Beth, "Greg Felton at VPL," *The (Unofficial) BCLA Intellectual Freedom Committee Blog* (blog), February 26, 2008, https://bclaifc.wordpress.com/2008/02/26/greg-felton-at-vpl/.

Felton approached the library to request that they host a reading event for his latest book, *The Host and the Parasite: How Israel's Fifth Column Consumed America*. The library agreed to host the event on February 25, because they deemed it "a book that people might not feel free to read," according to VPL Director of youth services and community relations Janice Douglas.[188] The event caught the eye of writer and journalist Terry Glavin, who wrote an opinion piece in the *Vancouver Sun* that sparked the public debate surrounding the event. He accused Felton of antisemitism (as well as anti-Israel views) and the library of making an error in judgment by providing its Freedom To Read Week platform to someone of such dubious reputation and affiliations, which he described as "neo-Nazi websites, conspiracy-theory bulletin boards, and sometimes even in pamphlets of the Marxist-Leninist sort."[189] He also mocked the publisher of the book, Dandelion Books, for publishing titles about "the lost continent of Atlantis, space aliens, New Age mysticism, mind control, 9-11 conspiracies," implying further bad judgment by the library for not vetting the book according to better standards.[190] I will note here that a *Library Journal* article reported that the book was not reviewed by mainstream media and had very limited library holdings, according to WorldCat, with five ordered to VPL at that time.[191] My last check of WorldCat showed only 19 libraries with holdings of the book's two editions, and VPL's catalogue now shows just one copy in one branch.

VPL City Librarian Paul Whitney replied to Glavin's opinion in a letter to the editor the following day and his first statement was one of library neutrality, affirming that while the library is hosting Felton, it "is in no way agreeing with his positions."[192] Then he went on to defend the library's decision, arguing, "it appeared to us that his book was provocative but not hateful and we have found no information indicating the book is subject to any legal action," before focusing on the issue of intellectual freedom: "We were aware of the freedom-of-expression

---

188 Terry Glavin, "Does Our Library Know There's Another Word For Anti-Semitism," *Vancouver Sun*, February 12, 2008, A17, ProQuest.

189 Glavin, "Does Our Library Know There's Another Word For Anti-Semitism."

190 Glavin.

191 Norman Oder, "Vancouver Library Under Fire for Hosting Controversial Author Called Anti-Semitic," *Library Journal*, February 15, 2008, https://www.libraryjournal.com/story/vancouver-library-under-fire-for-hosting-controversial-authorcalled-anti-semitic.

192 Paul Whitney, letter to the editor, *Vancouver Sun*, February 13, 2008, ProQuest.

debate surrounding Felton's departure from the *Vancouver Courier*, where he was a columnist, and therefore felt his reading was relevant for Freedom to Read Week."[193] But Glavin remained unconvinced and wrote a lengthy blog post in which he suggested confusion in the library's decision making. He said that library staff told him they had only read an excerpt of the book and the library had no copies yet, so he asked how Whitney could determine the book was not hateful and if he was directly involved in the decision.[194] To this point, library spokesperson Jean Kavanagh explained that, in the time between Glavin speaking to Douglas and Whitney's letter to the editor, several staff members had read the book, informing the decision to proceed with the event.[195] Glavin also pointed out that when Whitney was the chief librarian at the Burnaby Public Library he banned a book titled *Against Pornography: The Evidence of Harm* in 1994, for which he was rebuked by the BCLA.[196] I am more willing than Glavin was to give Whitney the benefit of the doubt that he had learned and grown in the 14 years since banning that book, but it is important, as Glavin suggested, to think about the difference in impact between having a book that contains harmful images on a library shelf and hosting an event that contains harmful speech. He also argued that providing the Freedom To Read Week platform for Felton "has afforded legitimacy, and even a sanction of decency, to what is actually a grotesque infringement of free speech. It is a demand that we either dignify people like Felton by debating with them, or shut up."[197] And that last point aligns with other voices we've heard from in other examples, arguing that to debate hate gives it the privilege of being considered debatable and not simply despicable.

VPL received over 200 calls and emails, with most calling for the event to be cancelled,[198] but there was no record of political interventions,

---

193 Whitney, letter to the editor.

194 Terry Glavin, "Freedom-To-Be-Antisemitic Week In Vancouver: The City Librarian Explains Why," *Terry Glavin Chronicles & Dissent* (blog), February 13, 2008, https://transmontanus.blogspot.com/2008/02/freedom-to-be-antisemitic-week-in.html.

195 Oder, "Vancouver Library Under Fire for Hosting Controversial Author Called Anti-Semitic."

196 Glavin, "Freedom-To-Be-Antisemitic Week In Vancouver." The BCLA link that Glavin provides is currently timing out, but I had checked it previously and confirmed the information.

197 Glavin, "Freedom-To-Be-Antisemitic Week In Vancouver."

198 "What's that doing in my library? Intellectual Freedom Stories and Advice," in 2009 *BCLA Conference Session Summary* (Burnaby: BCLA, 2009), https://core.ac.uk/reader/290480280.

policy reviews, or consequences for the library. A few letters to the editor were published in the *Vancouver Sun* in support of the event on the basis of free speech. One letter called Felton "a crank" but erroneously argued that the alternative to hosting his event would be book burning,[199] while another asserted that "different opinions enrich us as people, and sustain us as a free society."[200] Another letter accused that "City Librarian Paul Whitney's defence of 'free speech' is disingenuous" because the library would not afford the same protection for groups espousing other kinds of discrimination, but protects free speech for antisemitic and anti-Christian rhetoric.[201] However, looking back to 1999 we see that VPL defended the CFSL's right to free speech in the library, and while Doug Collins was under fire at that time specifically for antisemitism, the CFSL on the whole is also known for a variety of other discriminatory views.

The Canadian Jewish Congress (CJC) worked with the Jewish Federation of Greater Vancouver and the Canada-Israel Committee to develop a response strategy.[202] They reached out to VPL and met with some senior staff to share their concerns and ask that the library cancel the event, admit they made a mistake, and condemn Felton's book.[203] The CJC also contacted the Diversity Relations Unit of the Vancouver Police Department and the BC Hate Crime Team to request that they attend if the event was not cancelled.[204] The group did not call for a protest at the event, as they believed it would be against their community's best interest and would generate more publicity for Felton, and they stated: "There is no advantage to engaging Mr. Felton in a debate, as there is no debating what he has to say. To do so would only legitimize his views and opinions."[205] However, they encouraged people to call or email the VPL board or City Librarian Whitney to voice their opposition

---

199   Paul Whitney, letter to the editor, *Vancouver Sun*, February 13, 2008, A12, ProQuest.

200   Dorian Rayn, letter to the editor, *Vancouver Sun,* February 16, 2008, C3, ProQuest.

201   Donald F. Davis, letter to the editor, *Vancouver Sun*, February 14, 2008, A18, ProQuest.

202   The CJC post is no longer available, but it was shared on the website of an American pro-Israel group called Librarians For Fairness. Gerry Cuttler and Romy Rittler, "Call to Action by the Canadian Jewish Congress, Pacific Region," Librarians for Fairness, February 23, 2008, http://librariansforfairness.org/news_post.asp?NPI=248.

203   Cuttler and Rittler, "Call to Action by the Canadian Jewish Congress."

204   Cuttler and Rittler,

205   Cuttler and Rittler.

to the event. They also provided a list of information points, including the argument that free speech protections do not entitle people to public fora at public institutions, the suggestion that VPL implement a vetting system for speakers, and questions about why they chose this particular controversial speaker and if other controversial topics would be included as part of Freedom To Read Week.[206]

The union representing some VPL staff, CUPE Local 391, released a statement on the day of the event stating that they were not consulted in the booking of it and that "[t]he Union does not endorse the event and would strongly condemn any anti-Semitic writings which constitute hate literature."[207] The statement goes on to confirm "the union's support for intellectual freedom," but suggests support for those arguing that this event should not have been legitimized as a freedom of speech issue.[208] They ended by inviting "members of the public to consider information available about Felton's writings and to think critically whether or not Felton's views actually support freedom of speech or have hateful content," and recommending that people who find Felton's material to be hateful not attend the event.[209] At the event there were no reports of protest, just some fiery debate in the presence of an RCMP officer from the hate crimes division.[210] The BCLA Intellectual Freedom Committee's unofficial blog published a post by committee member and VPL staffer Beth the following day, who affirmed that "In my mind, there is no question that the library should have gone ahead with this event" because "[f]reedom of expression means standing up for everyone's right to free speech" even if they speak repugnant views.[211] Beth did also lament that VPL had not participated in Freedom To Read Week for a few years and noted some irony that while VPL was defending the event that Felton initiated under the FTRW banner, the library was also hosting its own provocative series called Speak Up! "[t]hat's full of the kind of open-minded

---

206 Cuttler and Rittler.

207 "Vancouver Public Library's 'Freedom to Read' Week Controversy; February 25, 2008: 7.30 p.m.," CUPE 391, February 25, 2008, https://cupe391.ca/2008/02/25/vancouver-public-librarys-freedom-to-read-week-controversy-february-25-2008-7-30-p-m/. CUPE 391 Statement Feb 25, 2008.

208 "Vancouver Public Library's 'Freedom to Read' Week Controversy."

209 "Vancouver Public Library's 'Freedom to Read' Week Controversy."

210 "What's That Doing in my library?"

211 Beth, "Greg Felton at VPL."

debate that gives intellectual freedom a good name."[212] If VPL had promoted that series as a FTRW initiative they might have avoided some criticism and they would not have given Felton the distinction of being their only FTRW author, which Glavin warned would now allow Felton to describe his book "as the toast of Freedom To Read Week in Vancouver."[213]

2009 Vancouver, British Columbia

The following year in Vancouver, the public library faced another event controversy when an Australian-based right-to-die group, Exit International, booked a room at the main downtown branch for a workshop to be held on September 10, 2009. The library initially accepted the booking for the two-part seminar, with part one being a public discussion of right-to-die politics and part two a private presentation for people over age 55 about methods for suicide. However, the library then cancelled it based on legal advice pertaining to the second part of the seminar.[214] City Librarian Paul Whitney stated that the legal advice they sought from lawyers and the police indicated that the presentation would contravene the Criminal Code of Canada, which is against the library's policy for room bookings and would put the library at risk.[215] Whitney acknowledged that the library carries books holding the same kinds of information that would be shared at the seminar, but he said that holding the workshop "is more active" and could expose the library to legal liability.[216] It is interesting that he made this distinction for this topic about the difference in impact between books and events, but he and other librarians have not made this point for other controversial event issues, such as those involving discrimination against marginalized groups.

Exit International's director, Philip Nitschke, was the first doctor to legally assist a suicide in Australia before the law allowing it was

---

212 Beth.

213 Terry Glavin, "Some Free Speech is Less Worthy of Defence," *Ottawa Citizen,* February 29, 2008, A11, ProQuest.

214 Gerry Bellett, "Library Bans Assisted-Suicide Workshop," *Vancouver Sun,* September 22, 2009, A7, ProQuest.

215 James Keller, "Vancouver Library Bars Assisted-Suicide Group's How-To Workshop," *The Canadian Press,* September 21, 2009, ProQuest.

216 Keller, "Vancouver Library Bars Assisted-Suicide Group's How-To Workshop."

overturned, and he said that although his group's book had been banned in Australia, they had been holding these workshops for years without legal problems in Australia, New Zealand, and the United Kingdom, so he was "taken aback to find the suggestion that simply providing this accurate information is going to be any breach of Canadian law."[217] Wayne Sumner, a professor emeritus of Philosophy at the University of Toronto who has worked on the topic of euthanasia, disagreed with the library's position and said that providing information at a workshop was unlikely to cross any legal boundaries as long as the drugs themselves were not provided: "It's hard to see how any significant line is being crossed. The library has already spent public money to acquire this book and put it on the shelves, which isn't entirely passive."[218] And David Eby, Executive Director of the BC Civil Liberties Association criticized the library for inappropriately restricting free speech because, according to their review of the seminar materials, Exit International would not be breaking any laws.[219] The BCCLA and Exit International had a meeting with the library board in hope of changing the cancellation decision, but the board maintained its position based on legal counsel and maintained its neutrality about the issue at hand. As Whitney said: "The board made it clear that this does not in any way represent the board's position on assisted suicide as a public policy matter," but it was too legally risky for the library to host the workshop.[220]

Although I found no reports of the library receiving letters or calls on the issue, we might assume they did receive some, and some strong public opinions on the issue were presented in a variety of Canadian newspapers. Leonard Stern of the *Ottawa Citizen's* editorial board wrote what I have to call a bizarre editorial in which he voiced his support for the library's decision by calling the right-to-die movement "creepy" and the Exit International workshop "weird" and a "marketing event — for suicide," then said, "[t]he line between advocates and

---

217   Keller.

218   Keller, "Vancouver Library Bars Assisted-Suicide Group's How-To Workshop."

219   "B.C. Group Decries Ban on Suicide Seminar," *National Post,* September 22, 2009, A4, ProQuest.

220   Randy Shore, "Right-to-Die Group Fails to Convince Vancouver Library Board to Rent Space; Seminar to Discuss Suicide may Contravene Canadian Laws, Legal Advisers Tell VPL," *Vancouver Sun,* October 21, 2009, A6, ProQuest.

fetishists can look pretty blurry at times."[221] And self-described pro-life feminist Naomi Lakritz wrote an opinion piece in the *Calgary Herald* arguing that the library rejecting the seminar is not a suppression of free speech because "it is the library's prerogative to decide what things it will allow on its premises."[222] However, based on the examples that we've seen so far, many librarians would disagree with that argument. She also contended that if the library has a copy of *Mein Kampf* it is not obligated to rent rooms to neo-Nazi groups,[223] but some might argue that VPL had done so by allowing the CFSL to use its rooms a number of times.

On the other side of the issue, a *Vancouver Sun* letter to the editor from a Criminology professor criticized the library, saying that "[w]hen trusted institutions censor talk about suicide, not only do they undermine the core values on which they are built, they diminish our humanity."[224] Another letter to the editor in the *Vancouver Province* and an opinion piece in the *Kamloops Daily News* did not focus on the library or questions of freedom of speech, but did express support for the work of Exit International and the right-to-die movement.[225] In the end, a Unitarian Church hosted the workshop on November 4, 2009, with up to 100 attendees expected,[226] and–as expected by the church, Exit International, and the BCCLA–the workshops proceeded without legal incident.[227] Reverend Steven Epperson spoke about the reasoning behind the decision to host the event, explaining that, "[h]istorically, we have provided a forum, a space, for controversial, difficult ideas to be presented," and noting their neutrality: "It does not mean in any way endorsement."[228] These are the same

---

221 "The Pro-Death Lobby," *Ottawa Citizen*, September 23, 2009, A12, ProQuest.

222 Naomi Lakritz, "Booking Space to Help People Check Out Not a Right," *Calgary Herald*, September 23, 2009, A12, ProQuest.

223 Lakritz, "Booking Space to Help People Check Out Not a Right."

224 Russel Ogden, letter to the editor, *Vancouver Sun*, September 29, 2009, A6, ProQuest.

225 Mary Beaussart, letter to the editor, *The Province*, October 28, 2009, A17, ProQuest; David Charbonneau, "When Life is Intolerable, Why Not a Graceful Exit?" *Kamloops Daily News*, October 22, 2009, A7, ProQuest.

226 John Bermingham, "Church Hosts Right-to-Die Doctor; Library Rejects Assisted-Suicide Advocate on Advice from Lawyers," *The Province*, October 25, 2009, A3, ProQuest.

227 Les Perreaux, "Ad Campaign for Assisted Suicide Banned from Canadian Airwaves," *The Globe and Mail*, September 27, 2010, A6, ProQuest.

228 Bermingham, "Church Hosts Right-to-Die Doctor."

reasons we have heard from libraries in defending their decisions to allow controversial events in their spaces, as David Eby of the BCCLA pointed out: "Usually, librarians are our closest allies in this free-speech debate."[229]

As an aside, here's a little ditty about Exit International and the Toronto Public Library. On July 23, 2010, TPL refused a booking for an Exit International workshop at one of their branches.[230] Toronto Library Divisional Support Manager Heather Mathis informed the group via email that their booking was rejected based on legal counsel, as was the case in Vancouver the previous year, because it would be "contrary to the law or the Library's Rules of Conduct."[231] And again, like in Vancouver, they were able to book the event at a Unitarian Church instead.[232] There was no evidence of public outcry surrounding the workshop rejection by the library, which is why I am not discussing it in detail or counting it in my controversial event bookings, but there was opposition to an ad campaign by Exit International.[233] In response, Dr. Nitschke said: "The ban on the ad and the opposition to the presentation seems predicated on the idea that the only reason we remain on this planet is because we can't figure out a way out of it. It's a bizarre concept and extremely paternalistic."[234]

2012 Belleville, Ontario

The Belleville Public Library created a controversy with an event featuring *Globe and Mail* crime journalist Timothy Appleby set to speak about his book, *A New Kind of Monster*, on October 20, 2012. The book is about convicted murderer Colonel Russell Williams and the crimes he committed in the Belleville area the previous year, and the library's press release for the event invited attendees "to share Appleby's unique perspective on the dark and violent crimes that shocked

---

229 Bermingham.

230 Exit International, "Toronto Public Library Censors Euthanasia Meeting," August 22, 2010, https://exitinternational.net/media/MRCanada810.pdf.

231 "Toronto Public Library Censors Euthanasia Meeting."

232 Perreaux, "Ad Campaign for Assisted Suicide Banned from Canadian Airwaves."

233 Perreaux.

234 Perreaux, "Ad Campaign for Assisted Suicide Banned from Canadian Airwaves."

our community and the killer who perpetrated them."[235] Public outcry came in the form of phone calls and emails to the library asking them to cancel the event, suggesting it was insensitive and inappropriate for the library to book the author: "It just reopens the wounds of the families," said one library patron.[236] An informal online poll by *The Intelligencer* newspaper found 56% of the 250 voters were opposed to the event.[237] Andy Lloyd, whose sister Jessica was killed by Williams, said he also received calls from people who were not pleased with the library's planned event, and he met with the library board to discuss the issue.[238] City Councillor Egerton Boyce also expressed his desire for the event to be reconsidered, but fellow councillor and chair of the library board, Garnet Thompson was neutral on the subject, stating that the booking was an "operational matter" for which the library CEO and staff are responsible.[239]

The library initially tried to defend the event, as CEO Trevor Pross said that Appleby was approached by the previous library CEO prior to the publication of the book and the event was not meant to discuss the Williams case but would "examine different aspects of writing."[240] However, the press release for the event clearly states it is about the book and his investigation of the Williams crimes, so that explanation was widely rejected. Pross also noted that the library did receive some calls in support of the freedom of speech aspect of the controversy,[241] and an opinion piece in *The Intelligencer* was in favour of the event going forward because to cancel would be "small-minded censorship" and people have the choice not to attend.[242] *The Intelligencer* editors disagreed in an editorial, arguing that while Appleby has the

---

235 W. Brice McVicar, "Library Appearance may Get Rough Review," *The Intelligencer*, October 12, 2012, ProQuest.

236 McVicar, "Library Appearance may Get Rough Review"; Taylor Renkema, "Library Cancels Williams' Book Author's Appearance," QNet News, October 18, 2012, http://www.qnetnews.ca/?p=28502; W. Brice McVicar, "Author's Library Visit Called Off," *The Intelligencer*, October 19, 2012, ProQuest.

237 Glenn May-Anderson, "Who Decides what's Best for Us?" *The Intelligencer*, October 13, 2012, ProQuest.

238 McVicar, "Author's Library Visit Called Off."

239 McVicar, "Library Appearance may Get Rough Review."

240 McVicar, "Library Appearance may Get Rough Review."

241 McVicar, "Author's Library Visit Called Off."

242 May-Anderson, "Who Decides what's Best for Us?"

right to write and promote this book and the library has the right to hold this event, that does not mean it is the right thing to do: "As a facility not only funded by taxpayer dollars but one that aspires to be a community leader, the library has failed miserably in this case."[243]

The Belleville Public Library Board did consider the issue at their October 16 meeting, but after a lengthy debate, the motion to cancel the event was denied.[244] However, afterward CEO Trevor Pross made the decision to cancel it based on community feedback, and board chair Thompson supported the decision, asserting that the cancellation was not infringing on Appleby's freedom of speech because the library has his book available for circulation.[245] On that point, Pross said: "There's criticism we might face for turning an author away when we are a library that welcomes various viewpoints. That's not the main concern in this issue though, it's causing that pain to people. We just had to respect that."[246] That position and the concern expressed by the general public is quite the contrast from what we have seen in most of the other examples of controversial events where discrimination and hate were involved. In this case, great care and concern were being shown for the community's feelings and healing, which were prioritized. Interestingly, I was unable to find any library association or free speech advocacy statements on this issue. Is that because the library had the book in its collection so it was not limiting freedom of expression, as the library CEO argued? Is that because the event was booked by the library itself, so it was their right to cancel it without it being considered censorship by the professional library and free speech communities, as opposed to if the library cancelled a book event from a third party? Does that make the difference? Or was it too small a controversy and did not catch their attention?

---

243 "Library Again Shows It's Out of Touch," *The Intelligencer*, October 13, 2012, ProQuest.

244 The Minutes of the Regular Meeting of the Belleville Public Library Board, October 16, 2012, Belleville, https://www.bellevillelibrary.ca/photos/custom/Lib%20Documents/Minutes%20Regular%20Committee%2016%20Oct%202012.pdf; Renkema, "Library Cancels Williams' Book Author's Appearance."

245 Renkema, "Library Cancels Williams' Book Author's Appearance."

246 McVicar, "Author's Library Visit Called Off."

2013 Ottawa, Ontario

There was a protest outside the main branch of Ottawa Public Library (OPL) on February 4, 2013, over an event on the topic of blocking the construction of mosques. A group called ACT! For Canada, which describes itself as focusing on Canadian democratic values, organized the event featuring self-proclaimed "mosque-buster" Gavin Boby, a UK lawyer who promotes legal tactics to prevent the construction of mosques.[247] He claims to have successfully blocked 16 mosques out of 17 challenges using his strategy of focusing on municipal code issues and avoiding political issues that could lead to accusations of Islamophobia,[248] but he spoke freely about the reasons behind his opposition to mosques: "Increasingly what we are seeing now is self-declared Muslim areas where you get Muslim patrols saying you can't walk a dog, wear a skirt."[249] One of the ACT! event organizers, Janice Fiamengo (who we will see again later in 2018), wrote a letter to the editor in the *Ottawa Citizen* defending Boby as "a reasonable person concerned about community safety," but then went on to state that mosques ruin neighbourhoods by turning them into "Islamic no-go areas... where campaigns of harassment and bodily attack are directed against non-Muslim residents," and that "[m]any [mosques] are centres of jihadist activity."[250]

Boby failed to avoid accusations of Islamophobia, as the Canadian Council on American-Islamic Relations (CAIR-CAN) called him "openly Islamophobic" and an "anti-Muslim hate-monger" and called on the library to cancel his speaking engagement because it will violate the library's rules prohibiting violations of the Canadian Criminal Code and the Ontario Human Rights Code in library spaces.[251] CAIR-CAN's Executive Director Ihsaan Gardee also argued that, "[b]y affording someone like this who has this kind of message, a publicly-funded taxpayer

---

247 Glen McGregor, "Muslim Group Wants Lawyer's Speech Nixed; Controversial British 'Mosquebuster' Slated to Talk at Library," *Ottawa Citizen*, February 4, 2013, ProQuest.

248 McGregor, "Muslim Group Wants Lawyer's Speech Nixed."

249 "Anti-Mosque Lawyer Speaks in Ottawa Despite Protests," *CBC*, February 4, 2013, https://www.cbc.ca/news/canada/ottawa/anti-mosque-lawyer-speaks-in-ottawa-despite-protests-1.1300508.

250 Janice Fiamengo, "Gavin Boby Not Misguided," *Ottawa Citizen*, February 4, 2013, ProQuest.

251 McGregor, "Muslim Group Wants Lawyer's Speech Nixed."

venue, it adds and gives credibility to their message."[252] In response to CAIR-CAN's concerns, the library reminded ACT! of their policy and notified police of the event.[253] OPL CEO Danielle McDonald emphasized the library's neutral position: "We are not sponsoring this event, let's be clear on that,"[254] and library board chair Jan Harder affirmed the need to preserve freedom of speech and said the event could only be stopped if a law was broken.[255] But the public was not pleased, as the library received hundreds of emails demanding the event be cancelled.[256]

With the event proceeding, CAIR-CAN planned an interfaith gathering to speak out against Islamophobia in public institutions for 6 pm outside the library, including speakers representing Ottawa's Jewish, Quaker, Muslim, and United Church communities.[257] There were no reports of violence or disruption at the event, and inside between 40 and 60 people attended,[258] including some who opposed Boby's perspective. Lawyer Ernie Tannis spoke up during the Q&A period to ask why Boby does not focus on radicals, who he pointed out exist within all faith groups, instead of condemning all Muslims.[259] And Caryma Sa'd, a law student who was wearing a hijab along with two other audience members, described Boby's talk as "despicable" and said she was "disappointed" that the library allowed it.[260]

In looking for other public commentary on the event, I found an opinion piece in the *Ottawa Citizen* co-written by Fred Litwin, president of the Free Thinking Film Society, and author Salim Mansur, who were critical of Boby for conflating Islam with more radical Islamism, but

---

252 "Anti-Mosque Lawyer Speaks in Ottawa Despite Protests."

253 McGregor, "Muslim Group Wants Lawyer's Speech Nixed."

254 McGregor, "Muslim Group Wants Lawyer's Speech Nixed."

255 "Anti-Mosque Lawyer Speaks in Ottawa Despite Protests."

256 "Anti-Mosque Lawyer Speaks in Ottawa Despite Protests."

257 CAIR, "CAIR-CAN: Interfaith Community to Speak Out Against Islamophobic Speech at Public Institutions", *Facebook*, February 4, 2013, https://www.facebook.com/notes/10157988379592695/.

258 "Anti-Mosque Lawyer Speaks in Ottawa Despite Protests" says 40; Zev Singer, "Anti-Mosque Talk Causes No Fuss; British Lawyer Gavin Boby Draws Small Crowd," *Ottawa Citizen*, February 5, 2013, ProQuest says 60.

259 Singer, "Anti-Mosque Talk Causes No Fuss."

260 Singer.

they did not mention the library.[261] I also found a blog post containing the text of what is said to have been another *Ottawa Citizen* opinion, but I was unable to locate it at the source. That piece also did not have anything to say about the library, but accused CAIR-CAN of "hypocrisy," contending that "Non-Muslims pay taxes too. What if they want to hear the mosquebuster speech?"[262] A post on the blog *Islamophobia Watch* called the library's position on the matter "a disgrace" and suggested that Islamophobia is broadly accepted in Canada, arguing that "[i]f Boby's hate-propaganda was directed against the Jewish rather than the Muslim community, it is difficult to believe that the same shallow arguments about freedom of speech would be advanced in defence of his right to address a meeting at a publicly-funded institution."[263] However, we have seen historical examples of libraries using free speech arguments to allow events to proceed despite claims of antisemitic views being shared. A few weeks after the Boby event, a small group gathered for a different event at the OPL main branch, this time to hear Muslim missionaries speak, where they were critical of the library for allowing Boby to spread hate speech.[264]

2013 Guelph, Ontario

A *Guelph Mercury* opinion piece on April 17, 2013 that opposed Enbridge's proposed pipeline changes to Line 9 between Sarnia and Montreal, announced that there would be an "apply-a-thon" at the main branch of the Guelph Public Library the following day to assist members of the public in filling out the 10-page paperwork required to give feedback about the pipeline proposal to the National Energy Board.[265] That is how the library found out about this event that was set to take

---

261 Fred Litwin and Salim Mansur, "Mistaking Islamism for Islam; Too Many Who Oppose Fanaticism End Up Supporting the Islamist View that Muslims Cannot be Moderate," *Ottawa Citizen*, January 29, 2013, ProQuest.

262 KGS, "Op-Ed in Ottawa Citizen on CAIR-CAN Opposition to Gavin Boby: Smacks of Intimidation," *The Tundra Tabloids* (blog), February 5, 2013, https://tundratabloids.com/2013/02/05/op-ed-in-ottawa-citizen-on-cair-can-opposition-to-gavin-boby-smacks-of-intimidation/.

263 Bob Pitt, "Gavin Boby Addresses Small Meeting at Ottawa Public Library," *Islamophobia Watch* (blog), February 5, 2013, http://islamophobiawatch.co.uk/gavin-boby-addresses-small-meeting-at-ottowa-public-library/.

264 Vito Pilieci, "Muslim Missionaries Protest Boby's Speech; Lawyer's Criticisms Provocative, Clerics Say," *Ottawa Citizen*, February 25, 2013, ProQuest.

265 "Guelph Library to be Site of 'Apply-a-Thon'," *Guelph Mercury*, April 17, 2013, A6, ProQuest.

place at their branch, because a room had not been booked for it, and the event organizers, the Guelph Anti-Pipeline Action Group (GAP), had not notified nor requested permission from any library staff.[266]

News of the event prompted a small political debate around questions of politics in the public library and free speech. Former City Councillor David Birtwistle wrote an email to the mayor and city council and copied to the *Mercury* questioning whether such a political event was appropriate to take place in the library: "Surely such political activities do not fall within the (library's) mandate?"[267] And in an interview he asserted: "That's a political matter and it shouldn't be in the library. That ain't the place to protest."[268] Then Councillor Ian Findlay responded to that email arguing that "[t]he Guelph Public Library strongly supports free speech and critical thinking in our community. We would not welcome political interference or censorship." He added in an interview: "I encourage free speech throughout our community," and he had no problem with this or other events in the library, excluding those that "promot[e] hatred or violence."[269] However, in response to the planned event, the library's Assistant CEO Cathy McInnis affirmed that the library tries to maintain a neutral and non-partisan position by not allowing political messages or events, assuring: "If we had known [about the event], we probably would have said that's not something we would allow at the library. It definitely wouldn't be something we would have sanctioned."[270]

GAP swiftly moved the event to another venue "due to a perceived conflict of interest" in holding it at the library,[271] allowing all involved to avoid a bigger controversy. An editorial from the *Guelph Mercury* written afterward demonstrates how minor this controversy was, as its biggest argument was that the library should require users to request to use space for certain kinds of events and then review those

---

266 "Pipeline Protest Planned for Guelph Library Spurs Criticism," *Guelph Mercury*, April 17, 2013, https://www.guelphmercury.com/news-story/2785883-pipeline-protest-planned-for-guelph-library-spurs-criticism/.

267 "Pipeline Protest Planned for Guelph Library Spurs Criticism."

268 "Pipeline Protest Planned for Guelph Library Spurs Criticism."

269 "Pipeline Protest Planned for Guelph Library Spurs Criticism."

270 "Pipeline Protest Planned for Guelph Library Spurs Criticism."

271 "Pipeline Protest Planned for Guelph Library Spurs Criticism."

requests according to its policies.²⁷² It also said: "Our libraries should be a resource where thinking and intelligent discussion are promoted. But it needs to be a controlled community asset as well for a host of reasons."²⁷³ This response is quite mild when compared with some of the other strong opinions we have seen around issues of politics and free speech in the library, but it is also interesting and important to note that this local paper is going against the trend we have seen by arguing for firmer control over how the public uses the library space.

2013 Waterloo, Ontario

Governor General's Award-winning author David Gilmour was scheduled for a speaking engagement about his new and, at the time, Giller Prize long-listed book, *Extraordinary*, at the Waterloo Public Library on Sept 30, 2013, organized by a local bookstore called Words Worth Books.²⁷⁴ However, Gilmour sparked a controversy a few days earlier when he explained to Hazlitt magazine his lack of interest in reading or teaching the works of Chinese and women writers (except Virginia Woolf!) in his role as English instructor at the University of Toronto.²⁷⁵ He faced significant criticism for his offensive comments, including from some U of T professors, English Department Chair Paul Stevens, who was upset and appalled,²⁷⁶ and over 100 people who rallied at the university to protest Gilmour and highlight problems of inequality in academic reading lists.²⁷⁷ Yet some other faculty and authors, including Margaret Atwood, defended Gilmour's free speech rights.²⁷⁸ Gilm-

---

272   Phil Andrews, ed., "Library Can Learn Lesson From Protest Debate," *Guelph Mercury*, April 22, 2013, https://www.neighbourhoodgroup.com/downloads/local-food-has-great-legs.pdf.

273   Andrews, ed., "Library Can Learn Lesson From Protest Debate."

274   Liz Monteiro, "Gilmour Cancels Waterloo Event: Move Follows Outcry Over Hot-Button Remarks," *Waterloo Region Record*, September 28, 2013, ProQuest.

275   Emily M. Keeler, interview with David Gilmour, *Shelf Esteem*, Hazlitt, September 25, 2013, https://hazlitt.net/blog/gilmour-transcript.

276   Monteiro, "Gilmour Cancels Waterloo Event"; Holger Syme, "David Gilmour's No Colleague of Mine," *Huff Post* (blog), September 26, 2013, https://www.huffpost.com/archive/ca/entry/holger-syme-david-gilmour_b_3996818.

277   Sandro Contenta and Chown Oved Marco, "Students Rally in Protest of Gilmour's Reading Lists: Others Defend Academic Freedom as Fallout Continues from Professor's Remarks," *Toronto Star*, September 28, 2013, ProQuest.

278   Contenta and Marco, "Students Rally in Protest of Gilmour's Reading Lists."

our apologized for "the mess that this has caused" and for using words carelessly.[279]

This left the bookstore in a tricky situation, as Words Worth Books co-owner David Worsley was reluctant to cancel the event because "he was not in the business of censorship," but then announced that it was cancelled because "the timing is not right for an event."[280] Initially Worsley said that the bookstore and the library made the decision to cancel together, but later the same day he said it was the store's decision to ask Gilmour's publisher for him to "graciously decline" the speaking engagement given the circumstances, and the publisher agreed.[281] Worsley elaborated on the reasons behind the cancellation: "It would no longer be about books, arts and the humanities. It would just be a circus," and they could not afford to be associated with Gilmour's comments.[282]

There was not a big public outcry over the event cancellation and no political interventions or policy implications. One student from the University of Waterloo who was a coordinator for The Women's Centre on campus said that although she did not approve of Gilmour's comments, she also did not support banning him from speaking about his book.[283] Whereas a letter to the editor argued that it is up to the promoter who they choose to sponsor for speaking engagements and the bookstore was justified in cancelling and disassociating themselves from Gilmour.[284] This is an exceptional event, the only one where the organizer cancelled the event due to controversy. Since the bookstore booked it and then cancelled it, does that also cancel out the question of intellectual freedom being denied? The *Waterloo Region Record* did not think so, as they published an editorial criticizing Words Worth Books for the cancellation and suggesting the library had been involved in that "ridiculous decision."[285] In it they asked: "Isn't a free

---

279 Monteiro, "Gilmour Cancels Waterloo Event"

280 Monteiro.

281 Monteiro.

282 Monteiro.

283 Monteiro.

284 Jennifer Ghent-Fuller, letter to the editor, *Waterloo Region Record*, October 7, 2013, ProQuest.

285 "Gilmour Should Have Spoken Here," *Waterloo Region Record*, October 1, 2013, A6, ProQuest.

exchange of ideas worth defending for a bookstore and a library?" and offered that if the event had taken place and if protestors had showed up, "[m]aybe everyone could have had an intelligent discussion and come away with a better understanding of someone else's way of thinking."[286]

2013 Vancouver, British Columbia

To memorialize the 14 women engineering students who were killed in the misogynist École Polytechnique massacre of 1989, the Vancouver Rape Relief and Women's Shelter (VRR) held an annual event at the Vancouver Public Library. However, in 2013, their inclusion of Janice Raymond in the program with a talk titled "Prostitution: Not a Job, not a Choice"[287] generated a controversy. According to my research, this controversial event did not get covered by the mainstream media, but I did find online discussion about the issues involved as well as a lengthy statement from VPL, so I have chosen to include it, as the controversy was significant enough to prompt a public statement from the library.

Established in 1973, VRR is Canada's longest running rape crisis centre, and its transition house shelter opened in 1981.[288] It focuses its services on people who were "born females and raised as girls into our current womanhood" and engages in advocacy to end prostitution.[289] The centre is no stranger to controversy, as it was the subject of a BC Human Rights Tribunal complaint in 1995, which it ultimately won through appeal in the courts.[290] Janice Raymond, professor emerita of Women, Gender, Sexuality Studies at the University of

---

286 "Gilmour Should Have Spoken Here."

287 "Montreal Massacre Memorial 2013–Program," Vancouver Rape Relief & Women's Shelter, November 30, 2013, https://web.archive.org/web/20171021153903/http://www.rapereliefshelter.bc.ca/learn/resources/montreal-massacre-memorial-2013-program.

288 "What We Do and Who We Serve," Vancouver Rape Relief & Women's Shelter, n.d., https://rapereliefshelter.bc.ca/who-we-serve-and-what-we-do/.

289 "What We Do and Who We Serve."

290 Shannon Rupp, "Transsexual Loses Latest Bid to Counsel Victims of Rape," *The Globe and Mail*, December 8, 2005, https://www.theglobeandmail.com/news/national/transsexual-loses-latest-bid-to-counsel-victims-of-rape/article990772/. I will also note that in 2019, VRR did not receive municipal funding based on its policy of excluding trans women from its services; Emad Agahi, "Vancouver Cuts Funding to Rape Crisis Centre Over Policy Excluding Transgender Women," *CTV News*, March 16, 2019, https://bc.ctvnews.ca/vancouver-cuts-funding-to-rape-crisis-centre-over-policy-excluding-transgender-women-1.4339524.

Massachusetts Amherst,[291] is also a controversial figure for her trans-exclusionary views, having written and lectured against transgender rights, as well as against sex work and sex trafficking.

The first sign of opposition to Raymond speaking at this event in a library space came from someone known as El Feministo who sent an open letter to the VPL board and VRR, and posted it online on rabble.ca.[292] In the letter, El Feministo listed their many problems with VRR and Raymond, arguing that many of Raymond's controversial opinions have been widely criticized and debunked and accusing VRR of "a politics of exclusion reified into a praxis of hate."[293] However, the letter, "motivated by values promoting civil discourse in a vibrant public sphere," recognized the right of VRR to hold the event but asked that "space be made available to both transgender communities and sex work communities to respond to Ms. Raymond."[294] The letter writer referenced the library's meeting room policy's inclusion of the BC Human Rights Code and the library's Diversity and Inclusion statement to support the call for VPL to include voices that Raymond and VRR exclude.[295] In the comment discussion of the letter on rabble.ca, El Feministo went into more detail about their concerns that by having Raymond give this particular talk at an event meant to memorialize the victims of the École Polytechnique massacre, VRR "is exploiting a tragedy to promote its own political agenda." El Feministo, further asserted their appreciation of intellectual freedom.[296] They also added in the comments that they received a response from VPL that explained the

---

291 "Emeriti Faculty," University of Massachusetts Amherst, n.d., https://www.umass.edu/wgss/emeriti-faculty-wgss.

292 El Feministo, "Janice Raymond at Vancouver Public Library Montreal Massacre Memorial," Feminism, Rabble.ca, November 19, 2013, https://babble.rabble.ca/babble/feminism/janice-raymond-vancouver-public-library-montreal-massacre-memorial.

293 El Feministo, "Janice Raymond at Vancouver Public Library Montreal Massacre Memorial."

294 El Feministo, "Janice Raymond at Vancouver Public Library Montreal Massacre Memorial."

295 El Feministo, "Janice Raymond at Vancouver Public Library Montreal Massacre Memorial."

296 El Feministo, November 20, 2013 (9:36 p.m.), comment on Vancouver Rape Relief, "Vancouver Rape Relief is exploiting a tragedy to promote its own political agenda," https://babble.rabble.ca/babble/feminism/janice-raymond-vancouver-public-library-montreal-massacre-memorial#forum-topic-top.

VRR event was a third-party public space rental and the library does not endorse it, which they accepted.[297]

VPL Chief Librarian Sandra Singh also released a public statement that said: "there has been significant concern expressed to the library" about Raymond speaking, and went on to discuss the common explanations of library neutrality, freedom of speech, and the rules and legal codes in its room booking policy.[298] Singh said that, based on the concerns raised about the event, the library confirmed with VRR that they would not contravene the Canadian Criminal Code or BC Human Rights Code, which the library considers its "litmus tests for the limits of free speech because we have to make space for all ideas in our community as per the Charter of Rights and Freedoms."[299] And in responding to El Feministo's call for oppositional voices to be included, Singh affirmed that "VPL cares deeply about respecting the diversity of our community" and invited "any community group to propose a program partnership with VPL that they would like to see."[300] Perhaps the library could have done more to demonstrate their respect for community concerns by being proactive and initiating such partnerships with community groups to achieve diversity and inclusion.

VRR released a statement defending their choice to include Raymond's talk as part of their annual memorial event and noted that they had received many letters of support and donations in light of the event controversy.[301] They stated that the event features topics about "the most pressing issues," noting that the debate around prostitution was an important and current issue that the Supreme Court of Canada was deciding at the time, and because the event focuses on "end[ing] male

---

297 El Feministo, November 20, 2013 (3:49 p.m.), comment on Vancouver Public Library, "For VPL, this is essentially a room rental," https://babble.rabble.ca/babble/feminism/janice-raymond-vancouver-public-library-montreal-massacre-memorial#forum-topic-top.

298 "VPL Statement Regarding Speaker Janice Raymond at Vancouver Rape Relief Event at the Central Library," Vancouver Public Library, November 22, 2013, https://web.archive.org/web/20170421094531/https://www.vpl.ca/news/details/vpl_statement_regarding_speaker_janice_raymond_at_vancouver_rape_relief_eve.

299 "VPL Statement Regarding Speaker Janice Raymond at Vancouver Rape Relief Event at the Central Library."

300 "VPL Statement Regarding Speaker Janice Raymond at Vancouver Rape Relief Event at the Central Library."

301 "Statement Regarding Dr. Janice Raymond Speak at the Montreal Massacre Memorial," Vancouver Rape Relief & Women's Shelter, November 22, 2013, https://rapereliefshelter.bc.ca/statement-regarding-dr-janice-raymond-speak-at-the-montreal-massacre-memorial/.

violence against women," it was a valid choice to include Raymond "to speak about her extensive equality-seeking work on prostitution as a form of violence against women."[302] In a rabble.ca article about the controversy, one of the event organizers, Hilla Kerner, spoke more about the connection between the topic of prostitution and the memorial for victims of male violence against women, while a sex worker and sex work advocate named Katrina Caudle criticized Raymond's and VRR's approach to sex work, arguing that "[a]bolition removes my right to choose."[303]

I found no evidence of political debate around the event and very little from the library professional world. The unofficial blog of the BCLA Intellectual Freedom Committee had a post about the event, talking through the conflict that librarians can sometimes feel between intellectual freedom and other competing rights, using a series of tweets by VPL librarian Tara Robertson as the basis.[304] Tara had tweeted that she felt conflict between her professional value of intellectual freedom and her personal values that opposed Raymond's perspectives about trans people and sex work, and she decided to use her personal time to attend a protest of the event, exercising her own intellectual freedom.[305] The BCLA blogger appreciated Robertson's honesty and her decision, asserting that "[w]e librarians aren't neutral grey blocks of matter! We have values of our own!"[306] The blog argued that it is problematic how these public debates around preserving freedom of expression for controversial opinions remain academic:

> "Looking at the law as some sort of dispassionate arbitrator here works for privileged folks like myself, and I can take the intellectual freedom stuff as my primary value in the discussion. 'It's not illegal so it's fine!' I could say, dust off my hands and be done with it. For others, who see and feel the effects of speech that is hateful but

---

302 "Statement Regarding Dr. Janice Raymond Speak at the Montreal Massacre Memorial."

303 Mercedes Allen, "Memorial Draws Controversy Over Invitation of Speaker Janice Raymond," Rabble, November 29, 2013, https://rabble.ca/feminism/memorial-draws-controversy-over-invitation-speaker-janice-raymond/.

304 jjackunrau, "On Janice Raymond and the Value of More Speech," *The (Unofficial) BCLA Intellectual Freedom Committee Blog* (blog), November 29, 2008, https://bclaifc.wordpress.com/2013/11/29/on-janice-raymond-and-the-value-of-more-speech/.

305 jjackunrau, "On Janice Raymond and the Value of More Speech."

306 jjackunrau.

might not legally be hate speech this might not be just an academic issue, but something more."

And that is the point that marginalized groups protesting hateful speech, if not legally-deemed hate speech, have been trying to make in many of these stories. But the blog post ended in favour of intellectual freedom for both sides, thanked the library "for giving a space to all sorts of opinions," and encouraged librarians to "show up to listen/talk/shout."[307]

The event went ahead on November 30, 2013. There were some discussions of counter-events or public protests, including a planned video demonstration by activist Morgane Oger, but these discussions and plans were complicated by organizers' reluctance to protest the memorial out of respect for the massacre victims, and an unwillingness to participate in a similar political co-optation of that tragedy as VRR had been accused of.[308]

2017 Saskatoon, Saskatchewan

The Saskatoon public library generated some controversy when it cancelled an event booked for January 28, 2017 at its Alice Turner branch due to planned protests of the event. Saskatoon MP and Conservative leadership candidate Brad Trost was scheduled to speak about "respect for life" and other topics at an event organized by an anti-abortion group called the Campaign Life Coalition of Saskatchewan, so a Facebook event emerged to encourage abortion rights supporters to attend the event in protest, with about 50 people planning to attend.[309] According to the library, the event was originally booked by an unnamed group for "a day of reflection," and they only learned of the actual event plans from a protest organizer requesting they cancel the event based on the content, which they refused, citing freedom

---

307 jjackunrau.

308 Allen, "Memorial Draws Controversy Over Invitation of Speaker Janice Raymond."

309 Stephanie Levitz, "Saskatoon Library Refuses to Let MP Brad Trost Hold Anti-Abortion Meeting," *CBC*, January 26, 2017, https://www.cbc.ca/news/politics/saskatoon-library-brad-trost-anti-abortion-meeting-1.3954098.

of speech.[310] Trost's campaign said that the event evolved from him speaking as a guest of the anti-abortion group into a campaign event organized by his team.[311] However, the library was never notified about any of this. This is the first but not the last example we will see of a group booking a library meeting room without providing full details of who is booking the room and for what purpose. It could be seen as a tactic to delay or prevent attention to the event from the library and public.

When the library did find out, they decided to cancel the event because its "controversial nature" was going to cause protests that the library could not handle.[312] SPL CEO Carol Cooley said: "We're just not equipped with staff, security, space to manage a protest against Mr. Trost," and while she assured that "[i]t has nothing to do with his views; we definitely back intellectual freedom and the Charter of Rights and Freedoms," she also noted that if the library had known the nature of the event at the time of the booking, they might have refused it based on the likelihood of protest.[313] The library cited its "safe use bylaw," which forbids activities that have "the effect of disturbing other patrons or library staff or preventing or hindering their use and enjoyment of library facilities" in the cancellation decision.[314] Invoking this policy in this decision, thereby prioritizing library patron and staff safety over intellectual freedom is an interesting and uncommon approach, although it could be seen as similar to the Belleville Public Library's decision to prioritize the community's feelings over intellectual freedom (however, that was the library's own booking and not a third-party event). Both examples demonstrate libraries choosing to override the value of intellectual freedom, in one case based on logistics and safety, in the other based on community values.

---

310 "Statement Regarding Library Safe Use," Saskatchewan Public Library, January 27, 2017, https://web.archive.org/web/20190606070923/https://saskatoonlibrary.ca/sites/default/files/Statement%20on%20Library%20Safe%20Use%20January%2027.pdf; Levitz, "Saskatoon Library Refuses to Let MP Brad Trost Hold Anti-Abortion Meeting"; "Saskatoon Library Defends Cancelling Brad Trost's Anti-Abortion Meeting," *CBC*, January 27, 2017, https://www.cbc.ca/news/canada/saskatoon/mp-brad-trost-saskatoon-library-cancelling-1.3955605; "Saskatoon Public Library Responds to Cancellation of Brad Trost Campaign Event," 650 CKOM, January 27, 2017, https://www.ckom.com/2017/01/27/saskatoon-public-library-responds-to-cancellation-of-brad-trost-campaign-event/.

311 Levitz, "Saskatoon Library Refuses to Let MP Brad Trost Hold Anti-Abortion Meeting."

312 Levitz.

313 Levitz, "Saskatoon Library Refuses to Let MP Brad Trost Hold Anti-Abortion Meeting."

314 Levitz.

Trost did not accept the library's reasoning, however, and he argued that anti-abortion views were not very controversial in Saskatoon, so the event was unlikely to provoke an unmanageable protest.[315] And if security were such a concern, the library could have let his team know and they could have provided security.[316] He accused the library of playing politics and expressed frustration that his event was being cancelled when it was the protestors who were creating the security concerns: "It wasn't us that caused the security [problem], so why are we the ones being punished?"[317] Cooley did apologize for having used the phrase "controversial nature" to describe the event in her initial communication about the cancellation,[318] but the library stuck with its decision. University of Saskatchewan law professor Ken Norman said the library did not violate Trost's freedom of speech rights, because the cancellation was not based on the content of the event and they had a policy in place that supported their decision.[319]

The Campaign Life Coalition of Saskatchewan did not release any public statements about the library's cancellation that I could find, and the event was relocated to a Saskatoon hotel requiring advanced seat reservations.[320] The protest organizers planned to protest at the hotel, but would have to do it across the street since it is private property, and they encouraged protestors to use fake names to register and attend the event in order to bring a pro-choice perspective into the discussion.[321] In the end, there was not a protest at the event, according to the CBC, but some attendees did question Trost's views against abortion and same-sex marriage.[322] Trost then tweeted asking the library, "where is the disruption? Where is the security threat? Where

---

315 Levitz.

316 "Saskatoon Public Library Responds to Cancellation of Brad Trost Campaign Event."

317 "Saskatoon Public Library Responds to Cancellation of Brad Trost Campaign Event."

318 "Statement Regarding Library Safe Use."

319 "Saskatoon Library Didn't Violate Brad Trost's Freedom of Speech, Says U of S Prof," *CBC*, January 30, 2017, https://www.cbc.ca/news/canada/saskatoon/brad-trost-freedom-of-speech-1.3958652.

320 "Saskatoon Library Defends Cancelling Brad Trost's Anti-Abortion Meeting."

321 Levitz, "Saskatoon Library Refuses to Let MP Brad Trost Hold Anti-Abortion Meeting."

322 "No Protests As Brad Trost Meets With Anti-Abortion Supporters," *CBC*, January 28, 2017, https://www.cbc.ca/news/canada/saskatoon/brad-trost-anti-abortion-no-protest-1.3957044.

is our apology?"[323] But I did not find any public record of an apology from the library, nor any discussion of policy changes in light of the controversy.

2017 Edmonton, Alberta

Edmonton Public Library hosted two controversial speakers as part of their 2017 Forward Thinking Speaker Series, but neither speaker was controversial when they were originally booked.[324] Joseph Boyden had been booked for an event to take place on April 27 as part of the EPL series when news broke in December of 2016 challenging his claims to Indigenous ancestry and accusing him of cultural appropriation and identity fraud in exploiting Indigenous experiences as the basis for his literary success.[325] The City of Edmonton had also booked Boyden to speak at their Winter Cities Shake-Up Conference in February, but in light of the news, the city consulted with local Indigenous leaders and decided to cancel his appearance so as not to distract from the focus of the conference.[326] The library, on the other hand, kept Boyden's speaking engagement, stating that they had consulted with the community, including their Indigenous relations advisor and incoming Elder-in-residence, and they asserted that Boyden was not invited "as an authoritative voice on Indigenous issues, but rather as a celebrated Canadian author."[327] It is interesting that the library was able to separate those two facets of Boyden given that his celebrated writing was considered an authoritative voice on Indigenous issues.

---

323 "No Protests As Brad Trost Meets With Anti-Abortion Supporters."

324 Alvin M. Schrader, "Can Public Libraries Maintain Their Commitment to Intellectual Freedom in the Face of Outrage over Unpopular Speakers?" Centre for Free Expression (blog), August 15, 2019, https://cfe.ryerson.ca/blog/2019/08/can-public-libraries-maintain-their-commitment-intellectual-freedom-face-outrage-over. Alvin Schrader lists Salman Rushdie's lecture in the 2016 Forward Thinking Speaker Series as a controversial event, but I was unable to find any reports or comments of that controversy in my newspaper database and internet searching, so I was unable to include it in this history.

325 Jorge Barrera, "Author Joseph Boyden's Shape-Shifting Indigenous Identity," *APTN News*, December 23, 2016, https://www.aptnnews.ca/national-news/author-joseph-boydens-shape-shifting-indigenous-identity/.

326 Victoria Ahearn, "City of Edmonton Scraps Joseph Boyden's Speaking Slot At Culture Event," *CBC*, January 19, 2017, https://www.cbc.ca/news/canada/edmonton/joseph-boyden-edmonton-1.3943534.

327 Ahearn, "City of Edmonton Scraps Joseph Boyden's Speaking Slot At Culture Event."

Facing pressure to cancel the event, EPL CEO Pillar Martinez argued that "[i]t's really important to recognize that the library's role is to promote intellectual freedom and freedom of expression," and having Boyden speak was "a great opportunity for our community to get together to listen to Joseph Boyden, to have a conversation."[328] Implicit in that conversation suggestion, once again, is the academic nature of the issue at hand for those making the decisions. Martinez thinks the community (who or what that means is a big and loaded question) can benefit from listening to and talking with Boyden, but perhaps some Indigenous people whose identity and voice he had appropriated do not want to hear what he has to say. Not to mention the fact that he had already been given a big public platform and his voice had already been heard, and they saw how he used it and the harm it had caused. Presenting the issue as an opportunity for conversation undermines valid concerns and overlooks real harm. Ironically, the library also hosted two Truth and Reconciliation Commissioners to speak about the TRC process as part of the same speaker series that February. The goal of that event was to "help foster reconciliation and healing."[329]

Indigenous author Aaron Paquette questioned the library's reasoning for going ahead with the Boyden booking: "I think it's odd to call it intellectual freedom when what we're talking about is someone who has completely misrepresented themselves to many people and many (sic) different ways."[330] But he added that he hoped Boyden would answer some hard questions at the event, and he might even attend to see if Boyden "finally steps up and takes responsibility to the communities from which he's gained so much but has, at this point, returned so little."[331] I did not find evidence of much outcry from the library world about the event, but the Library Association of Alberta's spring conference featured Joseph Boyden as a keynote speaker (the session was sponsored by EPL), and he spoke on a conference panel called

---

328 Wallis Snowdon, "Amid Ancestry Controversy, Edmonton Library Defends Joseph Boyden Event," *CBC*, January 20, 2017, https://www.cbc.ca/news/canada/edmonton/amid-ancestry-controversy-edmonton-library-defends-joseph-boyden-event-1.3944855.

329 "Forward Thinking Speaker Series: A Conversation About Reconciliation," Global News, February 28, 2017, https://globalnews.ca/event/3220011/forward-thinking-speaker-series-a-conversation-about-reconciliation/

330 Snowdon, "Amid Ancestry Controversy."

331 Snowdon.

"Sharing Indigenous Perspectives."[332] According to the Ex Libris Association newsletter, Boyden's appearances for EPL and the library conference were well attended.[333]

Later that year, George Takei was scheduled for a Forward Thinking Speaker Series event to take place on Nov 29, which was also a fundraiser for a new downtown library building, when news broke earlier that month of a sexual assault allegation against Takei for an incident in 1981.[334] EPL CEO Martinez acknowledged that the library was in a difficult position: "We know this is very serious. But so far, this is just one allegation, which Mr. Takei is denying," so the first decision that the library and event sponsor Edmonton Community Foundation made was to wait until the end of the week to see if any new information came to light that might influence the final decision.[335] An opinion piece in the *Edmonton Journal* explored some of the implications that could be involved in cancelling or proceeding with the event, such as censorship and homophobia, but it ended by suggesting that this controversy provided another opportunity for a difficult public discussion: "we can't just give him a platform to deliver a pat speech. He has to face tough questions. Rather than shutting down speech, perhaps this is just the vital moment to have a hard and public conversation."[336]

That opinion piece noted that the library had heard little in the way of public concern about the Takei event, but perhaps complaints increased as the news spread and the event drew closer, because the Ex Libris Association newsletter said that the library "resisted bitter public pressure to cancel it."[337] Ex Libris also reported that 1300 people attended and there were no protests or incidents.[338] Martinez explained that going ahead with the event "was not an easy or comfortable

---

332 "ALC Libraries More Than Ever," *Alberta Library Conference*, (Jasper: ALC, 2017), https://www.laa.ca/alc2017/documents/ALC2017SaturdayFinal.PDF.

333 Alvin M. Schrader, "Prairies News," *ELAN: The Ex Libris Association Newsletter*, Fall, 2017, 14, https://www.exlibris.ca/lib/exe/fetch.php?media=newsletters:elan_issue_62_fall_2017.pdf.

334 Paula Simons, "If Takei is Allowed to Speak, He should have to Say Something," *Edmonton Journal*, November 16, 2017, A1, ProQuest.

335 Simons, "If Takei is Allowed to Speak."

336 Simons.

337 Simons; Alvin M. Schrader, "Prairies News," *ELAN: The Ex Libris Association Newsletter*, Spring, 2018, 13, https://www.exlibris.ca/lib/exe/fetch.php?media=newsletters:elan_issue_63_spring_2018.pdf.

338 Schrader, "Prairies News," 2018.

decision," but the library believed in the "presumption of innocence" and the important role the library plays as a public space "to be part of the process of critical thinking, to ask questions."[339] In the aftermath of these controversies, Martinez spoke on a panel called "Intellectual Freedom: Sustaining a Core Value" at the Canadian Federation of Library Associations (CFLA) National Forum in May 2018, where she reflected on the events and affirmed EPL's position of protecting freedom of expression and encouraging a diversity of opinions. According to a summary of the panel discussion, all of the panelists agreed that intellectual freedom must be upheld without restrictions other than the limitations of Canadian law, but some did acknowledge a growing discomfort among some library professionals with unmitigated free speech that might make the library an unsafe space for marginalized community members.[340]

2017 Toronto, Ontario

A memorial to honour lawyer Barbara Kulaszka held at the Toronto Public Library (TPL) Richview branch on July 12, 2017 created a considerable controversy and led to library policy change. The event had been booked 3 weeks earlier by white nationalist Paul Fromm, but the library did not realize who had booked the room and for what purpose until the day before the event.[341] As word spread, the library quickly received hundreds of complaints calling for it to cancel the memorial for the lawyer known for defending white nationalists against hate crime charges, including Holocaust-denier Ernst Zundel, and for

---

339 Curtis Gillespie, "Warning," *Edify*, January 30, 2018, https://edifyedmonton.com/urban/community/warning/.

340 "Artificial Intelligence and Intellectual Freedom, Key Policy Concerns for Canadian Libraries," *Canadian Federation of Library Associations / Fédération Canadienne Des Associations De Bibliothèques*, May 2, 2018, http://cfla-fcab.ca/wp-content/uploads/2018/07/CFLA-FCAB-2018-National-Forum-Paper-final.pdf, 8.

341 Ainslie Cruickshank, "Memorial Goes Ahead at Toronto Library for Lawyer Who Represented Far-Right Extremists," *Toronto Star*, July 12, 2017, ProQuest; "Statement From City Librarian Vickery Bowles on Last Evening's Event at Richview Library," Cision Canada, July 13, 2017, https://www.newswire.ca/news-releases/statement-from-city-librarian-vickery-bowles-on-last-evenings-event-at-richview-library-634362023.html.

undoing Canada's law against false news.[342] Those complaints came from human rights advocates, local politicians, and union representatives. Bernie Farber, former Head of the Canadian Jewish Congress and then Executive Director of the Mosaic Institute, said that Kulaszka's legacy "is one of increasing and permitting hatred in Canada" and that allowing the event in their space "certainly will discredit the Toronto library system."[343] Nathan Leipciger, an 89-yr-old survivor of Nazi concentration camps emailed the library to express his outrage that TPL had rented space to known white nationalist leaders like Paul Fromm and Marc Lemire "despite their long record of promoting bigotry and their disturbing ties to the neo-Nazi movement."[344] Human rights lawyer Richard Warman pointed out that Fromm had been barred from speaking in federal Parliament and Lemire is the last known leader of the Heritage Front: "If that's not good enough for the Toronto Public Library to say, 'No, thanks' then what could be?"[345]

Mayor John Tory was "deeply concerned" about the event and asked the library to consider cancelling the booking,[346] as did City Councillor James Pasternak, who said "it is truly shocking" that such individuals would be allowed to host an event in the library.[347] Another City Councillor, John Campbell, expressed his disappointment with the library booking, noting: "There's a fine line between freedom of speech and hate speech."[348] From the library labour perspective, Maureen O'Reilly, President of the Toronto Public Library Workers Union CUPE Local 4948, said that the decision to hold the event "failed their regular

---

342 Cruickshank, "Memorial Goes Ahead at Toronto Library for Lawyer Who Represented Far-Right Extremists;" "Statement From City Librarian Vickery Bowles on Last Evening's Event at Richview Library;" "Toronto Library Defends Allowing Controversial Memorial Service to Go Ahead," *CBC*, July 13, 2017, https://www.cbc.ca/news/canada/toronto/toronto-library-controversial-memorial-1.4202658; Joseph Brean, "Fringe-Right Champion Victorious in Death, Too; Memorial for Controversial Lawyer to Proceed Unabated," *National Post,* July 13, 2017, A3, ProQuest.

343 Cruickshank, "Memorial Goes Ahead at Toronto Library for Lawyer Who Represented Far-Right Extremists."

344 Cruickshank.

345 Brean, "Fringe-Right Champion Victorious in Death."

346 John Tory (@JohnTory), "My statement on tonight's meeting at the Richview Library," Twitter, July 12, 2017, 5:28 p.m., https://twitter.com/JohnTory/status/885249533302759424.

347 Cruickshank, "Memorial Goes Ahead at Toronto Library for Lawyer Who Represented Far-Right Extremists."

348 "Toronto Library Defends Allowing Controversial Memorial Service to Go Ahead."

patrons"[349] by not taking a stand against hate. She later argued that the library's own policy could have allowed them to cancel the booking, since it had originally been booked under a fake name and attendees were charged a fee, neither of which, she said, were permitted by TPL.[350]

The library said it heard the concerns from the public and was taking them very seriously, but they sought legal advice which informed their decision that they could not cancel the booking because it did not break any laws, and to do so would contravene the Canadian Charter of Rights and Freedoms, the principles of intellectual freedom, and the library's own mission and values.[351] City Librarian Vickery Bowles said: "We preserve our democratic society by making it available to people with a wide range of ideas and viewpoints including those which some consider unacceptable," and added, "[t]his was a memorial service. If this had been a white supremacist rally we wouldn't have allowed it."[352] The library had extra security guards on site for the event. Furthermore, a library staff member spoke to the meeting organizers and attendees to reiterate the meeting room terms of use, reminding them of the library's code of conduct and the Canadian Human Rights Act, and the staff member stayed in the room to monitor the event.[353] About 20 people attended the memorial, including one wearing the t-shirt of a neo-Nazi group, but media were not allowed inside, and there were 3 silent people in the parking lot wearing black clothing and dark masks who refused to talk to the media, not identifying themselves as supporters or protesters.[354] Paul Fromm accused those who called for the memorial to be cancelled of being "opponents of free speech," while attendee Max French said: "There was no Holocaust denial going on in there, and if there was, what of it?"[355]

---

349 "Toronto Library Defends Allowing Controversial Memorial Service to Go Ahead."

350 Haseena Manek, "When Hate Goes Public," *Our Times*, August 17, 2017, https://ourtimes.ca/article/when-hate-goes-public.

351 Cruickshank, "Memorial Goes Ahead at Toronto Library for Lawyer Who Represented Far-Right Extremists;" "Toronto Library Defends Allowing Controversial Memorial Service to Go Ahead."

352 "Toronto Library Defends Allowing Controversial Memorial Service to Go Ahead."

353 Brean, "Fringe-Right Champion Victorious in Death."

354 Cruickshank, "Memorial Goes Ahead at Toronto Library for Lawyer Who Represented Far-Right Extremists"; Brean, "Fringe-Right Champion Victorious in Death."

355 Cruickshank.

Bowles released a statement affirming the library's dedication to ensuring "legal rights to gather and to freedom of speech while protecting against discrimination, harassment and hate speech," and confirming that the event did not violate any laws.[356] In light of the controversy, Mayor Tory requested the library board review the room booking policy, which Bowles indicated would occur that fall.[357] And in the days following the memorial, opinion pieces were published in newspapers representing both sides of the debate. A *Globe and Mail* opinion argued that "[f]ree speech is the cardinal right–the right that underpins all others," and that "[l]ibraries, in particular, should be havens for free expression."[358] It went on to praise libraries' neutral approach to space booking and recommended, as we have seen suggested before, that people "simply turn away" from the "offensive opinions" of "Canada's white nationalists and Holocaust deniers."[359] The *Toronto Sun* also had an opinion piece defending the library's decision, noting the value of neutrality and protecting free speech.[360] On the other side, Bernie Farber wrote an editorial in the *Toronto Sun* describing his childhood experience of the library as a "sanctuary," "a safe place," a "haven" where he did not have to worry about antisemitism; he refuted the library's reasoning for allowing the Kulaszka memorial to be held in their space, and said that TPL's decision "has forever shattered the symbolism of Canadian libraries."[361]

Over the course of that fall, the library board reviewed its room booking policy, relevant City of Toronto policies, and feedback from community members and stakeholders, which led to proposed policy changes aimed at limiting the potential for hate speech in the library to be voted on at the December 11 board meeting.[362] The library notified police in advance of the meeting at the downtown Toronto

---

356 "Statement From City Librarian Vickery Bowles on Last Evening's Event at Richview Library."

357 "Statement From City Librarian Vickery Bowles on Last Evening's Event at Richview Library."

358 Marcus Gee, "Banning Ideas from Public Spaces is Not the Way to Dispute them," *The Globe and Mail,* July 14, 2017, A7, ProQuest.

359 Gee, "Banning Ideas from Public Spaces is Not the Way to Dispute them."

360 Liz Braun, "Don't Blame the Library; Beleaguered Facility Not at Fault for Hate Gathering," *Toronto Sun,* July 14, 2017, A12, ProQuest.

361 Bernie Farber, "Library no Longer Haven; Neo-Nazis Should Have Been Barred," *Toronto Sun,* July 16, 2017, A20, ProQuest.

362 Samantha Beattie, "Toronto Library Bars Hate Groups From Renting Space," *Toronto Star,* December 11, 2017, ProQuest.

Reference Library as a precaution due to the hot topic being discussed and the fact that Paul Fromm was on the docket to speak in opposition to the proposed changes, along with Bernie Farber, Madi Murariu of the Centre for Israel and Jewish Affairs, and Mohammed Hashim of the Toronto and York Regional Labour Council, who were in favour of the changes.[363] Fromm was there to argue that the proposed changes were "an affront to free speech" and that the library "belongs to all citizens and should be open to use, including rental of rooms for meetings, to all citizens, without discrimination, if for no other reason than all taxpayers pay for it."[364] (He seemed to be overlooking the facts that the memorial he organized required an entrance fee and banned the media from attending.) While Farber spoke more about the library as a safe space and encouraged the board to "[r]eject hate, embrace diversity."[365]

Similar to library policy changes we have seen considered and rejected in Victoria but would come to be implemented in other library systems, the proposed changes for TPL would allow the library to deny or cancel bookings they deemed "likely to promote, or would have the effect of promoting discrimination, contempt or hatred for any group or person" on the basis of a number of factors including race, ethnic origin, religion, age, and sexual orientation.[366] The updated policy would also clearly state that the Canadian Criminal Code and Ontario Human Rights Code are not to be contravened by those booking library space, and any appeals about booking decisions would go to the City Librarian, whose decision would be final.[367] Many library associations and other stakeholders had submitted feedback in writing to the board,

---

363 Beattie, "Toronto Library Bars Hate Groups From Renting Space"; Samantha Beattie, "Board Bars Hate Groups from Renting Library Space: Monday's Unanimous Decision Lets Staff Deny Or Cancel Bookings," *Toronto Star,* December 12, 2017, https://www.thestar.com/news/city_hall/2017/12/11/toronto-library-looks-at-barring-hate-groups-from-renting-space.html.

364 Beattie, "Toronto Library Bars Hate Groups From Renting Space."

365 Beattie, "Toronto Library Bars Hate Groups From Renting Space"; Beattie, "Board Bars Hate Groups from Renting Library Space."

366 Beattie, "Toronto Library Bars Hate Groups From Renting Space."

367 Beattie, "Toronto Library Bars Hate Groups From Renting Space"; "Toronto Library Staff Can Now Refuse Event Bookings 'Likely' to Promote Hate," *CBC,* December 11, 2017, https://www.cbc.ca/news/canada/toronto/toronto-library-board-hate-room-booking-1.4443914.

with the majority in support of the changes.[368] The Federation of Ontario Public Libraries, OLA, CFLA, ALA Office for Intellectual Freedom, Urban Libraries Council, and Canadian Urban Libraries Council all wrote in support of the proposed changes, and many also voiced support for the library's position in allowing the memorial to happen.[369] Other groups such as East Enders Against Racism and the Centre for Israel and Jewish Affairs also wrote in support of the proposed changes.[370] However, James L. Turk, Director of the Centre for Free Expression at Toronto Metropolitan University (formerly Ryerson University), wrote in support of the library's decision to allow the memorial and urged the board to continue TPL's "long and proud commitment to intellectual freedom" and public accessibility "by keeping rental fees modest and by imposing minimal restriction on who can use the library facilities."[371]

The board approved the policy changes in a unanimous vote.[372] Bowles assured that under the new policy the library would "continue making our booking decisions based on the purpose of the booking," and, accordingly, the Kulaszka memorial would likely still have been approved because "[t]here was no reason to believe there was going to be hate or discrimination at that meeting."[373] In fact, the library did deny a booking request from Fromm that October, for a lecture and Q&A by Victor Fletcher, editor of *Toronto Street News*, which was described by a *National Post* columnist as "a compendium of bigoted conspiracy theories."[374] Bowles said that in contrast to a memorial where there was unlikely to be hate speech, it was reasonable to

---

[368] Toronto Public Library, *Toronto Public Library Board Meeting No. 10*, (Toronto, ON: Toronto Public Library, 2017), https://www.torontopubliclibrary.ca/content/about-the-library/pdfs/board/meetings/2017/dec11/B20171211-full-agenda-revised.pdf; TPLWU CUPE Local 4948 had previously submitted written feedback in September to request a change in policy: Toronto Public Library, Toronto Public Library Board Meeting, (Toronto, ON: Toronto Public Library, 2017), https://www.torontopubliclibrary.ca/content/about-the-library/pdfs/board/meetings/2017/sep25/09-communications-combined.pdf.

[369] Toronto Public Library, *Toronto Public Library Board Meeting No. 10*.

[370] Toronto Public Library.

[371] Toronto Public Library.

[372] "Toronto Library Staff Can Now Refuse Event Bookings 'Likely' to Promote Hate."

[373] "Toronto Library Staff Can Now Refuse Event Bookings 'Likely' to Promote Hate."

[374] Chris Selley, "Toronto's Public Libraries Make an Imperfect but Brave Stand for Free Speech," *National Post*, December 15, 2017, https://nationalpost.com/opinion/chris-selley-torontos-public-libraries-make-an-imperfect-but-brave-stand-for-free-speech.

expect that there would be hate speech at this event, and TPL's legal counsel backed the decision.[375] I found no evidence of public controversy for this denied booking.

Responding to the new policy, the BC Library Association posted a blog entry written by BC Civil Liberties Association policy Director, Micheal Vonn, who opposed the changes, arguing "that in requiring library staff to sort anticipated 'good' speech from anticipated 'bad' speech, the new policy is antithetical to the unique and critical mission of libraries to provide universal access to a broad range of information and ideas, including the offensive ones."[376] In speculating about what might or might not be allowed under the new policy, Vonn anticipated TPL's (and VPL's) next big controversy when he wondered: "For example, will gender-critical feminist speakers be denied access to room rentals on the grounds that their views could promote contempt for transgendered persons?"[377] (We will soon find out the answer.) However, constitutional lawyer Bruce Ryder said that the new policy was an improvement on the old and would be more Charter-proof if challenged, but he suggested a "cautious approach to denying space" and recognized that the library would likely still face criticism from the public for future rentals and refusals.[378] Then in 2018, OLA awarded Bowles with the Les Fowlie Intellectual Freedom Award for her work around the event and policy changes.[379]

2017 Ottawa, Ontario

The group ACT! For Canada, which hosted "mosquebuster" Gavin Boby at OPL in 2013, had booked a room at the main branch of OPL for November 25, 2017 to screen a controversial anti-Islam documentary called *Killing Europe*. However, this event was cancelled by the library

---

[375] Selley, "Toronto's Public Libraries Make an Imperfect but Brave Stand for Free Speech." I did not find any record of public controversy around that Fromm/Fletcher event being denied.

[376] Micheal Vonn, "The Toronto Public Library's New Community Room Booking Policy," British Columbia Library Association, March 5, 2018, https://bclaconnect.ca/perspectives/2018/03/05/the-toronto-public-librarys-new-community-room-booking-policy/.

[377] Vonn, "The Toronto Public Library's New Community Room Booking Policy."

[378] Selley, "Toronto's Public Libraries Make an Imperfect but Brave Stand for Free Speech."

[379] "Vickery Bowles Wins Ola's Les Fowlie Intellectual Freedom Award," Freedom to Read, February 3, 2018, https://www.freedomtoread.ca/2018/02/vickery-bowles-wins-olas-les-fowlie-intellectual-freedom-award/.

in response to an email campaign of community complaints.³⁸⁰ Activist Fareed Khan, who organized the campaign against the film screening, argued that the film content would violate the library's policy against discrimination and that public spaces should not be used to promote hatred: "Groups that go out and promote hate against any identifiable group should never be allowed to use public facilities."³⁸¹ In response to the estimated hundreds of complaints sent to the library and city council, councillor and library board member Catherine McKenney looked into the film and brought the issue to the board because she agreed that it promoted discrimination.³⁸² Library board chair Tim Tierney said he heard concerns from "the Ottawa District Labour Council, unions, residents, board members and friends," prompting him to ask the OPL CEO to review the booking, which resulted in its cancellation.³⁸³

Even with the screening being cancelled, Khan expressed concern that the booking had been accepted at all, calling for a better room booking review system to ensure that OPL policies are being followed by groups who use their spaces, and Councillor McKenney also suggested revisiting the policy.³⁸⁴ Human rights lawyer Richard Warman, who identified himself as being "firmly in the camp of defending freedom of expression," supported the library's decision but also emphasized the obligation of the library to do at least a quick check into the group or event purpose, as he noted that a "30-second Google search" on the film would have found it "in clear violation" of the library's room booking policy.³⁸⁵ In 2013, OPL allowed the Boby event to proceed because their policy at the time only prohibited users from contravening Canada's Criminal Code and Ontario's Human Rights Code, but by 2017

---

380 "Library Cancels Anti-Islam Film Screening," *CBC*, November 25, 2017, https://www.cbc.ca/news/canada/ottawa/ottawa-public-library-central-branch-islam-islamophobia-public-protest-film-1.4418229.

381 "Library Cancels Anti-Islam Film Screening."

382 "Library Cancels Anti-Islam Film Screening."

383 "Library Cancels Anti-Islam Film Screening."

384 "Library Cancels Anti-Islam Film Screening." I did not find any evidence that a policy change occurred.

385 Blair Crawford, "Ottawa Library Cancels Planned Screening of Controversial 'Killing Europe' Doc," *Ottawa Citizen*, November 24, 2017, https://ottawacitizen.com/news/local-news/ottawa-library-cancels-planned-screening-of-controversial-hate-speech-film.

the library now also had an anti-discrimination policy similar to TPL's 2017 policy update.[386]

ACT! spokesperson Alexandra Belaire responded to the cancellation by calling the City of Ottawa and the library "tools of institutionalized oppression," and argued that by cancelling the world premiere screening of the film that they were perpetuating the kinds of abuses the film is exposing, such as homophobia, antisemitism, and rape-culture.[387] A protest that was organized by Ottawa Against Fascism and Solidarity Ottawa before the cancellation was announced went ahead as planned outside the library to demonstrate public support against Islamophobia, with speakers including a member of the Muslim community and Ottawa Labour Council president Sean McKenney.[388]

The controversy died down until the following June, when the screening organizer Madeline Weld, who is a member of ACT! and founder of Canadian Citizens for Charter Rights and Freedoms, applied for a judicial review of the library's decision to cancel the film screening.[389] Weld argued that the library "acted arbitrarily and unreasonably" and "violated [her] constitutional right to free expression" and the rights of the audience to see the film.[390] The Justice Centre for Constitutional Freedoms (JCCF) filed the court application on behalf of Weld, and in their statement they presented more details around the event booking than had previously been reported in the 2017 news coverage. According to JCCF, OPL informed Weld on October 27, 2017 that her event booking had been "reviewed and confirmed" so the rental contract was

---

386 "Library Cancels Anti-Islam Film Screening." The CBC reported that this was in OPL's policy, however, in its current version (there are no dates provided on the site about versions or approvals) the Meeting Room Booking Policy makes no mention of rules against discrimination, you must go to the Terms and Conditions when booking the room, where the rules against discrimination are listed in the section on cancellations. Both documents are referenced here: "Meeting Room Booking Policy," Ottawa Public Library, n.d., https://biblioottawalibrary.ca/en/meeting-room-booking-policy; "Terms and Conditions." Ottawa Public Library, n.d. https://biblioottawalibrary.ca/en/terms-and-conditions-0.

387 Crawford, "Ottawa Library Cancels Planned Screening of Controversial 'Killing Europe' Doc"; Chantal Sundaram, "Ottawa Shuts Down Far-Right 'ACT! for Canada'," Socialist, November 26, 2017, http://www.socialist.ca/node/3489.

388 Sundaram, "Ottawa Shuts Down Far-Right 'ACT! for Canada'."

389 "Library Faces Court Challenge Over Cancellation of Controversial Film," *Ottawa Citizen*, June 13, 2018, ProQuest; Weld v. Ottawa Public Library, Application to Divisional Court for Judicial Review, (2010), https://www.jccf.ca/wp-content/uploads/2018/06/Weld-v-OPL-filed-application.pdf.

390 "Library Faces Court Challenge Over Cancellation of Controversial Film."

made and the booking fee was paid by Weld.[391] Then on Nov 14, OPL Senior Manager Catherine Seaman contacted Weld for confirmation that the film would not contravene criminal or human rights codes and to let her know that the library was "anticipating disruptions" so she was required to pay for security, and Weld agreed to both points.[392] And on November 24, OPL CEO Danielle McDonald emailed Weld to inform her that based on the significant complaints received, the library undertook further review of the film and determined that it fell "within the category of material that the Library is not prepared to have displayed or screened on its property."[393] These details add weight to the earlier calls for better review of booking requests, but they also fail to mention the rule against promoting discrimination that is included in the rental contract terms and conditions.

In September 2019, the Ontario Court of Justice ruled that the library was within its rights to cancel the film screening because the library was not acting as a public body in renting the room for a ticketed event.[394] According to the ruling: "The Ottawa Public Library has no obligation to make its extraneous space available or to enter into a contract with any particular person" and "[p]ublicizing the availability of rooms for the community and the general public does not imply any legal obligation on the board or confer any right on the applicants or any other members of the public."[395] Essentially this ruling stated that the library is not acting in its role as a public institution when it rents rooms for private events, thus there is no obligation to protect intellectual freedom in those room bookings. Unhappy with this result, the JCCF sought to appeal the decision, but in February 2020 the

---

[391] "Ottawa Public Library Sued for Cancelling Controversial Documentary," Justice Centre for Constitutional Freedoms, June 13, 2018, https://www.jccf.ca/ottawa-public-library-sued-for-cancelling-controversial-documentary/.

[392] "Ottawa Public Library Sued for Cancelling Controversial Documentary."

[393] "Ottawa Public Library Sued for Cancelling Controversial Documentary."

[394] Blair Crawford, "Court Upholds Public Library's Decision to Cancel Screening of Controversial Film," *Ottawa Citizen*, September 19, 2019, https://ottawacitizen.com/news/local-news/court-upholds-librarys-decision-to-cancel-screening-of-controversial-film.

[395] Crawford, "Court Upholds Public Library's Decision to Cancel Screening of Controversial Film"; for further examination of the ruling see this article from the Canadian Bar Association: Christopher Wirth and Sakshi Chadha, "Court Rules That Termination of Rental Agreement by Public Library Is Not Subject to Judicial Review," The Canadian Bar Association, November 29, 2019, https://www.cba.org/Sections/Administrative-Law/Articles/2019/Court-rules.

Ontario Court of Appeal denied the appeal request,[396] which closed the issue. In light of this legal decision, moving forward I would expect that groups organizing potentially controversial events at public libraries might be careful to avoid making those events private or charging for tickets, which would make it easier for libraries to deny or cancel bookings.

2018 Ottawa, Ontario

The University of Ottawa's Students for Free Speech group had booked a speaking event at the Ottawa Public Library for March 24, 2018, featuring uOttawa English professor and self-described "contrarian, anti-feminist, defender of free speech and the right to dissent" Janice Fiamengo.[397] The talk, which was titled "Is the University About the Pursuit of Truth or the Protection of Approved Ideologies?" was booked at the library because, according to event organizer and uOttawa student Elijah Bedassie, his Students for Free Speech group had problems holding events on campus and being recognized as a student club. Explaining his goals, Bedassie said: "What we really want to do is open dialogue between people and honestly just try to protect free speech."[398] However, a group called Ottawa Against Fascism accused Fiamengo of being "anti-Muslim and anti-immigrant" and of "using her platform to whip up hatred against marginalized communities," so on their Facebook page the group called for a protest at the event.[399] In response to that protest call, Bedassie's group paid to have extra security in attendance.[400]

I was unable to find any media coverage, library statements, or political or public comments leading up to the event, but afterward, the *Ottawa Citizen* reported that the library spoke to lawyers and the police before approving the event, in order to avoid the kind of controversy

---

396 "Weld V. Ottawa Public Library," Justice Centre for Constitutional Freedoms, October 10, 2019, https://www.jccf.ca/court_cases/weld-v-ottawa-public-library/.

397 Blair Crawford, "Protesters Disrupt Lecture by UOttawa 'Anti-Feminist' at Ottawa Public Library," *Ottawa Citizen*, March 27, 2018, https://ottawacitizen.com/news/local-news/protesters-disrupt-lecture-by-uottawa-anti-feminist-at-ottawa-public-library. This happened before the Ontario court ruling in Sept 2019 that I just discussed.

398 Crawford, "Protesters Disrupt Lecture by UOttawa 'Anti-Feminist' at Ottawa Public Library."

399 Crawford.

400 Crawford.

they went through the previous year with the film event.[401] According to the advice they received, Fiamengo was not on law enforcement's radar and the event seemed unlikely to contravene the Canadian Criminal Code and the Ontario Human Rights Code, which are in the library's booking policy.[402] There was no mention in the sources I found for this event of the policy against promoting discrimination that was invoked in the 2017 OPL film cancellation, so we might assume that it was not seen to be relevant given the broad topic of the planned talk. OPL CEO Monique Désormeaux affirmed the importance of free speech but also noted that, "we always look in terms of what the purpose of the event is going to be" when reviewing bookings.[403]

About 20 demonstrators gathered outside the library, many wearing black clothing and face coverings and chanting: "No Debate! No platform for hate!"[404] They tried to block Fiamengo from entering the library, and when she did get inside, someone pulled the fire alarm, which caused the building to be evacuated and the event to be cancelled.[405] Videos showed some scuffling, including punches exchanged and a protester being handcuffed by the police, but the police would not confirm if any charges had been laid.[406] In the aftermath, Bedassie worried that this would "normaliz[e] violence" in response to disagreement and he was looking for a new venue to reschedule the talk, while Fiamengo denounced the protestors as scared and "weak-minded bullies."[407] Fiamengo's husband, David Soloway, wrote a blog post about the event in which he disparaged the protestors, but also criticized the police and hired security guards for using "'soft' or 'selective' policing."[408] And I was unable to find statements from the library about what happened.

---

401 Crawford.

402 Crawford.

403 Crawford.

404 Crawford.

405 Crawford.

406 Crawford.

407 Crawford.

408 David Soloway, "Confronting the Borg," *SAFS Newsletter*, April, 2018, 53–57, https://www.safs.ca/newsletters/issues/nl79.pdf.

2019 Vancouver, British Columbia

We return to Vancouver for an event at the VPL featuring another controversial, trans-exclusionary, self-identified feminist. Writer and founder of the Feminist Current website Meghan Murphy, who I mentioned in my introduction, booked a room to give a talk on "gender identity, ideology and women's rights" at the downtown branch on January 10, 2019, but the library began facing public backlash two months before, in November 2018.[409] As reported in the *Toronto Star*, Vice President of the BC NDP party and transgender woman Morgane Oger tweeted her criticism of the library for allowing the event in its space, arguing that Murphy's talk is likely to hurt trans people because her other talks and videos on the topic have contributed to spreading discrimination against trans people.[410] Oger also said: "It's inconceivable that the VPL would allow religious hatred, or racial hatred, or anti-Indigenous hatred to be spoken on its property and has policies stopping such events from happening."[411] However, as we have seen, VPL's policies have not prevented such events from happening, as all of the contested events we've looked at have been allowed, except for the assisted suicide lecture. And the policy changes made in 2000 noted the requirement to comply with the criminal code and human rights code, but VPL policy did not include a provision to prevent discrimination or hatred. Poet jaye simpson was also critical of the library on Twitter and asked VPL to cancel the event, and when they refused, simpson cancelled their participation in VPL's Open Book: A Trans, Gender Variant and Two Spirit Reading Circle. simpson then said they faced attacks on Twitter noting: "I've warned VPL this would happen, and because I spoke up it's happening to me, it's speaking to the fact this is a very real thing."[412] The queer resource centre Qmunity also asked the library to cancel the event and stated that, "Murphy's trans-exclusionary beliefs are well known and contribute to a climate

---

409 Cherise Seucharan, "Trans Advocates Criticize Vancouver Public Library for Welcoming Controversial Speaker," Toronto Star, November 28, 2018, https://www.thestar.com/vancouver/2018/11/28/trans-advocates-criticize-vancouver-public-library-for-welcoming-controversial-speaker.html.

410 Seucharan, "Trans Advocates Criticize Vancouver Public Library for Welcoming Controversial Speaker."

411 Seucharan.

412 Seucharan.

of hatred, fear, discrimination, and violence against trans people."[413] Moreover, Qmunity raised the point in their statement that has been an underlying and unifying point for the majority of these controversies: "we know all too well that speech does not have to meet a legal test for criminality to cause harm."[414] Another form of community protest was an online petition calling for VPL to no longer be permitted to participate in the Safe Place program and to remove their Safe Place stickers if they allowed the event to proceed.[415]

According to VPL's Feminist Current Event Report, VPL received notice that they would face legal action if they cancelled the booking, so their legal counsel advised them of the risks and the library board discussed the situation, then decided to allow the booking, but shift the timing to after the library closed to minimize disruption to users and impact on staff.[416] Publicly, VPL defended its decision to allow Murphy's talk based on arguments of library neutrality and intellectual freedom. Chief Librarian Christina de Castell released a statement that VPL is "not endorsing, or hosting this event," and that "[w]hile it is difficult for us as individuals and staff to accept a rental from an organization whose perspectives we disagree with, the fundamental role of libraries as a place for free speech and intellectual freedom must be upheld."[417] Her statement also noted that they had informed Vancouver Police to monitor the talk in case the criminal code was breached.[418] This decision to have police attend the event is surprising to me, since it does not seem to be in the spirit of intellectual freedom that the library believes in and it begs some questions. For instance,

---

413 Craig Takeuchi, "LGBT Activists and Organizations Concerned About Vancouver Public Library Event Featuring Controversial Speaker," *The Georgia Straight*, November 29, 2018, https://www.straight.com/life/1171981/lgbt-activists-and-organizations-concerned-about-vancouver-public-library-event.

414 Takeuchi, "LGBT Activists and Organizations Concerned About Vancouver Public Library Event Featuring Controversial Speaker."

415 Takeuchi, "LGBT Activists and Organizations Concerned About Vancouver Public Library Event Featuring Controversial Speaker." The Safe Place program, launched in 2016 by the Vancouver Police Department, designates places where 2SLGBTQIA+ people can seek help.

416 Referenced in Deborah A. Thomas, "Intellectual Freedom and Inclusivity: Opposites or Partners?," Journal of Intellectual Freedom and Privacy 4, no. 3 (2019), https://doi.org/ https://doi.org/10.5860/jifp.v4i3.7129. I was unable to access the report itself online.

417 Vancouver Public Library (@VPL), "Statement regarding Feminist Current Event," Twitter, November 28, 2018, 5:58 p.m., https://twitter.com/VPL/status/1067915660401885185.

418 Takeuchi, "LGBT Activists and Organizations Concerned About Vancouver Public Library Event Featuring Controversial Speaker."

how does the library determine which events require police monitoring? Some libraries have made the argument that their staff should not be in a position to decide which events or speakers are likely to promote discrimination, and I wonder how they would argue this situation is different.

I was unable to find any statements about the issue from CUPE Local 391, which represents library staff, but the BC Teachers' Federation tweeted its opposition in response to the VPL statement on Twitter, arguing that "[w]e need to ensure that public institutions in BC are not used to promote hate in any way, at any time."[419] In the library professional association arena, the Chair of the Canadian Federation of Library Associations, Alix-Rae Stefanko, wrote a letter of support to de Castell that was shared on the CFLA website, commending VPL for protecting the principle of free speech and keeping the library safe from hate.[420] Subsequently, the president of the BCLA, Shirley Lew, wrote a letter to the CFLA not in opposition to VPL's decision, but to let CFLA know that they overstepped beyond their scope and perhaps unintentionally shut down an important conversation about library values.[421]

Murphy responded to calls for VPL to cancel her event by denying that her beliefs are discriminatory or hateful and arguing that "[t]rans people are not marginalized because they have control over public discourse."[422] She said her event was "intended to be a conversation" about "feminist concern and critique" around gender identity legislation and policies that allow "males" into women-only spaces.[423] Meanwhile, Murphy was permanently suspended from Twitter, which does not have a history of handing out suspensions liberally, for "violating rules against hateful conduct."[424] Then on December 2 2018, news

---

419   BCTF (@BCTF), "We need to ensure that public institutions in BC are not used to promote hate in any way", Twitter, November 29, 2018, 8:31 p.m., https://twitter.com/bctf/status/1068316546408210432.

420   Alix-Rae Stefanko to Christina De Castell, "RE: Feminist Current Event at VPL," January 15, 2019, http://cfla-fcab.ca/wp-content/uploads/2019/01/VPL-Letter-of-Support-190115.pdf.

421   Shirley Lew to Alix-Rae Stefanko, April 1, 2019, https://bclaconnect.ca/wp-uploads/2019/10/Letter-to-CFLA-President-and-Board.pdf.

422   Seucharan, "Trans Advocates Criticize Vancouver Public Library for Welcoming Controversial Speaker."

423   Seucharan, "Trans Advocates Criticize Vancouver Public Library for Welcoming Controversial Speaker."

424   Takeuchi, "LGBT Activists and Organizations Concerned About Vancouver Public Library Event Featuring Controversial Speaker."

outlets received a fake email that appeared to be from Murphy announcing that she was cancelling the event due to the public outcry.[425] When notified, Murphy said she had not sent the message and that she was going ahead with the event: "I'm not going to stop talking about this, I'm not cancelling the event, I'm not going to be bullied... into submission."[426]

At the event, Murphy spoke to a full room while a crowd protested outside of the library, and there were no reports of any incidents or arrests.[427] *The Georgia Straight* reported that Qmunity organized a 2SLGBTQIA+-inclusive feminist event held the next day.[428] But the controversy did not end there, as the library board began reviewing the meeting room policy in the following months in order to "adapt and evolve to better listen to the voices of those who are most subject to discrimination."[429] At the library board's April 24, 2019 meeting, a number of community members and organization representatives who were opposed to the Murphy event shared their perspectives and recommendations for VPL. Tami Starlight of the Coalition Against Trans Antagonism (CATA) made a number of requests of VPL, including making a formal apology to acknowledge the harm caused by the event, improving the room rental policy to prevent anti-trans and anti-sex worker platforming, providing annual trans and sex worker sensitivity training for library staff and board, co-hosting trans and sex worker community dialogues with CATA for library staff and board, and providing free rental space for trans and sex worker events as

---

425 John Copsey, "Meghan Murphy's Gender Identity Talk at Vancouver Public Library Not Cancelled," *Global News*, December 2, 2018, https://globalnews.ca/news/4720183/controversial-feminist-speaker-meghan-murphy-cancels-vancouver-public-library-appearance/; Perrin Grauer, "Cancellation of Event at Vancouver Public Library Featuring Controversial Speaker Was Faked, Speaker Says," *Toronto Star*, December 2, 2018, https://www.thestar.com/vancouver/2018/12/02/cancellation-of-event-at-vancouver-public-library-featuring-controversial-speaker-was-faked-speaker-says.html.

426 Grauer, "Cancellation of Event at Vancouver Public Library Featuring Controversial Speaker Was Faked."

427 "Trans Advocates Rally Against Controversial Feminist Speaker Meghan Murphy," *CTV News*, January 11, 2019, https://bc.ctvnews.ca/trans-advocates-rally-against-controversial-feminist-speaker-meghan-murphy-1.4249890.

428 Carlito Pablo, "Proposed Vancouver Public Library Rental Policy Affirms Commitment to Intellectual Freedom," *The Georgia Straight*, September 23, 2019, https://www.straight.com/news/1305711/proposed-vancouver-public-library-rental-policy-affirms-commitment-intellectual-freedom.

429 "Trans Advocates Rally Against Controversial Feminist Speaker Meghan Murphy."

reparations.[430] Representatives from Vancouver Dyke March, WAVAW Rape Crisis Centre, Downtown Eastside Women's Centre, and Qmunity all spoke in support of the CATA recommendations.[431] Meenakshi Mannoe of the Pivot Legal Society also urged the board to consider those recommendations and encouraged the library to conduct a stigma audit on all of its policies that affect patrons.[432] Morgane Oger requested that VPL adopt policy changes like TPL did in December 2017 to deny bookings for purposes that are likely to promote discrimination and hatred.[433] However, we will soon see that TPL did not deny a Murphy event even with those policy changes in effect, and VPL would see Murphy again in 2020.

As the library board continued its policy review,[434] community stakeholders were also working on the issue. On June 25, 2019, Vancouver Pride Society (VPS) and other community organizations signed a letter written by CATA outlining concerns with the policy and requests for changes to be made.[435] But as the Pride Festival grew closer and no policy changes had been made, VPS informed VPL on July 15, "that lack of change to the room rental policies would preclude them from participating in the 2019 Pride Parade."[436] The VPS statement made it clear that individuals from VPL were still allowed to walk in the parade with the city or their union, but the institution of VPL would not be permitted to march.[437] They acknowledged that VPL had done some recent work to improve trans inclusion, but encouraged them to continue working on engagement and consultation in order to "rebuild trust with our communities so that the public library can be a place

---

430 VPL Board Regular Meeting Minutes, April 24, 2019, Vancouver, https://www.vpl.ca/sites/vpl/public/BrdMinutes2019-04-24.pdf, 2.

431 VPL Board Regular Meeting Minutes, 3.

432 VPL Board Regular Meeting Minutes, 3.

433 VPL Board Regular Meeting Minutes, 2.

434 In May 2019 they released a discussion draft as part of their review of the Public Meeting Rooms & Facilities Use Policy: "Public Meeting Rooms & Facilities Use Policy Discussion Draft," Vancouver Public LIbrary, May 27, 2019, https://www.vpl.ca/sites/vpl/public/DiscussionDraftPublicMeetingRoomsFacilitiesUsePolicy2019-05-27.pdf.

435 "VPS Statement on VPLS Entry in the 2019 Pride Parade," VPS Statement On VPLs Entry In The 2019 Pride Parade, May 26, 2020, https://vancouverpride.ca/news/vps-statement-on-vpls-entry-in-the-2019-pride-parade/.

436 "VPS Statement on VPLS Entry in the 2019 Pride Parade."

437 "VPS Statement on VPLS Entry in the 2019 Pride Parade." UBC was also denied participation in the Pride Parade that year, similarly for allowing a transphobic event on campus.

of safety for all of us."[438] Then they also recommended that VPL follow TPL's policy changes.[439]

VPL responded to being denied participation in the Pride Parade with disappointment, but maintained its commitment "to providing a venue where diverse ideas and opinions can be shared" alongside its "longstanding commitment to promoting dialogue and raising marginalized voices through [its] programs and services."[440] An opinion piece in the *National Post* voiced its support for the library defending free speech,[441] as did some letters to the editor in *The Province* and the *Vancouver Sun*.[442] Federal Conservative candidate for Vancouver Centre David Cavey announced that he would not participate in the pride parade based on the "shameful behaviour" of VPS barring UBC and VPL.[443] He said that VPS "should not be playing politics with the taxpayers' money."[444] But VPS Executive Director Andrea Arnot countered that "Pride is political," and affirmed that "[t]he Pride Parade is for queer, trans, and two-spirit people to be accepted in the rest of society, so we don't have to invite people to our parade who are transphobic or homophobic."[445]

In September, the library board approved proposed changes to the room booking policy that maintained the library's commitment to intellectual freedom and a position of neutrality toward events in its space, while expanding the references to the Criminal Code and

---

438 "VPS Statement on VPLS Entry in the 2019 Pride Parade."

439 "VPS Statement on VPLS Entry in the 2019 Pride Parade."

440 "Vancouver Public Library Banned from Pride Parade After Allowing Controversial Speaker," *The News*, July 23, 2019, ProQuest.

441 Chris Selley, "Libraries Are No Enemy of Pride, but They Are the Original Free Speech 'Safe Spaces,'" *National Post*, July 25, 2019, https://nationalpost.com/opinion/chris-selley-libraries-are-no-enemy-of-pride-but-they-are-the-original-free-speech-safe-spaces.

442 Dave Brown, letter to the editor, *The Province*, July 31, 2019, ProQuest; Jack Herman, letter to the editor, *Vancouver Sun,* August 3, 2019, ProQuest.

443 Dan Fumano, "'Pride Is Political'–Despite Progress, Vancouver Pride Still Fighting," *Vancouver Sun*, July 29, 2019, https://vancouversun.com/news/local-news/dan-fumano-pride-is-political-despite-progress-vancouver-pride-still-fighting.

444 Fumano.

445 Fumano.

Human Rights Code violations.[446] The updated policy did not include a section like TPL's update to prevent discrimination, which community groups had asked for, but it did include a new pre-screening process to look into event organizers and speakers and their affiliations, which is "intended to limit the likelihood that prohibited activities, including hate speech (as defined by law), will take place on library premises."[447] Speaking about the policy changes, de Castell said the library would consult with the BC Human Rights Commissioner to prevent discrimination, and she affirmed: "We are a place for everyone in Vancouver and that means we don't exclude one group in order to include another."[448]

The library world continued to grapple with the issues involved in the controversy. In an article in the ALA's *Journal of Intellectual Freedom and Privacy*, Deborah A. Thomas was thinking through the challenge of how to "hono[r] both intellectual freedom and inclusion."[449] She asked difficult questions like: "How would the final decision be made as to whether someone's dignity or safety is at 'material risk' and when that trumps the need for a plurality of ideas? What is the involvement of the community served by the library in making the decision and in potentially challenging it? What controversial ideas will we silence to support a world where everyone feels safe and included?"[450] She anonymously cited a "noted trans author" who made the important distinction between books on shelves and speaking events: "Platforming hate speech against my community renders the space itself unsafe for me, personally, before, during and after, and you (in my mind) can't stick rainbow stickers up in the same space as hate speech against trans people is being platformed. It's one or the other."[451]

---

446 Simon Little, "VPL Revises Room Booking Policy After Controversial Speaker Draws Protests," *Global News*, September 27, 2019, https://globalnews.ca/news/5961345/vpl-revises-room-booking-policy-meghan-murphy-protests/.

447 Alyse Kotyk and Regan Hasegawa, "Vancouver Public Library Changes Booking Policies for Events," *CTV News*, September 30, 2019, https://bc.ctvnews.ca/vancouver-public-library-changes-booking-policies-for-events-1.4617675; "Public Meeting Rooms & Facilities Use," Vancouver Public Library, September 25, 2019, https://www.vpl.ca/policy/public-meeting-rooms-facilities-use.

448 Kotyk and Hasegawa, "Vancouver Public Library Changes Booking Policies for Events."

449 Thomas, "Intellectual Freedom and Inclusivity."

450 Thomas.

451 Thomas.

Thomas also acknowledged the risks of harm and discrimination but then suggested that the library should not be a safe place.[452]

The BCLA website posted a roundtable discussion online featuring five transgender library workers in the Vancouver area discussing their perspectives and experiences of being trans in the library world.[453] Roundtable participant Shelby noted that the Murphy event generated "a lot of workplace discussion about issues facing trans employees" and led to her building a network of queer and ally coworkers, with Leah adding that "this network has provided a place to debrief, discuss, and support one another during the challenges we are facing as queer and trans VPL staff."[454] Both Hazel and Allison expressed disappointment that the annual BCLA conference did not take the initiative to include a panel discussion similar to this roundtable in their conference program.[455] Hazel also said: "I was deeply disheartened by the lack of pushback from librarians (particularly academic librarians in positions of power, who have academic freedom) in the face of transphobia. I recognize that you can't take on every battle, but trans people are literally dying because of the views espoused by so-called "gender critical" activists."[456] And Hazel made the point, echoed by syr, that "We all know libraries aren't (and shouldn't be) neutral."[457]

2019 Halifax, Nova Scotia

Mount Saint Vincent University professor Alex Khasnabish organized the Radical Imagination Film and Discussion Series for over 4 years at the central branch of Halifax Public Libraries (HPL), with the library co-sponsoring the event series by providing the room free of rental charge. In 2019, however, the library found the programming to be

---

452 Thomas.

453 Allison Jones et al., "Not Cis in LIS: A Roundtable Discussion About Being Trans in Libraries," British Columbia Library Association, September 5, 2019, https://bclaconnect.ca/perspectives/2019/09/05/not-cis-in-lis-a-roundtable-discussion-about-being-trans-in-libraries/.

454 Allison Jones et al., "Not Cis in LIS."

455 Allison Jones et al.

456 Allison Jones et al.

457 Allison Jones et al.

problematic.[458] Two of the films planned for that fall, *Profiled* and *Trouble 19: ACAB*, were on the topics of racial profiling and police violence, issues of local significance, and they raised concern among library management, who then asked Khasnabish to include a police officer in the panel discussion of the event.[459] HPL CEO Asa Kachan explained that the library made this suggestion in order to facilitate "open and uncensored community conversation around the issues of policing, injustice and violence," and because the library aims to provide access to a variety of viewpoints: "Libraries are democratic, inclusive spaces."[460] Khasnabish countered that "having police vet public events at the library seems a lot like censorship and that having police present as a formal part of the program would inhibit important community discussions."[461] He also pointed out that in his previous years of programming the film series that included topics such as climate change and decolonization, the library had never before intervened to require representation of both sides of the issue participate in the panel discussion.[462] When Khasnabish refused the library's suggestion, they said he might include a representative from the Halifax Regional Municipality instead of a police officer, or he could still use the library space for his event, but they would no longer provide sponsorship in the form of a free room, so he opted to try finding a new venue.[463]

Khasnabish wrote about this experience in the *Halifax Examiner*, explaining the importance of public access to free spaces and his disappointment and frustration with the library's approach to this event. He said that it was important for him to hold this series in space outside the university campus and to keep it free in order to encourage broader and more diverse attendance, so to lose the library's sponsorship

---

458 Alex Khasnabish, "Library's Insistence That Police Be Invited to Speak Spells End of Popular Film and Discussion Series," *The Nova Scotia Advocate*, June 27, 2019, https://nsadvocate.org/2019/06/27/librarys-insistence-that-police-be-invited-to-speak-spells-end-of-popular-film-and-discussion-series/.

459 Khasnabish, "Library's Insistence That Police Be Invited to Speak Spells End of Popular Film and Discussion Series"; Mairin Prentiss, "Library Won't Partner with Group Planning to Screen Films About Police Brutality," *CBC*, June 29, 2019, https://www.cbc.ca/news/canada/nova-scotia/halifax-library-rejects-police-film-screenings-1.5195260.

460 Prentiss, "Library Won't Partner with Group Planning to Screen Films About Police Brutality."

461 Khasnabish, "Library's Insistence That Police Be Invited to Speak Spells End of Popular Film and Discussion Series."

462 Khasnabish.

463 Prentiss, "Library Won't Partner with Group Planning to Screen Films About Police Brutality."

would be difficult, but he could not give in to their speaker requirements, which would create "a chilling of critical conversation and debate."[464] He argued that:

> "this is what censorship and deplatforming look like on a daily basis… it is the liberal, bureaucratic, plausibly deniable choking out of dissent and alternatives in the service of the status quo and the interests it represents that has been the most common face of censorship in a society like ours. It is a quiet, polite, and impersonal denial of the right to have difficult discussions in spaces not colonized by the powerful and their agents. I am sure senior library staff would never describe their intent in these terms, but the effect is the same."

Khasnabish was critical of the power dynamics at play, suggesting that as a powerful and celebrated social institution, the police have sufficient platforms and do not need to be featured in an event that seeks to promote the voices and experiences of people from marginalized communities.[465]

I did not find any evidence in the media of public outcry against the event or supporting police participation that informed the library's position, but from the library management's perspective, they saw the film screening event "as an opportunity to work toward solutions, healing and change as a community."[466] HPL Manager of Program Development, Karen Dahl, said that while the library had not previously suggested speakers for Khasnabish's programming, they felt it appropriate in this case given "how important and sensitive this issue is in our community right now," so having police participation would be "more inclusive" and facilitate their participation in change.[467] And she countered the accusation of censorship by explaining that the library is a "safe democratic space for our communities to work through things and sometimes that means bringing diverse and even opposing

---

464 Alex Khasnabish, "Policing the Radical Imagination," *Halifax Examiner*, July 1, 2019, https://www.halifaxexaminer.ca/featured/policing-the-radical-imagination/.

465 Khasnabish, "Policing the Radical Imagination"; Nicole Munro, "Man Refuses to Let Police Officer Speak, Loses Program Partnership With Halifax Public Libraries," *The Chronicle Herald*, July 2, 2019, https://www.saltwire.com/nova-scotia/news/man-refuses-to-let-police-officer-speak-loses-program-partnership-with-halifax-public-libraries-328251/.

466 Munro, "Man Refuses to Let Police Officer Speak."

467 Munro.

voices into a space."[468] Here Dahl seems to be contorting the concepts of inclusion and diversity to justify prioritizing powerful voices, and she ignores the very real threat that police pose to the safety of marginalized people, meaning that the library is no longer a safe space for them with police there. As an opinion in the *Halifax Examiner* pointed out in response to the library's statement about the controversy: "Using the language of creating 'a safe and welcoming public space' to insist that police should provide their perspective on profiling — a subject they have fallen down on horribly over the last several months — is absurd."[469]

Public outcry did come in support of Khasnabish through a petition and letter-writing campaign to the library, which prompted Kachan to request a meeting with Khasnabish to discuss a solution.[470] They decided that the event would proceed as originally planned and then the library would host its own separate event to discuss policing issues.[471] Khasnabish expressed appreciation for the library's willingness to collaborate on a solution, and the library released a statement that indicated some growth in understanding Khasnabish's and the community's concerns around policing and power and safety.[472] HPL affirmed the need to provide safe spaces where people, "especially those who experience marginalization, can speak freely and openly about the issues that affect them," and said that "[w]here policing is concerned, this is particularly true for members of our Indigenous, African Nova Scotian, and LGBTQ+ communities," and that the library "acknowledge[s] these concerns and the statistics related to likelihood of involvement in the justice system, and the power imbalance that many experience."[473]

---

468 Munro.

469 Philip Moscovitch, "Diminishing Dissent," *Halifax Examiner*, July 2, 2019, https://www.halifaxexaminer.ca/featured/diminishing-dissent/.

470 Nicole Munro, "Series Back at Halifax Library; Films on Racial Profiling to be shown with 'no Strings Attached'," *The Chronicle Herald*, July 8, 2019, ProQuest.

471 Robert Devet, "Radical Imagination Series Back at the Halifax Central Library Where It Belongs," *Nova Scotia Advocate*, July 5, 2019, https://nsadvocate.org/2019/07/05/radical-imagination-series-back-at-the-halifax-central-library-where-it-belongs/.

472 Devet, "Radical Imagination Series Back at the Halifax Central Library Where It Belongs"; Munro, "Series Back at Halifax Library."

473 Munro, "Series Back at Halifax Library."

2019 Kelowna, British Columbia

Storytime events featuring drag artists reading books to children have become popular in public libraries and other venues over the last 10 years. There had been some rumblings of conservative opposition to them (for example, right-wing Christians blogging against them in Toronto in 2018[474]), but in 2019 a public controversy broke out about the Okanagan Regional Library (ORL)'s Drag Queen Storytime in downtown Kelowna. ORL Youth Services Librarian Ashley Machum proposed the idea of having a drag queen storytime to ORL Head Librarian Chris Stephenson, who anticipated that there would be public pushback against the programming, but he approved two of the events for that fall because "[i]t's a no-brainer that kids and their families really love this stuff."[475] Moreover, Machum felt it was important programming for the library because "[t]here are many different ways that information is presented from different viewpoints, different communities, different cultures, different people," and, "[e]verybody has their own right [and] intellectual freedom to their own beliefs."[476] The library's website described the programming as helping "children develop empathy, learn about gender diversity and difference and tap into their own creativity," and local drag queen Freida Whales, also known as Tyson Cook, described that the agenda for the event was "to read stories to kids, just have a great time making anyone happy and entertaining anybody."[477] When the events were announced, the library faced criticism online with some commenters using hateful homophobic stereotypes as arguments against the events, but the first drag queen storytime on September 14, 2019, was very popular, with over 160 attendees,

---

[474] Sima Shakeri, "Christian Website Accuses Toronto Drag Queen Storytime Of Trying To 'Indoctrinate Kids,'" *Huffington Post Canada*, July 21, 2018, https://www.huffpost.com/archive/ca/entry/drag-queen-storytime-at-toronto-public-library-tries-to-indoctrinate-kids-lifesitenews_ca_5cd55bb1e4b07bc729775a95.

[475] Tahiat Mahboob, "How a B.C. Library's Drag Queen Story Hour Turned into a Nationwide Fight for Intellectual Freedom," *CBC*, November 7, 2020, https://www.cbc.ca/radio/docproject/how-a-b-c-library-s-drag-queen-story-hour-turned-into-a-nationwide-fight-for-intellectual-freedom-1.5786657.

[476] Mahboob, "How a B.C. Library's Drag Queen Story Hour Turned into a Nationwide Fight for Intellectual Freedom."

[477] "Drag Queen Storytime Is 'Controversial' and 'Potentially Divisive,' Says Okanagan Library CEO," *CBC*, September 20, 2019, https://www.cbc.ca/news/canada/british-columbia/kelowna-drag-queen-story-time-1.5292257.

including kids dressed in costumes who sang and danced along, and no protestors present.[478]

However, there was concern about the programming brewing in the library board, which fed the controversy and raised questions around librarians' professional autonomy vs the authority of the library board. ORL CEO Don Nettleton, who had received complaint letters and calls about the events,[479] wrote a memo on September 9 to the library board expressing his concerns that the events "will be offensive to a significant segment of our society" and could cause the library to lose broad public support.[480] He was also worried that this programming might be inappropriate for young children and could "reposition [the library] away from being an accepted, middle of the road, non-controversial (neutral) and safe environment for children's programming."[481] Nettleton noted the board's split response to the drag storytime, with half in support, who see "the library as a front-line agent to affect social change," and the other half, including himself, who prefer the library to be a "safe and neutral environment" rather than being "needlessly divisive" and "pushing a liberal political agenda." [482] Interestingly, for Nettleton, neutrality meant limiting intellectual freedom, which is a different approach than we've seen in most examples when the one principle typically supports the other. To him, that neutrality, which also seems to mean straight, was more important than making the library an inclusive space for gender and sexual diversity, and his idea of a "safe environment" meant preserving the status quo, rather than ensuring the library is what many in 2SLGBTQIA+ communities commonly understand as a "safe space." He ended the memo by recommending that a policy be developed that would direct children's programming staff to avoid "controversial and/or potentially divisive community issues."[483] The Kelowna Pride Society released a statement on September 17 in response to the memo thanking the

---

478 Mahboob, "How a B.C. Library's Drag Queen Story Hour Turned into a Nationwide Fight for Intellectual Freedom."

479 "Drag Queen Storytime Is 'Controversial' and 'Potentially Divisive'."

480 Okanagan Regional Library, *Notice of Meeting*, (Okanagan, BC: Okanagan Regional Library, 2019), 34, https://orl.bc.ca/docs/default-source/library_board/meeting_agendas/bod-agd_18sep19.pdf?sfvrsn=0.

481 Okanagan Regional Library, *Notice of Meeting*, 34.

482 Okanagan Regional Library.

483 Okanagan Regional Library, *Notice of Meeting*, 34.

library for hosting these diversifying events and noting that based on the attendance, "[i]t seems clear that the ORL provided a space for something the community was missing."[484] They also expressed hope that the board would disregard the memo and "[l]eave programming to the librarians."[485]

While the library board reviewed the memo and gathered feedback,[486] the next drag queen storytime went ahead on November 16, this time with about 300 attendees inside and two protestors outside the event who favoured "traditional values" and were against people treating their children like "social experiments."[487] ORL Public Services Director Monica Gaucher was happy with the events, arguing: "We are a space of freedom of information and freedom to access information." Central Okanagan school board trustee Norah Bowman expressed her support of the programming, "I trust our librarians, and I knew that our librarians would stand up for literacy and inclusivity."[488] When the board met on November 20 they had received about 350 pieces of correspondence representing both sides of the debate, including an email complaint from a library staff member who opposed the library "promoting adult agendas and ideologies, no matter how in vogue they may be," and another letter writer worried that "children could become confused by such behavior," describing drag as unacceptable.[489] Whereas a retired librarian commented that "[p]arents are responsible for what their children borrow, what they look at on the internet, what programs they go to" and "[l]ibraries… don't act in the place of a parent."[490] The BCLA also voiced support for drag storytimes, noting

---

484 "ORL Discussing Changes to Policy to Prevent Drag Queen Story Time," *Kelowna Pride*, September 17, 2019, https://www.kelownapride.com/post/orl-discussing-changes-to-policy-to-prevent-drag-queen-story-time.

485 "ORL Discussing Changes to Policy to Prevent Drag Queen Story Time."

486 "Drag Queen Storytime Is 'Controversial' and 'Potentially Divisive'."

487 Jules Knox, "Despite Controversy, Kelowna Library's Drag Queen Story Time Grows in Popularity," *Global News*, November 16, 2019, https://globalnews.ca/news/6179357/kelowna-library-drag-queen-story-time-popularity/.

488 Knox, "Despite Controversy."

489 Megan Turcato, "Okanagan library board won't intervene in Kelowna's Drag Queen Story Time," *Global News*, November 20, 2019, https://globalnews.ca/news/6195547/okanagan-library-board-drag-queen-story-time/.

490 Turcato, "Okanagan library board won't intervene."

the evidence that "discussions about gender identities are beneficial for children's health development."[491]

The board decided against Nettleton's call for an overarching children's programming policy, instead supporting professional and parental autonomy.[492] Kelowna city councillor and ORL board member Lloyd Wooldridge explained the reason for the board's decision: "We believe that librarians in communities throughout the region know their communities best to choose the programming that is appropriate."[493] The board also recommended that Nettleton and all senior staff take sensitivity and diversity training, which they did in December 2019, and Nettleton sent an apology letter to library staff.[494] The following summer, the BCLA awarded Ashley Machum and Christopher Stephenson with the Champion of Intellectual Freedom Award for their work "convinc[ing] skeptics that the tenets of Intellectual Freedom meant that a Drag Queen story time should be a welcome part of library programming."[495] In this case, intellectual freedom aligned with inclusion against discrimination.

2019 Toronto, Ontario

A group called Radical Feminists Unite rented a room at the Palmerston branch of Toronto Public Library for Meghan Murphy to speak at an event called "Gender Identity: What Does It Mean for Society, the Law and Women" on October 29, 2019. To get in front of the anticipated public outcry, City Librarian Vickery Bowles released a statement on October 12 indicating that the booking was in line with TPL policies, which had been updated in 2017, and that TPL "cannot deny access to a room rental on the basis of views that the third party holds if the request meets criteria set out in our policy."[496] She also noted

---

491 Turcato, "Okanagan library board won't intervene."

492 Turcato.

493 Turcato.

494 Mahboob, "How a B.C. Library's Drag Queen Story Hour Turned into a Nationwide Fight for Intellectual Freedom."

495 "BCLA Announces Recipients of 2020 Awards," Librarianship.ca, July 2, 2020, https://librarianship.ca/news/bcla-2020-awards/.

496 "Statement from City Librarian on Room Rental Event," Toronto Public Library, October 12, 2019, https://torontopubliclibrary.typepad.com/news_releases/2019/10/statement-from-city-librarian-on-room-rental-event.html.

the core value of intellectual freedom, the library's position of neutrality, and its commitment to equity and diversity.[497] Then three days later, Bowles released another longer statement in response to "significant discussion and negative feedback."[498] In this one, Bowles provided more detail on the decision-making, noting that TPL reviews the stated purpose of third-party events, and since this event's stated purpose was "[t]o have an educational and open discussion on the concept of gender identity and its legislation ramifications on women in Canada," and Murphy had never been charged with or convicted of hate speech, there was no policy or legal basis to deny the booking.[499] However, hate speech was no longer the bar to be met after the 2017 policy changes, which allow bookings to be denied if they "would have the effect of promoting discrimination, contempt or hatred."[500] Bowles also said that "TPL encourages public debate and discussion about differing ideas, we also encourage those with opposing or conflicting viewpoints to respectfully challenge each other's ideas and not the library's democratic mandate to provide free speech to both ."[501] This reads as though TPL was okay with people challenging views and ideas, just not those that the library deems off limits, as if "the library's democratic mandate to provide free speech" is not just another socially-constructed idea but a naturally occurring and infallible phenomenon. And she ended the statement with what I would describe as a patronizing suggestion to literary community members that "engaging in respectful civil discourse with people of opposing views may be a more productive strategy than abstaining from public library events."[502] So in addition to suggesting limits on what the public can criticize the library for, she also suggested limits on how the public should enact their criticism of the library. Unsurprisingly, a lot of the public did not accept these suggestions.

---

497 "Statement from City Librarian on Room Rental Event."

498 "City Librarian Statement on Upcoming Third-Party Room Rental Event," Toronto Public Library, October 15, 2019, https://torontopubliclibrary.typepad.com/news_releases/2019/10/city-librarian-statement-on-upcoming-third-party-room-rental-event-.html.

499 "City Librarian Statement on Upcoming Third-Party Room Rental Event."

500 "Community and Event Space Rental," Toronto Public Library, January 1, 2018, https://www.torontopubliclibrary.ca/terms-of-use/library-policies/community-and-event-space.jsp.

501 "City Librarian Statement on Upcoming Third-Party Room Rental Event."

502 "City Librarian Statement on Upcoming Third-Party Room Rental Event."

What Bowles was responding to from the literary community was an online petition started by writers Alicia Elliott, Catherine Hernandez, and Carianne Leung that called for TPL to cancel the event, stating that if the event happened there would be a protest at the library, and the petition signees would no longer participate in TPL events.[503] Within a few days, more than 2000 people had signed the petition,[504] which argued that "[o]ffering Murphy a platform means denying the resources and promise of safe and equitable space to trans communities."[505] In response to the library's reasoning for allowing the event booking, the petition states:

> "[t]hose who want to disseminate hate speech today know that they can misrepresent, then weaponize the phrase 'freedom of speech' in order to get what they want: an audience, and space to speak to and then mobilize that audience against marginalized communities... There is a difference between denying free speech—and what is known as deplatforming, which is when you refuse to allow hate speech to be disseminated in your facility."[506]

Discussing the petition they started, Hernandez said, "[o]ur hope is that a boycott will send a clear message that transphobic rhetoric leads to transphobic violence,"[507] and Elliott tweeted, "[t]his is a difficult decision to make, as we all love the TPL, but we love our trans friends and family more."[508] Another online petition was made by a group of artists, writers, and scientists who had been collaborators with TPL and often used their spaces for events, calling on the library

---

503 Alicia Elliot, Catherine Hernandez, and Carrianne Leung, "Stop Hate Speech from Being Spread at the Toronto Public Library," Change.org, accessed April, 2021, https://www.change.org/p/toronto-public-library-request-for-tpl-to-cancel-rental-booking-for-transphobic-event-at-palmerston-library.

504 At the time of writing there are over 9650 signatures.

505 Elliot, Hernandez, and Leung, "Stop Hate Speech from Being Spread at the Toronto Public Library."

506 Elliot, Hernandez, and Leung.

507 Becky Robertson, "Local Authors Are Now Boycotting the Toronto Public Library," blogTO, October 15, 2019, https://www.blogto.com/arts/2019/10/local-authors-boycotting-toronto-public-library/.

508 Alicia Elliott (@WordsandGuitar), "This is a difficult decision to make," Twitter, October 15, 2019, 10:01 a.m., https://twitter.com/WordsandGuitar/status/1184107074009075713.

to cancel the event, and if they did not, the signees would reconsider future partnerships with TPL.[509]

The group hosting the event, Radical Feminists Unite, released a statement that asserted, "[w]e are not a hate group, and we do not espouse hate speech, or advocate for the removal of rights from any marginalized group," and they described theirs and Murphy's ideas as being about gender identity and concerns for the rights of women and girls, which, to them, do not include transgender women.[510] Murphy also refuted accusations against her, arguing: "What I am saying is not controversial, and certainly is not hateful … We deserve space for this conversation and our concerns deserve respect."[511] The Canadian Civil Liberties Association (CCLA) supported TPL's decision to allow the event, as spokesperson Cara Zwibel noted the high legal threshold for hate speech and said: "She has the same rights to free expression as anyone else. Those rights can be limited but only for compelling reasons and in a proportional way. On the facts as I understand them, there isn't a basis for preventing her from speaking."[512] Opinion pieces in the *Globe and Mail* and *Toronto Sun* both wrote in favour of the library's decision to defend free speech,[513] however a second *Globe and Mail* opinion piece challenged Murphy's views as transphobic and anti-feminist.[514] In the *National Post*, Jonathan Kay defended Murphy as victim of "a modern red scare, with 'TERF' (trans-exclusionary

---

509   Al Donato et al., "Toronto Public Library Collaborators Condemn TPL's Decision On Meghan Murphy Talk," Change.org, accessed April, 2021, https://www.change.org/p/toronto-public-library-toronto-public-library-collaborators-condemn-tpl-s-decision-on-meghan-murphy-talk. At the time of writing there are over 500 signatures.

510   The Oct 17, 2019 statement was originally posted on the Radical Feminists Unite website, which I accessed in April 2021, but is now private. The statement is also posted in full on a blog called Dead Wild Roses: "RFU statement on Meghan Murphy event at Toronto Public Library," *Dead Wild Roses* (blog), October 24, 2019, https://deadwildroses.com/2019/10/24/rfu-statement-on-meghan-murphy-event-at-toronto-public-library/.

511   Julia Knope, "Tory 'Disappointed' in Toronto Public Library for Hosting Speaker Accused of Transphobia," *CBC*, October 17, 2019, https://www.cbc.ca/news/canada/toronto/toronto-public-library-tory-speaker-transphobia-1.5324218.

512   Francine Kopun, "Authors Warn They'll Boycott Toronto Public Library Over Speaker Accused of Being Anti-Transgender," *Toronto Star*, October 16, 2019, ProQuest.

513   Marcus Gee, "A Librarian's Stirring Call for Free Speech: Toronto Public Library Head Vickery Bowles was Right to Refuse Calls to Ban Controversial Speaker and Journalist Meghan Murphy," *The Globe and Mail*, October 19, 2019, ProQuest; Lorrie Goldstein, "City Librarian Vickery Bowles Defends Free Speech," *Toronto Sun*, October 17, 2019, ProQuest.

514   Denise Balkissoon, "The Targeting of Other Women Shows Meghan Murphy Is No Feminist," *The Globe and Mail*, October 28, 2019, https://www.theglobeandmail.com/opinion/article-the-targeting-of-other-women-shows-meghan-murphy-is-no-feminist/.

radical feminist) replacing 'commie' as the preferred term of abuse."[515] His mother, Barbara Kay, also wrote an opinion in the *National Post* in agreement with Murphy's "rational and reasonable boundary" that transgender people should "fall into a new and unique social category," and she argued that locker rooms and women's prisons should be "safe spaces" for women according to sex assigned at birth.[516] That's right, she was suggesting that prisons are an otherwise safe space for women, as long as they do not have trans women there. There was also an online petition in support of TPL.[517]

Some local politicians began speaking out against the library's decision, including Mayor John Tory, who had also been critical of TPL for allowing the Kulaszka memorial in 2017. This time he did not call for any policy changes, but he did contact Bowles to ask her to reconsider, and he shared with the press his disappointment that TPL was allowing "offensive commentary that is going to cause harm and cause hurt to others in the community."[518] Toronto-St. Paul's NDP MPP and NDP Culture Critic Jill Andrew expressed her dismay with the decision: "a person who publicly espouses hate speech should not be given a platform to disseminate their views at a publicly funded institution such as the TPL."[519] The Toronto Public Library Workers Union Local 4948 was also openly critical of the TPL decision. Their president Brendan Haley wrote a letter to Bowles arguing that Murphy's description of the event was "disingenuous, to say the least," and said:

> "Her views do, in fact, target highly vulnerable and marginalized communities not only in our workplace, but among library users in Toronto and beyond ... The work that staff have done to reach out

---

515 Jonathan Kay, "Campaign to Silence Feminist a Disgrace; Trans Activists Seek to De-Platform Meghan Murphy," *National Post*, October 18, 2019, ProQuest.

516 Barbara Kay, "How Feminist Meghan Murphy Fell Victim to Progressives' Double Standards," *National Post*, October 24, 2019, ProQuest.

517 Valerie Bernham, "Support for Toronto Public Library," Change.org, accessed April, 2021, https://www.change.org/p/toronto-public-library-support-for-toronto-public-library?signed=true. At the time of writing there are over 1700 signatures.

518 David Rider, "John Tory 'Disappointed' Toronto Library Allowing Event with Writer Accused of Being Anti-Transgender," *Toronto Star*, October 17, 2019, https://www.thestar.com/news/city_hall/2019/10/17/john-tory-disappointed-toronto-library-allowing-event-with-writer-accused-of-being-anti-transgender.html.

519 "NDP Culture Critic Responds to Toronto Public Library's Refusal to Cancel Event Featuring Meghan Murphy," Ontario NDP, October 17, 2019, https://www.ontariondp.ca/news/ndp-culture-critic-responds-toronto-public-library-s-refusal-cancel-event-featuring-meghan.

to community members, and to build trust and partnerships, has now been compromised to some extent by this decision. For many, the library might no longer represent a safe and inclusive space."[520]

Community organizations also joined the calls for the event to be cancelled. The Toronto Comic Arts Festival (TCAF) made a statement urging TPL to cancel the event, stating: "While we also support the ideals of free speech, the prior and likely future actions and speech of this speaker are incredibly harmful, and fall outside the bounds of protected speech due to their hateful and dehumanizing nature."[521] The group Canadian Parents of Trans, Two-Spirit & Gender Diverse Kids wrote a powerful open letter to the chair of the library board expressing deep disappointment "to see the TPL failing our children and our community."[522] It went on to say:

> "Additionally, in the past few weeks we have witnessed the TPL's dismissiveness toward the transgender community. Given that trans women face alarmingly high risk of harassment and violence, it is disingenuous of the TPL to say that we can all engage in civil debate about trans rights at an event that draws together Murphy's supporters. Further, TPL is sending the hurtful message to our children and youth that they do not deserve safety in the library's public spaces, while it is simultaneously sending an encouraging signal to those who wish to further marginalize and harm transgender people."[523]

And Pride Toronto weighed in with their opposition, saying in their statement: "It was our belief that the TPL was committed to creating library spaces that are inclusive, safe and welcoming. The recent decision to allow the event with Meghan Murphy is a betrayal to our

---

520   The Local 4948 letter is no longer available on their website, but can be found on pg. 4–5 of: Toronto Public Library Board Meeting, October 22, 2019, Toronto, https://www.torontopubliclibrary.ca/content/about-the-library/pdfs/board/meetings/2019/oct22/09-communications-combined.pdf.

521   TCAF The Toronto Comic Arts Festival (@TorontoComics), "While we also support the ideals of free speech," Twitter, October 16, 2019, 3:42 p.m., https://twitter.com/TorontoComics/status/1184555231503364097.

522   CdnParentsTransKids (@CPoTGDK), "Our statement on @torontolibrary renting space," Twitter, October 22, 2019, 9:39 a.m., https://twitter.com/CPoTGDK/status/1186638263118958593.

523   CdnParentsTransKids, "Our Statement on @torontolibrary renting space."

LGBT2SQ+ communities."[524] Pride argued that Murphy's viewpoints constitute "denial of the lives, experiences and identities of Trans people," and that "[i]t is clear that the Meghan Murphy event will violate both the spirit and the letter of TPL's anti-discrimination policy," then ended by saying that if theirs and the many other public appeals for the event to be cancelled are denied, "there will be consequences to our relationship for this betrayal."[525] These organizations were all arguing the point that transphobic views do real harm to trans people so the library can no longer claim to support and welcome the 2SLGBTQIA+ community when it supports and welcomes those who are causing that harm.

Despite these criticisms and appeals, Bowles stood firm on the decision. In an interview on the CBC's "As It Happens" radio program, host Carol Off asked tough questions and Bowles reaffirmed her arguments and reasoning around intellectual freedom and hate speech. She also brought in the concept of library neutrality and suggested that the library approaches collections and event bookings in the same neutral way:

> "We use the same principles in making decisions about room bookings as we do for our collections, Carol. We have a broad diversity of information and ideas and perspectives that are represented in all the books in our collections, and some of those ideas and perspectives people would find hurtful and painful. But we're not going to remove those books from our collection. And we are not going to eliminate programs from our branches that are controversial. And we're not going to shut down room bookings because the speaker in the room booking has controversial ideas."[526]

Of course, we have seen some people make the point that library collection methods are not actually neutral, and others have pointed out the differences in power and impact between having books on

---

524 Pride Toronto (@PrideToronto), "Pride Toronto's Board of Directors public statement," Twitter, October 18, 2019, 12:40 p.m., https://twitter.com/PrideToronto/status/1185234099998543874.

525 Pride Toronto, "Pride Toronto's Board of Directors public statement."

526 Sheena Goodyear, "'I'm Not Going to Reconsider': Toronto's Top Librarian Refuses to Bar Speaker Critical of Transgender Rights," *CBC*, October 17, 2019, https://www.cbc.ca/radio/asithappens/as-it-happens-thursday-edition-1.5324424/i-m-not-going-to-reconsider-toronto-s-top-librarian-refuses-to-bar-speaker-critical-of-transgender-rights-1.5324431.

your shelf and holding events in your space. Bowles also noted that the library had heard from members of the public who supported the event, including trans people, but most asked that their communications be kept in confidence to avoid reprisal.[527]

On October 22, the TPL board meeting heard from members of the public about the upcoming event. Public attendance at the meeting filled the board room and necessitated an overflow room with a livestream for about 120 people, and there were extra security guards and police present for part of the meeting.[528] By the time of the meeting, TPL and the board had received letters from 5 organizations supporting their decision: the Canadian Civil Liberties Association (CCLA), Canadian Federation of Library Associations (CFLA), Canadian Urban Libraries Council, Urban Libraries Council, and the Centre for Free Expression, and letters from 5 organizations requesting that the event be cancelled, including 4 that I have mentioned as well as 1 from the Trans Women's Association.[529] They also reported receiving 8 letters in support and 4 letters in opposition from individuals, as well as 389 emails in support and 69 in opposition, and 8 phone calls in support and 8 in opposition.[530] And the *Toronto Star* reported that at least 3 TPL room bookings had been cancelled at this point, citing opposition to the Murphy event as the reason.[531]

At the meeting, over 20 people gave deputations to the board to share their perspectives on the event booking, including trans people, community organization representatives, librarians, and other members

---

527 Goodyear, "'I'm Not Going to Reconsider.'"

528 Samantha Edwards, "Pride to Hold Trans Rally on the Night of Meghan Murphy Event," *NOW Magazine*, October 23, 2019, https://nowtoronto.com/culture/books-culture/pride-trans-rally-toronto-public-library-meghan-murphy.

529 Toronto Public Library, *Community Space Rental at Palmerston*, (Toronto: Toronto Public Library, 2019), https://www.torontopubliclibrary.ca/content/about-the-library/pdfs/board/meetings/2019/oct22/10a-community-space-rental-at.Palmerston.pdf; The letters can be found in: Toronto Public Library Board Meeting, October 22, 2019. https://www.torontopubliclibrary.ca/content/about-the-library/pdfs/board/meetings/2019/oct22/09-communications-combined.pdf.

530 Toronto Public Library, *Community Space Rental at Palmerston*.

531 Francine Kopun, "After Trans Rights Protest at Controversial Event, Toronto Votes to Review Community Space Policies," *Toronto Star*, October 30, 2019, https://www.thestar.com/news/city_hall/2019/10/30/after-trans-rights-protest-at-library-toronto-votes-to-review-community-space-policies.html.

of the public.[532] Pride TO Executive Director Olivia Nuamah spoke about the violence that many trans people experience and the responsibility that the library board will have for the negative social impacts of platforming transphobia. She further made the point that: "The gatekeepers of the definition of free speech are never subject to the unintended consequences of their desire to foster open intellectual discourse."[533] We have seen this important point raised before, that those in positions of power to make these decisions are approaching them academically because they are usually not at risk of experiencing the negative consequences of psychological or physical harm. Trans writer Gwen Benaway talked about her experiences of discrimination and called on the library to do more to protect trans rights.[534] Academic librarian Jane Schmidt shared that "there are a good number of librarians and library workers who believe that intellectual freedom must not trump the lives of real people. Ideology must never come before people and that is exactly the message that TPL is sending to the queer and trans community right now."[535] She also spoke about how the library wasted an opportunity to learn from VPL's experience with a Murphy event to consider context in their decision making, instead turning it into "a crusade for freedom of speech above all else."[536] Among the speakers who supported the library's decision was a 2SLGBTQIA+ community member named Benji who said: "I don't agree with everything Meghan Murphy says, but I believe we should have a platform to discuss these things in a nuanced and respectful way."[537]

The board made no motion to reconsider Bowles' decision. After the meeting, board member and Toronto Councillor Gord Perks said it is important to think about "the broader implication[s]" and that the

---

532   There was a lot of discussion of the board meeting on Twitter, too much for me to find and digest, but here are two threads of live-tweeting from the meeting: Ziya Jones (@ZiyaJonesA), "At the TPL public board meeting," Twitter, October 22, 2019, 6:00 p.m., https://twitter.com/ZiyaJonesA/status/1186764328151724032; Julia Duchesne (@juliamusing), "I'll be attending this meeting as an observer," Twitter, October 22, 2019, https://twitter.com/juliamusing/status/1186711470391857153.

533   Edwards, "Pride to Hold Trans Rally on the Night of Meghan Murphy Event."

534   Edwards.

535   Jane Schmidt, "My Remarks to the TPL Board," *The Incidental Academic Librarian* (blog), October 22, 2019, https://incidentalacademic.wordpress.com/2019/10/22/my-remarks-to-the-tpl-board/. Full disclosure: Jane is a friend and respected colleague of mine.

536   Schmidt, "My Remarks to the TPL Board."

537   Edwards, "Pride to Hold Trans Rally on the Night of Meghan Murphy Event."

board's role is to ensure library policy is being followed.[538] Referring to City Librarian Bowles, Perks said: "I don't have to agree with her decision. I just have to agree that she did the work."[539] Another board member and city councillor, Paul Ainslie, said the board cannot "get into the weeds" and overturn TPL staff decisions, adding that "we [the board] pride ourselves on being a forum where people can speak about things, and you can agree or disagree with them." In the meantime, a coalition of organizations including Pride TO, The 519, Artists for Climate and Migrant Justice and Indigenous Sovereignty, Fight for $15 & Fairness, Climate Justice Toronto, Maggies: Toronto Sex Workers Action Project, SURJ Toronto, No More Silence, IfNotNow Toronto, Workers' Action Centre, and New Socialists began organizing protests for the day of the event, which were endorsed by TPLWU Local 4948.[540] Also, two city councillors, Kristyn Wong-Tam and Mike Layton, reacted to the decision by proposing a motion that would be considered at the next city council meeting to strengthen policies for using community spaces to proactively identify and deny bookings for those who contravene the City of Toronto's Vision Statement on Access, Equity and Diversity as well as the city's Anti-Harassment/Discrimination policy.[541]

More public statements were released by TPL partners and other stakeholders. Glad Day Bookshop released a lengthy statement announcing a boycott of TPL, with whom they had partnered previously on a variety of initiatives, noting the "damage, harm and hate the TPL will be causing and fueling by allowing the event to take place at the library."[542] The statement also asked: "How can the Toronto Public Library leadership make amends for sacrificing its partnerships, ignoring authors, dismissing its workers, shattering community relationships and causing harm to Trans people?" It then offered, "we have an

---

538 Edwards.

539 Edwards, "Pride to Hold Trans Rally on the Night of Meghan Murphy Event."

540 "Community Groups Stage Protest in Support of Trans Lives" *Canada NewsWire*, October 28, 2019.

541 Francine Kopun, "Councillors Seek Tighter Control Over Library: Controversial Feminist's Right to Speak on Gender Identity Drives Debate," *Toronto Star,* October 25, 2019, ProQuest; Revised Member Motion MM11.14, October 29, 2019, City of Toronto, https://www.toronto.ca/legdocs/mmis/2019/mm/bgrd/backgroundfile-139260.pdf.

542 Glad Day Bookshop (@GDBooks), "Glad Day's statement on the @torontolibrary's failure," Twitter, October 29, 2019, 3:37 p.m., https://twitter.com/GDBooks/status/1189265035278929921.

idea of how you can start: at the top."⁵⁴³ Al Donato, a non-binary artist and journalist, stepped down as artist-in-residence at TPL's Oakwood branch, noting that the library no longer felt safe.⁵⁴⁴ Another rebuke of the library came from Kaleb Robertson, aka Fluffy Souffle, one half of the duo Fay and Fluffy, who had been doing a drag storytime with TPL for over 3 years. Robertson announced that the pair was ending their relationship with TPL over the Murphy event, stating:

> "I am a trans man who is fiercely protective of trans kids and women. I could not call myself an ally and fighter for my community if I continue a relationship with a space that will host someone who is actively fighting to take away my legal rights as a human. Trans people existing and having rights to employment, housing, and safety is not a discussion."⁵⁴⁵

Robertson also spoke to City News and said that freedom of speech should not be protected at the cost of other people's freedoms, and that Fay and Fluffy's Storytime would continue at other Toronto venues.⁵⁴⁶

PEN Canada's statement said it supports TPL's decision because "Murphy's opinions do not meet a legal threshold for exclusion under the library's rental policy, though they are clearly at odds with the inclusive spirit which should inform its enforcement."⁵⁴⁷ But it also went on to say that "Advocating for trans people to be barred from gendered public spaces although it contravenes no laws, clearly fosters discrimination against them."⁵⁴⁸ It is confusing that PEN Canada admits these views that Murphy holds and speaks often publicly "clearly foste[r] discrimination," while also asserting that TPL had no legal policy justification to cancel the booking even though TPL's policy allows

---

543 Glad Day Bookshop, "Glad Day's statement on the @torontolibrary's failure."

544 Edwards, "Pride to Hold Trans Rally on the Night of Meghan Murphy Event."

545 Kaleb Robertson (@uncle_kaleb), "I am writing to let you know," Instagram, October 29, 2019, https://www.instagram.com/p/B4NPpLbglYb/.

546 Dilshad Burman, "Fay and Fluffy's Storytime Ends Toronto Public Library Affiliation Over Meghan Murphy Talk," City News, October 29, 2019, https://toronto.citynews.ca/2019/10/29/fay-and-fluffys-library-storytime-cancelled-meghan-murphy-event/.

547 "Public Libraries and Freedom of Expression," PEN Canada, October 28, 2019, https://pencanada.ca/news/public-libraries-and-freedom-of-expression/.

548 "Public Libraries and Freedom of Expression."

for bookings to be denied or cancelled if they are likely to promote discrimination.[549] Murphy herself said she had received "a ton of support throughout Canada" in response to the event controversy, and the demand for tickets exceeded the event's capacity.[550] She said that people are "very angry about the way these writers and politicians are trying to silence free speech, silence women, and bully the library into not upholding their mandate."[551] In an interview with *Toronto Star*, the City Librarian once again defended TPL's decision, and offered that "we seem to be in a place where there is less tolerance for a diversity of viewpoints and civil discourse is discouraged in some instances, which I think is very challenging." She went on to say, "I believe that this has been a valuable debate and I know it's been hurtful for the transgender community," then said that the library will work hard with the 2SLGBTQIA+ community to offer programs and services that meet their needs.[552] But evidently not their need to be protected from transphobia in the library.

On October 29, 2019, about 100 people gathered at Barbara Hall park in the Gay Village for a rally, then moved over to the Palmerston TPL branch in The Annex neighbourhood where a crowd of 1000 protested outside the event.[553] Inside the library, a sold-out crowd of about 100 attended the discussion and listened to Murphy say things like, "[i]f you're born male, you remain male for life," and the "trans-activist movement has made for the erasure of women."[554] Outside, there were about 30 police officers monitoring the protest, but there were no serious incidents or arrests.[555] The protest, which included a read-

---

549 "Community and Event Space Rental," Toronto Public Library, January 1, 2018, https://www.torontopubliclibrary.ca/terms-of-use/library-policies/community-and-event-space.jsp. See section 4.4.a.1.

550 Joseph Brean, "Meghan Murphy, the Woman Behind Trans Wars Breaking Out at the Public Library," *National Post*, October 28, 2019, https://nationalpost.com/news/meghan-murphy-the-woman-behind-trans-wars-breaking-out-at-the-public-library.

551 Brean, "Meghan Murphy."

552 Francine Kopun, "'This Has Been a Valuable Debate': Toronto Librarian Says Some Good Has Come From Meghan Murphy Controversy," *Toronto Star*, October 29, 2019, ProQuest.

553 KC Hoard, "Hundreds Protest Controversial Toronto Public Library Event Featuring Meghan Murphy," *The Globe and Mail*, October 29, 2019, ProQuest; Francine, "'This Has Been a Valuable Debate'."

554 Liam Casey, "Hundreds Gather Outside Toronto Library to Protest Gender Identity Speaker," *The Canadian Press*, October 29, 2019, ProQuest.

555 Francine, "'This Has Been a Valuable Debate'."

in of works by trans authors, brought together trans individuals and activists, 2SLGBTQIA+ advocates, library workers from TPL and beyond, politicians, and many other members of the public chanting "[t]rans rights are human rights!" and other slogans, holding signs with messages like, "[n]o hate, no fear," and "[t]rans rights are not debatable."[556] The crowd also booed and jeered the event attendees who left through the front door when it ended, so the police escorted the rest out of the back door.[557] At that point some protestors also entered the front of the library, which prompted library staff and police to lock the front doors, despite the library still being open, to prevent others from entering.[558]

By the time of the event and protest, the online petition initiated by the group of local authors had over 8600 signatures,[559] 12 events had been cancelled at TPL in protest,[560] and Bowles reported that comments on social media and in person at the board meeting were overwhelmingly negative, but over 90% of the emails, calls, and letters that TPL received, as well as the majority of newspaper opinions, supported TPL's decision.[561] I also found that the majority of letters to the editor after the event supported the library, with only a couple in opposition.[562] Public outcry and media coverage did not quiet down in the weeks following the event. Speaking to *Global News*, trans writer

---

556 Francine, "'This Has Been a Valuable Debate'"; Pride Toronto (@PrideToronto), "What amazing turn out tonight to declare no to hate," Twitter, October 29, 2019, 6:33 p.m., https://twitter.com/PrideToronto/status/1189309293629267969.

557 Casey, "Hundreds Gather Outside Toronto Library to Protest Gender Identity Speaker"; Arvin Joaquin, Cameron Perrier, and Erica Lenti, "Meghan Murphy, the Toronto Public Library and Fighting Transphobia: an Explainer," *Xtra Magazine*, October 30, 2019, https://xtramagazine.com/power/meghan-murphy-toronto-library-transphobia-163924; "Meghan Murphy: Canadian Feminist's Trans Talk Sparks Uproar," *BBC*, October 30, 2019, https://www.bbc.com/news/world-us-canada-50214381.

558 Joaquin, Perrier, and Lenti, "Meghan Murphy."

559 Casey, "Hundreds Gather Outside Toronto Library to Protest Gender Identity Speaker."

560 Kopun, "After Trans Rights Protest at Controversial Event."

561 Lisa Peet, "Meeting Room Policy Protests in Toronto, Vancouver," Library Journal, December 5, 2019, https://www.libraryjournal.com/story/Meeting-Room-Policy-Protests-in-Toronto-Vancouver.

562 "Library Talk Stirs Free-Speech Debate," letters to the editor, *Toronto Star*, October 30, 2019, ProQuest; Robert Girvan, "Lend an Ear," *The Globe and Mail,* October 31, 2019, ProQuest; "Megan Murphy Transgender Controversy Raises Questions About the Limits of Free Speech," letters to the editor, *Toronto Star*, November 2, 2019, ProQuest; Simon Rosenblum, letter to the editor, *Toronto Star,* November 4, 2019; Paul Kahnert, letter to the editor, Toronto Star, November 4, 2019, ProQuest.

Niko Stratis suggested that TPL was acting in bad faith: "They're clearly not interested in listening to trans people. They want to be able to hold us up as a paragon of them being inclusive, but their actions don't line up to their words."[563] And Gwen Benaway said that for TPL to frame this as a free speech issue deflects from the real issue of putting trans peoples' identities and rights up for debate and the harm that can cause: "The average Canadian isn't seeing the whole picture. The free speech thing takes us away from what's actually going on — it's that these events really do organize and coordinate active harassment campaigns against trans folk in public life."[564] University of Toronto Women and Gender Studies professor Alissa Trotz agreed that given the context of discrimination and violence that many trans people experience,[565] free speech should not apply when what's being discussed is dehumanization.[566] There were also discussions of the legalities in a *Toronto Star* article in which University of Ottawa Law professor Carissima Mathen suggested that Murphy's speech would be unlikely to meet the high threshold of hate speech.[567] However, University of Toronto Law professor Brenda Cossman noted that according to TPL's policy against promoting or having the effect of promoting discrimination, the bar for banning the event is lower.[568] She noted that cancelling an event based on that element of library policy could generate a Charter challenge, but there were no examples for that happening yet.[569] And neither law professor brought up the relevant September 2019 Ontario Court ruling about Ottawa Public Library,[570] which determined that the library could deny a room rental for a

---

563 Rachael D'Amore, "'Canadians Aren't Seeing the Whole Picture': The Meghan Murphy Event and Trans Rights," *Global News*, October 30, 2019, https://globalnews.ca/news/6102791/toronto-library-meghan-murphy-trans-community/. Full disclosure: I know and admire Niko.

564 D'Amore, "'Canadians Aren't Seeing the Whole Picture'."

565 Abigail Curlew, "Transgender Hate Crimes Are on the Rise Even in Canada," *The Conversation*, August 20, 2020, https://theconversation.com/transgender-hate-crimes-are-on-the-rise-even-in-canada-121541.

566 D'Amore, "'Canadians Aren't Seeing the Whole Picture'."

567 Jacques Gallant, "Setting the Record Straight on Freedom of Speech: Cultural Debates Reveal Common Misconceptions about Legal Rights and their Limits, Experts Say," *Toronto Star,* November 24, 2019, ProQuest.

568 Gallant, "Setting the Record Straight on Freedom of Speech."

569 Gallant, "Setting the Record Straight on Freedom of Speech."

570 Crawford, "Court Upholds Public Library's Decision to Cancel Screening of Controversial Film"; for further examination of the ruling see: Wirth and Sakshi Chadha, "Court Rules That Termination of Rental Agreement by Public Library Is Not Subject to Judicial Review."

private ticketed event.[571] In a blog post written before the event and protest, academic librarian Kris Joseph was critical of TPL's room booking policy, and its policymakers including Bowles, for failing to include strategies to handle controversial events:

> "The options are 'let it happen' or 'cancel it,' with no guidance in the policy on contextualizing the event, consulting or engaging with the community, suggesting alternatives, or mitigating risk of harming the welcoming and supportive environment praised in the 'Purpose' section. Instead, the policy prioritizes the lens of intellectual freedom-perhaps supplemented by the value of access-when determining how to handle a request for a controversial room rental. This is a policy failure."[572]

And the incoming president of TPLWU Local 4948 told *Library Journal* that the TPL administration should not have focused only on free speech: "They should have looked at what it means if you're offering a library as a safe, welcoming space and at the same time you're allowing these individuals to come into the library and pretty much call into question somebody's entire existence in the world."[573] However, Bowles maintained that "[t]hrough our rules of conduct we will make sure that you are not harassed or discriminated against" and "we will welcome everyone without judgment."[574]

Newspaper opinion pieces continued to voice support for the library decision, most on the basis of the free speech argument, although some went further in echoing and agreeing with Murphy's language

---

571 A poster for the event, pictured in this tweet, shows that tickets for the event were $5. Ziya Jones (@ZiyaJonesA), "Hey@torontolibrary," Twitter, October 11, 2019, 5:43 p.m., https://twitter.com/ZiyaJonesA/status/1182773784492871680?s=20.

572 Kris Joseph, "The Curious Case of Free-Speech-Loving Librarians Who Don't Think the Toronto Public Library Should Provide Space for Meghan Murphy: Part One," *Kris Joseph* (blog), October 23, 2019, https://krisjoseph.ca/2019/10/tpl-mm-part-one/.

573 Peet, "Meeting Room Policy Protests in Toronto, Vancouver."

574 Peet.

and ideas.[575] I found one opinion opposed to the library's decision, and both the *Toronto Star* and the *National Post* featured lengthy debates exploring both sides of the controversy.[576] I must also note that in December, the *Toronto Star* named City Librarian Vickery Bowles on its list of "Best People of 2019."[577] And I could not help but notice that in their write up for her, they adopted some problematic language, referring to transgender people as "self-identified transgender people."[578] This is the kind of language that does not appear transphobic at quick glance, but it implies a subtle challenge to transgender identity and separates trans women from other women. I see this as evidence of the normalization of transphobia that critics of Murphy and the library decision were worried about.

Many of the newspaper opinions that supported the library also expressed opposition to city council's latest intervention into library policy. At the city council meeting the day after the Murphy event, council voted 20-1 in favour of Councillors Wong-Tam and Layton's motion to review the city's, including the library's, third-party community space policies to ensure that they reflect the city's policies around equity, diversity, and protection from discrimination.[579] The review process would involve the city manager, city lawyer, and include consultations with members of the 2SLGBTQIA+ community.[580] Stephen Holyday was the lone opposing vote because he felt it inappropriate for city

---

575 Kopun, "After Trans Rights Protest at Controversial Event"; "Chris Selley: Attack on Public Libraries for Letting Meghan Murphy Speak Is a Nauseating Spectacle," *National Post*, October 30, 2019, ProQuest; Sue-Ann Levy, "Sad State of Free Speech; Intolerant Radicals and their Meghan Murphy Circus," *Toronto Sun*, October 30, 2019, ProQuest; Sue-Ann Levy, "Council's Thought Police Jump on Meghan Murphy Issue," *Toronto Sun*, October 31, 2019, ProQuest; Star Editorial Board, "Toronto City Council Falls Short on Free Speech," *Toronto Star*, November 2, 2019, ProQuest; Rex Murphy, "Toronto Library Holds the Line on Free Speech," *National Post*, October 31, 2019, ProQuest; Lorne Gunter, "Meghan Murphy Saga Shows How Extreme Political Correctness Has Become," *Toronto Sun*, November 2, 2019, ProQuest; "Free Speech Too Important to Be Left to Politicians," *Toronto Sun*, November 3, 2019, ProQuest.

576 Shree Paradkar, "Shree Paradkar: Cancel Culture Accompanied By an Eye Roll Is Usually an Excuse to Duck Accountability," *Toronto Star*, November 5, 2019, ProQuest; Cara Zwibel and Joan Moriarity, "Should Meghan Murphy Have Been Allowed to Speak at the Toronto Public Library?," *Toronto Star*, November 5, 2019, ProQuest; Jonathan Kay and Mercedes Allen, "Speaking of Gender: A National Post Debate About Gender Identity and Free Speech," *National Post*, December 2, 2019, ProQuest.

577 Heather Mallick, "The Best People of 2019," *Toronto Star*, December 23, 2019, https://www.thestar.com/opinion/star-columnists/2019/12/23/the-best-people-of-2019.html.

578 Mallick, "The Best People of 2019."

579 Kopun, "After Trans Rights Protest at Controversial Event."

580 Kopun.

council to challenge the autonomy of the library board, and he said that he "regarded this motion as an attack on the City Librarian who stood her ground on the decision."[581] However, Councillor Joe Cressy offered the perspective that "if we have a policy that's allowing discrimination to flourish in our libraries, we need to review and change that policy."[582]

Commentary from the library profession continued into November, with the librarians and archivists of the York University Faculty Association writing an open letter to the TPL board to condemn their position of neutrality and stated that the decision to allow the event "was poorly considered and very hurtful" and suggested it "has damaging consequences for our profession as a whole."[583] Edmonton Public Library's CEO, Pillar Martinez, released a statement in support of TPL on the basis of protecting intellectual freedom and freedom of expression, arguing that it is possible to champion those principles while also advocating "for equity, diversity and inclusion." She ended with a personal expression of neutrality, proudly declaring, "I am not anti-anyone. I am pro free speech."[584] Speaking to *Library Journal* about EPL conducting a meeting room policy review, Martinez said: "I don't know that we could promise that library spaces will not have people who say offensive things. We can't guarantee that. That's the beauty of the public library–the diversity of our users, the diversity of opinions and beliefs."[585] As we saw in Halifax, here Martinez is distorting the spirit behind the idea of diversity, a concept originally intended to promote inclusion of marginalized and oppressed people, to accommodate offensive opinions that discriminate against those same marginalized people.

---

581 Kopun.

582 Natalie Johnson, "Council Calls for Review of Toronto Facility Permits in Wake of Controversial Speech at Library," *CTV News*, October 30, 2019, https://toronto.ctvnews.ca/council-calls-for-review-of-toronto-facility-permits-in-wake-of-controversial-speech-at-library-1.4662934.

583 William Denton and Art Redding to Sue Graham-Nutter and Vickery Bowles, Toronto, November 8, 2019, https://krisjosephca.files.wordpress.com/2019/11/yufa-letter-room-booking-20191108.pdf.

584 Pilar Martinez, "EPL and Freedom of Expression," *Edmonton Public Library* (blog), November 1, 2019, https://www.epl.ca/blogs/post/epl-and-freedom-of-expression/.

585 Peet, "Meeting Room Policy Protests in Toronto."

Martinez's position prompted EPL's writer-in-residence at the time, Matthew Stepanic, to speak out in opposition because part of his role was to create a safe and inclusive space for writers from marginalized groups.[586] He asserted that "Free speech does not mean you have the right to get a public forum for whatever you want to say."[587] EPL board trustee Jill Scheyk responded to Martinez directly through email to express her disappointment with Martinez's statement and asked Martinez to apologize to the trans community.[588] She also tweeted to encourage public attendance at an upcoming EPL board meeting and referenced EPL's meeting room policy.[589] Subsequently, Scheyk received a formal letter saying that her recent conduct "warrants assessment" as a breach of policy and that her "Twitter activity overall provided a catalyst for anonymous and extremely disrespectful input towards our CEO and EPL in general."[590] Scheyk then wrote a letter to defend her actions and apologized for tweeting an internal document, but on Jan 15, 2020 she received a letter from the board asking her to resign for publicly "present[ing] a negative and biased opinion,"[591] and she did so on February 10.[592] Martinez would not comment on the resignation because it was a board matter. Also in Alberta, the Library Association of Alberta released a neutral statement in November 2019 that recognized both sides of the TPL controversy and urged "that we continue a respectful and thoughtful discourse to hold ourselves accountable to our communities."[593] Whereas, in BC, the Creston Public Library Chief Librarian Saara Itkonen released a powerful

---

586 Omar Mosleh, "Edmonton Writer in Residence Calls Out Library CEO for Supporting Space Rental to Meghan Murphy," *Toronto Star*, November 2, 2019, ProQuest.

587 Mosleh, "Edmonton Writer in Residence Calls Out Library CEO for Supporting Space Rental to Meghan Murphy."

588 Omar Mosleh, "The Toronto Library Hosted Meghan Murphy. Now an Edmonton Library Trustee Says She's Paying a Price for Speaking Out," *Toronto Star*, February 11, 2020, https://www.thestar.com/edmonton/2020/02/11/the-toronto-library-hosted-meghan-murphy-now-an-edmonton-library-trustee-says-shes-paying-a-price-for-speaking-out.html.

589 Mosleh, "The Toronto Library Hosted Meghan Murphy."

590 Mosleh, "The Toronto Library Hosted Meghan Murphy."

591 Lauren Boothby, "Edmonton Library Trustee Says She Was Forced to Resign in Dispute Over Free Speech, Tweets," *Edmonton Journal*, February 12, 2020, https://edmontonjournal.com/news/local-news/edmonton-library-trustee-says-she-was-forced-to-resign-in-dispute-over-free-speech-tweets.

592 Mosleh, "The Toronto Library Hosted Meghan Murphy."

593 "LAA Statement on Toronto Public Library," Library Association of Alberta, November 12, 2019, https://www.laa.ca/page/news/ezlist_item_ef11602c-54e4-48ad-8771-e4b9ecc04210.aspx.

statement, asserting that "Creston Library is not neutral and we will not provide a platform for hate speech."[594] She acknowledged the importance of freedom of information and speech in libraries, but said: "I don't want anyone to feel that they aren't welcome at our library unless they are coming to the library to harm others. If you are then please stay away."[595]

In January 2020, Another Story Bookshop and other community partners organized a teach-in and dialogue for trans people and allies, to discuss trans rights issues around identity and public space access, as well as topics like allyship, community, and advocacy.[596] The teach-in was held at The 519, facilitated by author Kai Cheng Thom, and included writer Gwen Benaway, outreach worker Monica Forrester, and activist Chanelle Gallant.[597] Originally the event had been pitched to TPL, who offered space and speaker honoraria. However, there were delays in TPL's communications for confirming dates, so the organizers found a different venue to partner with.[598] A TPL spokesperson stated that the delay was based on their desire to involve TPL's staff Pride Alliance in planning the event, but the community organizers felt there was more urgency to the event.[599] The TPL statement also noted that the library was working on community outreach to develop programming that would highlight trans voices and stories.[600]

Meanwhile, the city reviewed its policies governing the use of city facilities by people promoting intolerance or discrimination, and the resulting report, which included TPL's response to the review as an

---

594 Saara Itkonen, "Libraries Aren't Neutral," *Creston Valley Advance*, November 14, 2019, https://www.crestonvalleyadvance.ca/news/libraries-arent-neutral/.

595 Itkonen, "Libraries Aren't Neutral."

596 Michael Rancic, "After Protesting the Library, Trans Activists Host a Teach-In," *NOW Magazine*, January 23, 2020, https://nowtoronto.com/culture/books-culture/trans-teach-in-kai-cheng-thom-library.

597 Rancic, "After Protesting the Library."

598 Rancic.

599 Rancic.

600 Rancic.

attachment,[601] came back to city council on March 3, 2021,[602] where it was referred to the Lesbian, Gay, Bisexual, Transgender, Queer and Two-Spirit Advisory Committee[603] for consideration at their June 2021 meeting.[604] At that meeting,[605] the committee voted in favour of recommending that city council adopt the report's recommendations with amendments, including one for the library board to request the City Librarian report back to the committee about their progress in 2022.[606] Also at that meeting, Vickery Bowles reinforced that room bookings are reviewed based on stated purpose and that if Murphy were to book a TPL room again for the same purpose, the library would again allow it, which was not received well by the committee.[607] Then in October 2021, Toronto city council adopted the amended recommendations for reviewing the use of city spaces,[608] but evidently the library's review resulted in no changes because when the library reported back to the committee in May 2022, the 2017-updated library booking policies and procedures remained intact.[609] Despite some newly developed service

---

601 Vickery Bowles to Chris Murray, Toronto, January 6, 2021, in *Attachment 1: Toronto Public Library Response to MM 11.14*, https://www.toronto.ca/legdocs/mmis/2021/cc/bgrd/backgroundfile-164697.pdf.

602 City Manager and Chief People Officer, People & Equity, *Reviewing City of Toronto Policies Governing the Use of Libraries and City Facilities by Individuals and Groups Promoting Intolerance or Discrimination*, (Toronto, ON: City of Toronto, 2021), https://www.toronto.ca/legdocs/mmis/2021/cc/bgrd/backgroundfile-164696.pdf.

603 City of Toronto, *City Council Consideration on March 10, 2021* (Toronto, ON: City of Toronto, 2021), http://app.toronto.ca/tmmis/viewAgendaItemHistory.do?item=2021.CC30.2.

604 City of Toronto Two-Spirit, Lesbian, Gay, Bisexual, Transgender and Queer Advisory Committee Meeting Agenda, June 22, 2021, Toronto, https://secure.toronto.ca/council/report.do?meeting=2021.QS2&type=agenda.

605 City of Toronto Two-Spirit, Lesbian, Gay, Bisexual, Transgender and Queer Advisory Committee Meeting, June 22, 2021, Toronto, https://www.youtube.com/live/dDpzKOkYkgM.

606 City of Toronto Two-Spirit, Lesbian, Gay, Bisexual, Transgender and Queer Advisory Committee–Decision Letter, June 22, 2021, Toronto, https://www.toronto.ca/legdocs/mmis/2021/ex/bgrd/backgroundfile-170677.pdf.

607 City of Toronto 2SLGBTQ Advisory Committee Meeting, June 22, 2021.

608 City of Toronto, *City Council Consideration on October 1, 2021* (Toronto, ON: City of Toronto, 2021), https://secure.toronto.ca/council/agenda-item.do?item=2021.EX26.14.

609 Vickery Bowles, *Letter to City of Toronto 2SLGBTQ Advisory Committee*, May 19, 2022, https://www.toronto.ca/legdocs/mmis/2022/qs/bgrd/backgroundfile-225883.pdf.

initiatives for the 2SLGBTQIA+ communities,[610] the policy at the core of the conflict was maintained.[611]

2020 Grand Prairie and Medicine Hat, Alberta

In January 2020, before COVID-19 was declared a global pandemic and the rush to develop vaccines for it had yet to begin, a controversial documentary called *Vaxxed II: The People's Truth*, sequel to discredited doctor Andrew Wakefield's 2016 *Vaxxed*, was having small screenings in some theatres and libraries in Alberta.[612] The anti-vaccine non-profit group Canadians for Vaccine Choice hosted the screenings at the Grande Prairie Public Library to an audience of 8, including 3 of the event organizers, and at the Medicine Hat Public Library to an unknown audience size.[613] Grand Prairie PL Director Deb Cryderman offered the reasoning of freedom of expression for allowing the film screenings: "Even if information is controversial or doesn't correlate with our beliefs or we don't agree with it, we can still offer a room rental,"[614] but she also noted that allowing event bookings does not constitute endorsement of the ideas freely expressed at those events.[615] Medicine Hat PL Chief Librarian Ken Feser echoed the freedom of expression sentiment, as both libraries' room booking policies allow for intellectual freedom but prohibit contravention of the Criminal Code of Canada and the Canadian Charter of Rights and Freedoms.[616]

---

610 Toronto Public Library, 2SLGBTQ+ Advisory Committee Report-Back: Toronto Public Library Update, May 19, 2022, https://www.toronto.ca/legdocs/mmis/2022/qs/bgrd/backgroundfile-225831.pdf.

611 TPL also updated its Equity Statement and Intellectual Freedom Statement in December 2022, with the latter including a section on "Intellectual Freedom & Equity." We'll see how those statements are deployed in future conflicts. https://www.torontopubliclibrary.ca/terms-of-use/library-policies/equity-statement.jsp; https://www.torontopubliclibrary.ca/terms-of-use/library-policies/intellectual-freedom-statement.jsp.

612 Jordan Omstead, "Alberta Health Advocates Alarmed by Anti-Vaxx Documentary Screened in Theatres, Libraries," *CBC*, January 28, 2020, https://www.cbc.ca/news/canada/edmonton/anti-vaxx-documentary-misinformation-alberta-1.5442573.

613 Omstead.

614 Omstead.

615 Rumneek Johal, "Anti-Vaccine Documentary Being Screened in Alberta Theatres, Libraries," *Daily Hive*, January 28, 2020, https://dailyhive.com/edmonton/anti-vaccine-documentary-alberta-theatres-libraries.

616 Omstead, "Alberta Health Advocates Alarmed by Anti-Vaxx Documentary Screened in Theatres"; Johal, "Anti-Vaccine Documentary Being Screened in Alberta Theatres."

The screenings did not generate much public interest in attendance or outcry, but public health experts spoke out against the film and the library. Dr. Joan Robinson, a pediatric infectious diseases specialist at the University of Alberta said: "It's not scientific at all. It's total propaganda based on people's emotions," and, "I think it's very disappointing that it would be shown in a public forum, especially by the public library."[617] While Timothy Caulfield, Canada Research Chair in Health Law and Policy at the University of Alberta argued: "This is not about an open debate and freedom of expression. This is really about the spreading of harmful information that can really erode public confidence in vaccines."[618] Caulfield also expressed concern that having these kinds of films screened at public libraries gives them more legitimacy in the public eye, which can impact vaccine hesitancy and cause greater physical harm.[619] I did also find one opinion piece in the University of Manitoba student newspaper, *The Manitoban*, suggesting that spreading medical misinformation that "threatens the well-being of our society as a whole" should not be the kind of speech that is protected by the Charter of Rights and Freedoms.[620]

Interestingly, in this case one library did something we have not seen in other examples of event controversies. Instead of relying on a neutral position, Grand Prairie PL made an effort to highlight an oppositional perspective to the anti-vaccine film screening with a display about vaccinations outside the meeting room for over a week. Deb Cryderman explained that the library partnered with Alberta Health Services to create the display because "[she] believe[s] that it is the duty of libraries to provide the public with full access to information."[621] Based on the low attendance numbers for the film screening, I would assume that more people were exposed to the display than to the film, so this proactive example of counterprogramming could be seen as a success.

---

617 Omstead, "Alberta Health Advocates Alarmed by Anti-Vaxx Documentary Screened in Theatres."

618 Omstead.

619 Omstead; Emily Keller, "Anti-Vaccination Film Screenings Cause Controversy," *Everything GP*, January 29, 2020, https://everythinggp.com/2020/01/29/anti-vaccination-film-screenings-cause-controversy/.

620 Meagan Hughes, "Misleading Public Health Propaganda Must Be Stopped," *The Manitoban*, February 24, 2020, https://web.archive.org/web/20201202210842/http://www.themanitoban.com/2020/02/misleading-public-health-propaganda-must-be-stopped/39151/.

621 Johal, "Anti-Vaccine Documentary Being Screened in Alberta Theatres."

2020 Vancouver, British Columbia

A few months after the TPL controversy, and less than a year after VPL revised its meeting room policy in the wake of the Feminist Current event, a group called Gender Identity YVR requested to book a room at the downtown central branch of VPL for Meghan Murphy to speak at an event on March 21, 2020.[622] As per the updated room booking policy, VPL needed to conduct a pre-screening and risk assessment, so they did not immediately accept the booking request, which prompted Murphy to threaten legal action if the request was denied.[623] Once the VPL board had conducted the review, which included seeking legal counsel and advice from the Vancouver Police Department, VPL Chief Librarian Christina de Castell released a statement indicating that despite many calls from the public for the request to be denied, and "[a]fter a difficult and emotional discussion, a majority of the Board decided to accept the rental request," as their risk assessment had found that that event was unlikely to breach criminal or human rights codes.[624] The statement affirmed a position of neutrality and commitment to freedom of expression, while noting the work that VPL has done toward "fostering inclusion and reducing discrimination."[625] It also noted that the event would be held after the library closed as a safety precaution.[626] De Castell ended by acknowledging "that decisions like this have caused a loss of trust for some," but that she hoped the library could "continue to work with these communities to promote dialogue and raise marginalized voices through our programs and services, and we continue to welcome ideas for ways to do this within the current policy and legal environment."[627]

---

622 Andrew Weichel, "Meghan Murphy Threatens Legal Action If Vancouver Library Rejects March Event," *CTV News*, January 28, 2020, https://bc.ctvnews.ca/meghan-murphy-threatens-legal-action-if-vancouver-library-rejects-march-event-1.4759505. The event was originally titled "For Females Only: Sports, Spaces, and Safety," but later changed to "Women's Places & Spaces: sports, Prisons, and Shelters" because it had caused confusion that the event itself was "for females only" to attend; Simon Little, "Event Featuring Controversial Speaker Meghan Murphy to Go Ahead at Vancouver Library," *Global News*, January 27, 2020, https://globalnews.ca/news/6469847/controversial-event-megan-murphy-vancouver-library/.

623 Weichel, "Meghan Murphy Threatens Legal Action If Vancouver Library Rejects March Event."

624 "Statement From VPL's Chief Librarian Regarding March 21 GIDYVR Event," Vancouver Public Library, January 27, 2020, https://www.vpl.ca/statement-on-gidyvr-event.

625 "Statement From VPL's Chief Librarian Regarding March 21 GIDYVR Event."

626 "Statement From VPL's Chief Librarian Regarding March 21 GIDYVR Event."

627 "Statement From VPL's Chief Librarian Regarding March 21 GIDYVR Event."

I did not find as many sources for this Murphy event as I did for the last one at VPL, but it is safe to assume that many of the same parties were supporting and opposing it. This time, however, CUPE Local 391, representing library workers, released a statement to disagree with the board's decision. The statement noted the stress that many of its members experienced with the previous Murphy event, including "symptoms of anxiety, fear, anger, and depression in both their professional and personal lives," as well as targeted social media attacks from the public, and argued that these health and safety concerns have "the potential for long-term damage that cannot be ignored."[628]

Although the library had approved the event, an oncoming global pandemic had other plans. Due to COVID-19, the library, and everything else, had to close their doors and cancel public events, so Murphy was unable to speak at VPL in March 2020.

Historical Summary

As I wrote this in 2020–21, pandemic closures meant that no further in-person events had happened since March 2020. In sum, from 1960 to 2020, I found 33 controversial events at Canadian public libraries.[629] While there were only 4 that I found between 1960 and 1990, from the late 1990s onward public controversy and protest of events at public libraries became more common. One explanation for this upswing in the 90s could be that with the rise of the internet people were more aware of events happening at libraries and they were more connected with each other to coordinate protests. Of the 33 controversial events, 5 were library-planned events, 3 were partnerships between a third party and a library, and 25 were third-party bookings. And of those 33 events, 25 were allowed by the libraries to proceed (76%), and only 6 (18%) were cancelled by the libraries, while the 2013 anti-pipeline event in Guelph was moved by the third-party organizers, but likely would have been cancelled by the library, and the 2013 Gilmour event in Waterloo was ostensibly cancelled by the third-party

---

[628] Greg Taylor, "Statement from CUPE Local 391," CUPE BC, February 19, 2020, https://www.cupe.bc.ca/statement_from_cupe_local_391.

[629] I do not include the 2010 TPL refusal to book an Exit International event in my count, because I found no evidence of public protest, but I included it in my discussion for interest and thoroughness.

organizers.[630] Of the 6 events that were cancelled by libraries, 1 was a library-planned event (Belleville 2012) and 5 were booked by third parties (Mississauga 1978, Ottawa 1990, Vancouver 2009, Saskatoon 2017, Ottawa 2017).

For the 25 events allowed by the libraries to proceed, the reasons given were the protection of intellectual freedom and freedom of expression, often coupled with a lack of criminal hate speech record for the speakers, and assertions of library neutrality. For the 6 events that were cancelled by libraries, the reasons were: not wanting to promote homosexuality or expose minors to it (Mississauga 1978); racist views of the speakers (Ottawa 1990); legal risk for the library (Vancouver 2009); being too hurtful to the community (Belleville 2012); inability to operationally manage the expected protest (Saskatoon 2017); and the event would violate the library's anti-discrimination policy (Ottawa 2017). In terms of public opposition to controversial events, the most common source of public outcry was a concern about hate speech and promotion of discrimination, for 18 events (55%),[631] only 2 of which were cancelled (Ottawa 1990 and Ottawa 2017). Other event issues that the public opposed included communism, homosexuality, assisted suicide, environmental activism, an anti-choice politician, Indigenous identity fraud, drag storytimes, and anti-vaccine propaganda.

There were 5 controversial events that prompted political involvement in the form of discussions and/or motions in city council or provincial parliament: Mississauga 1978, GVPL 1996, North Vancouver 1999, Regina 2000, and Toronto 2019. None of those political interventions affected the decision of whether or not to cancel the event. Five other events prompted politicians to voice concerns, with one supporting an event: Guelph 2013; and four in opposition to events: GVPL 1998, Belleville 2012, TPL 2017, Ottawa 2017. As for policy implications, there were five controversial events that prompted libraries to change their policies: Mississauga expanded their section on film use and selection

---

[630] I do not include Ottawa 2018 and Vancouver 2020 in my count of cancelled events, because the libraries had decided they could happen, but then the reasons they didn't take place were based on specific safety circumstances outside of the libraries' control (fire alarm and pandemic, respectively), not due to public opposition.

[631] I did not include David Gilmour's 2013 controversy over racist and sexist comments because his event was not about this topic and because he is not engaged in the kinds of activism that others are who I included in that count. But I am open to discussion.

in 1978; GVPL resisted city council pressures for a bigger change, but did add references to the Canadian criminal code in 1996; similarly, in 1999 VPL added references to the criminal and human rights codes; TPL added language to prevent promotion of discrimination or hatred and added references the criminal and human rights codes in 2017; and in 2019 VPL expanded its references to the criminal and human rights codes and added a new pre-screening process.

The consequences faced by libraries for their decisions of whether or not to cancel controversial events included: one legal challenge, which went in favour of Ottawa Public Library cancelling ACT! for Canada's 2017 film screening; one library, VPL in 2019, was banned from participating in the Pride Festival, but it is very likely that TPL would have also been banned from Pride in 2020 if it had not been cancelled due to the pandemic; the Okanagan Regional Library CEO and senior staff were required to do sensitivity and diversity training in 2019; and TPL saw dozens of events and partnerships cancelled in 2019. On the other hand, three Intellectual Freedom awards were given to libraries or librarians from provincial library associations: GVPL in 1997, Bowles of TPL in 2018, and Machum and Stephenson of ORL in 2020.

In all, I would argue that the majority of public outcry, about 25 events, was based on what could commonly be understood as progressive politics,[632] with conservative politics generating opposition to six events, and then two events that I could not easily classify politically (See Table 1).[633] I break down the politics of the public protests in this way because when we look at the whole picture of these controversies in recent Canadian history, it is important to remember the underlying reasons behind the public outcry. Conservative politics were behind the opposition to events with morality or politics they disagreed with, such as homosexuality, pornography, communism, environmental activism, and assisted suicide. Whereas progressive politics were primarily concerned with the 18 events where hate speech and discrimination were the main issues, as well as seven other events. These

---

632   The London 1960 and Halifax 2019 events are included in my progressive count because, although conservative politics drove initial concerns, it was more significant progressive public outcry that prompted the library to reconsider and reschedule the events.

633   The two I could not classify politically were the Belleville 2012 crime book event, and the sex assault allegations against George Takei in Edmonton in 2017. Maybe the Belleville example is progressive by promoting community care? Maybe the Takei one is progressive, as part of #metoo? I don't feel strongly about the politics of either, but am open to discussion.

progressive politics were not simply arguing against events because they disagreed with the views of the speakers or they opposed open dialogue. Rather, they were addressing power imbalances and challenging the concept and value of dialogue with people who are seeking to deny one's human rights, identity, dignity, and safety. They were challenging the status quo of intellectual freedom and neutrality to argue for protection from hate, discrimination, and misinformation, for making libraries the spaces they claim to be: inclusive, welcoming, and safe community hubs that care about diversity.

If we compare these majority progressive challenges temporally to the conservative challenges, we see that the progressive challenges are consistent from the 1990s onward, whereas two of the six conservative challenges occurred in the 1970s, with the remaining four occurring very sporadically since then. The amount and the persistence of the progressive public challenges demonstrate that the public library as an institution is not as progressive as it claims to be, or thinks it wants to be. Over the course of their history, public libraries adopted the language of diversity and inclusion and developed some programs and services around those ideals, but failed to confront the underlying tensions and competing interests between those ideals and the libraries' traditions of neutrality and intellectual freedom. These regular public challenges to this state of contradiction have been calling out that hypocrisy and trying to force that reckoning. Now it is time to think about why and how neutrality resists these progressive appeals, and how to learn from this history to improve community, care, safety, and social justice in public libraries.

Contested Spaces
Whitney Kemble

Table 1.

Year	Library	Issue	What happened?	Protest Politics
1960	London	communist propaganda	happened (cancelled then rescheduled)	con then prog
1978	Mississauga	homosexuality	cancelled by library	conservative
1978	Oakville	homosexuality	happened	conservative
1990	Ottawa	hate/discrimination	cancelled by library	progressive
1996	GVPL (main)	hate/discrimination	happened	progressive
1998	GVPL (JdF)	hate/discrimination	happened	progressive
1999	GVPL (NMC)	hate/discrimination	happened	progressive
1999	GVPL (JdF)	hate/discrimination	happened	progressive
1999	GVPL (JdF)	hate/discrimination	happened	progressive
1997	West Vancouver	hate/discrimination	happened	progressive
1999	North Vancouver	hate/discrimination	happened	progressive
1999	Vancouver	hate/discrimination	happened	progressive
2000	Regina	homosexuality/pornography	happened	conservative
2008	Vancouver	hate/discrimination	happened	progressive
2009	Vancouver	assisted suicide	cancelled by library	conservative
2012	Belleville	crime book hurtful to community	cancelled by library	
2013	Ottawa	hate/discrimination	happened	progressive
2013	Guelph	anti-pipeline/environmental activism	moved by organizer	conservative
2013	Waterloo	sexist, racist comments	cancelled by organizer	progressive
2013	Vancouver	hate/discrimination	happened	progressive
2017	Saskatoon	anti-choice politician	cancelled by library	progressive
2017	Edmonton	Indigenous identity fraud	happened	progressive
2017	Edmonton	sexual assault allegations	happened	
2017	Toronto	hate/discrimination	happened	progressive
2017	Ottawa	hate/discrimination	cancelled by library	progressive
2018	Ottawa	hate/discrimination	happened (but disrupted by fire alarm)	progressive
2019	Vancouver	hate/discrimination	happened	progressive
2019	Halifax	critique of policing	happened (cancelled then rescheduled)	progressive
2019	Kelowna	drag queen storytime	happened	conservative
2019	Toronto	hate/discrimination	happened	progressive
2020	Grand Prairie	anti-vaccine propaganda	happened	progressive
2020	Medicine Hat	anti-vaccine propaganda	happened	progressive
2020	Vancouver	hate/discrimination	cancelled due to COVID-19	progressive

Part III

Terra Neutralis? Critiquing the False Narrative of Libraries as Neutral Spaces

The ongoing debate within the library profession about library neutrality has a long history that traces back at least as far as the late 1960s when the Social Responsibility Round Table (SRRT) of the American Library Association (ALA) was founded to challenge library neutrality and the conservative status quo of the ALA by providing a venue for exploring librarians' social and political concerns.[1] [2] Yet, libraries as institutions and the profession of librarianship have never been neutral.[3] As Mark Rosenzweig describes, libraries were developed from enlightenment ideology "as powerful instruments of social integration and control," and early librarianship was "primarily concerned with the regulation of literacy, the policing of literary taste,

---

1   Steven Joyce, "A Few Gates Redux: An Examination of the Social Responsibility Debate in the Early 1970s and 1990s," in *Questioning Library Neutrality*, ed. Alison M. Lewis (Duluth, MN: Library Juice Press, 2008). For a thorough historical examination of the development of the SRRT and its tensions with intellectual freedom and neutrality, see Toni Samek, *Intellectual Freedom and Social Responsibility in American Librarianship, 1967–1974*, Jefferson: McFarland, 2001.

2   I mention this development in the ALA because that association's size and scope has significantly impacted librarianship across North America and beyond. While similar challenges and conversations were happening within Canadian librarianship, the Canadian Library Association (CLA), before its dissolution in 2016, was smaller and it did not have a committee or round table comparable to the SRRT.

3   Here is a selection of titles to learn more about histories of librarians challenging the status quo: Norman G. Kester, *Liberating Minds: The Stories and Professional Lives of Gay, Lesbian, and Bisexual Librarians and Their Advocates*, Jefferson: McFarland, 1997; James V. Carmichael, *Daring to Find Our Names: The Search for Lesbigay Library History*, Westport: Greenwood Press, 1998; Mary Lee Bundy and Frederick J. Stielow, *Activism in American Librarianship: 1962–1973*, New York: Greenwood Press, 1987; E. J. Josey, *The Black Librarian in America Revisited*, Metuchen: Scarecrow Press, 1994; Wayne Wiegand and Shirley Wiegand, *The Desegregation of Public Libraries in The Jim Crow South: Civil Rights and Local Activism*, Baton Rouge: Louisiana State University Press, 2018.

and the propagation of a particular class culture with all its political, economic, and social prejudices."[4] Wayne Bivens-Tatum also locates the foundations of libraries within enlightenment ideology,[5] and nina de jesus engages with his work to argue that libraries embody enlightenment values, which are "steeped in and reinforce white supremacist settler state ideologies."[6]

Libraries, like other institutions, reflect and reinforce the social, economic, and political power structures they were built upon. While they can change over time, in line with social shifts, they remain tied to the existing dominant power structures and cultural hegemony, and the posturing and claims of neutrality mask the ways that power functions in libraries. The myth of neutrality assumes an equal footing, but as Steven Joyce argues: "Neutrality does not exist in a vacuum; rather, it is immersed in a largely taken-for-granted and unquestioned status quo, and that status quo is certainly not neutral."[7] In the context of Canada's liberal democracy, that status quo has generally focused on individual rights and freedoms, with most power held by white, settler, male, upper class, straight, cisgender, and able-bodied individuals. I find feminist philosopher Nancy Fraser's critique of Habermas' idealized bourgeois public sphere helpful here, as she argues that social inequalities cannot simply be overcome by ignoring them; rather, the so-called bracketing of social inequalities as if they do not exist "usually works to the advantage of dominant groups in society and to the disadvantage of subordinates."[8] Thus, the myth of neutrality protects the status quo and protects libraries from making progressive choices and changes that could shift power and create greater equity.

---

4   Mark Rosenzweig, "Politics and Anti-Politics in Librarianship," in *Questioning Library Neutrality*, ed. Alison M. Lewis (Duluth, MN: Library Juice Press, 2008), 5–6. Bruce Curtis identifies similar forces in "'Littery Merrit,' 'Useful Knowledge,' and the Organization of Township Libraries in Canada West, 1840–1860," Ontario History 78 (1986), 284–312.

5   Wayne Bivens-Tatum, *Libraries and The Enlightenment*, Los Angeles, CA: Library Juice Press, 2012.

6   nina de jesus, "Locating the Library in Institutional Oppression," *In the Library with the Lead Pipe*, September 14, 2014, https://www.inthelibrarywiththeleadpipe.org/2014/locating-the-library-in-institutional-oppression/.

7   Joyce, "A Few Gates Redux," 54.

8   Nancy Fraser, "Rethinking the Public Sphere: A Contribution to the Critique of Actually Existing Democracy," in *Public Space Reader*, ed. Miodrag Mitrasinovic and Vikas Mehta (New York: Routledge), https://doi.org/10.4324/9781351202558-6, 63–64. Thank you to Jonathan Cope's "The Labor of Informational Democracy: A Library and Information Science Framework for Evaluating the Democratic Potential in Socially-Generated Information" in *Progressive Community Action* for leading me to the Fraser piece.

The profession of librarianship also reflects existing power structures in the hierarchies of our library administrations and professional organizations. Christina Neigel points out that the people holding positions of power are not typically those working directly with marginalized communities and that "[p]ower structures in library organizations largely limit democratic decision-making *among the very people* who work in libraries… Thus, the voices representing the interests/views of Canadian libraries are those of the most powerful, not the most representative." (emphasis in original)[9] It is also very important to recognize the racial composition of librarianship as an overwhelmingly white profession. According to Statistics Canada, in 2016, 89% of librarians employed in Canada were white.[10] While I am not able to discuss all of the problems of whiteness and white supremacy in libraries here,[11] I raise the issue because the white demographic domination of librarianship is not an accident, but a reflection and result of white supremacy writ large in Canadian society. We must draw attention to and critique the normativity of whiteness in libraries, to challenge that normativity, which is fundamental to the facade of neutrality.[12]

Library neutrality is often discussed and celebrated as a mechanism for openness that ensures individuals have equal access to services, spaces, collections, and protection of intellectual freedom regardless of identity or opinion. At the 2018 ALA Midwinter President's Program

---

9   Christina Neigel, "Library Meetings Rooms & Librarianship's Existential Crisis?," *Resistant Librarian* (blog), October 26, 2019, https://resistantlibrarian.home.blog/2019/10/26/library-meetings-rooms-librarianships-existential-crisis/.

10 Josh Chan, "Beyond Tokenism: The Importance of Staff Diversity in Libraries" *BCLA Connect Perspectives Newsletter* 12, no. 1 (2020). https://bclaconnect.ca/perspectives/2020/11/30/beyond-tokenism-the-importance-of-staff-diversity-in-libraries.

11 There has been much written on these issues, but here is a selection of titles:
Karla J. Strand, "Disrupting Whiteness in Libraries and Librarianship: A Reading List," The Office of the Gender and Women's Studies Librarian, 2019, https://www.library.wisc.edu/gwslibrarian/bibliographies/disrupting-whiteness-in-libraries/;
Myrna Morales, Em Claire Knowles, and Chris Bourg, "Diversity, Social Justice, and the Future of Libraries," *Portal: Libraries and the Academy* 14, no. 3 (2014): 439–51. doi:10.1353/pla.2014.0017; Angela Galvan, "Soliciting Performance, Hiding Bias: Whiteness and Librarianship ," *In the Library With The Lead Pipe*, June 3, 2015, https://www.inthelibrarywiththeleadpipe.org/2015/soliciting-performance-hiding-bias-whiteness-and-librarianship/; Gina Schlesselman-Tarango, ed. *Topographies of Whiteness : Mapping Whiteness in Library and Information Science*, (Sacramento, CA: Library Juice Press, 2017).

12 For more on the normativity of whiteness in libraries see: Todd Honma, "Trippin' over the Color Line: The Invisibility of Race in Library and Information Studies," *InterActions: UCLA Journal of Education and Information Studies* 1, no. 2 (2005); and April Hathcock, "White Librarianship in Blackface: Diversity Initiatives in LIS," *In the Library With The Lead Pipe*, October 7, 2015, https://www.inthelibrarywiththeleadpipe.org/2015/lis-diversity/.

panel discussion, "Are Libraries Neutral?," James LaRue and Em Claire Knowles both made this argument in their pro-neutrality remarks.[13] However, panel members on the opposing side challenged that vision of neutrality as incorrect and inequitable. Emily Drabinski argued that: "In focusing such a conversation on an idealized notion of neutrality that none of us encounter in our real lives, we offer an alibi to those who have the power to define themselves and their worldviews as normal, as neutral, as apolitical. That isn't most of us."[14] Additionally, she said: "Those steeped in and rewarded by dominant ways of seeing the world don't have to know how intensely political the ostensibly neutral position is. If the white supremacists booking your meeting space are not after you, you don't have to know how dangerous they are."[15] That last point echoes arguments we have heard from those protesting library events where they feel their rights and safety are threatened, and it connects to the issue of white normativity in librarianship. In a similar vein, Chris Bourg brought up the example of providing a platform to Nazis, arguing that "allowing those who deny the humanity and basic dignity of others to co-opt the legitimacy of our libraries and our profession to spread their hatred and intimidation is not in any way a neutral choice."[16] R. David Lankes focused on the responsibilities that libraries have to the communities they serve, arguing that "[w]e have long ago rejected the notion that this means we treat all equally, and instead seek to serve equitably," adding that, "[e]quity is not neutrality. If you differentiate or prioritize service in any way to those you serve, you are not neutral."[17] Emily Knox made related points about the conflict between neutrality and community:

---

13   James LaRue, "Are Libraries Neutral?," *James LaRue–MyLiBlog* (blog), February 11, 2018, https://jaslarue.blogspot.com/2018/02/are-libraries-neutral.html; Em Claire Knowles, "Can Libraries Be Neutral? Should They Be Neutral?," *Simmons SLIS Blogs* (blog), March 26, 2018, https://slis.simmons.edu/blogs/emclaireknowles-publications/2018/03/26/can-libraries-be-neutral-should-they-strive-to-be-neutral/.

14   Emily Drabinski, "Are Libraries Neutral?" *emilydrabinski.com* (blog), February 12, 2018, http://www.emilydrabinski.com/are-libraries-neutral/.

15   Drabinski, "Are Libraries Neutral?"

16   Chris Bourg, "Debating Y/Our Humanity, or Are Libraries Neutral?," *Feral Librarian* (blog), February 11, 2018, https://chrisbourg.wordpress.com/2018/02/11/debating-y-our-humanity-or-are-libraries-neutral/.

17   R. David Lankes, "My Remarks on Library Neutrality for the ALA MidWinter President's Panel," *R. David Lankes* (blog), February 11, 2018, https://davidlankes.org/my-remarks-on-library-neutrality-for-the-ala-midwinter-presidents-panel/.

"Libraries, any library, cannot presume to be a hub for a community by being neutral. If libraries are about people then they must take people's lives seriously. Even when supporting those lives might court some controversy. Deciding not to support marginalized people is never neutral. It is always a choice."[18]

As we saw in most of the historical examples of Canadian public library event protests, the principles and rights of individual intellectual freedom and freedom of expression have become central elements of library neutrality. In the Canadian legal context there are some laws that limit freedom of expression, including sections 318 and 319 of the Criminal Code which address hate and are most relevant to our discussion.[19] I'm not a legal expert, so I will not be delving into the complex legal details of hate speech and free speech, nor am I interested in a carceral approach to this issue. Rather, as a long-time prison and police abolitionist I have spent many years reading, thinking, and imagining about the possibilities for actual justice that lay beyond our existing legal frameworks. Critical Race Theory (CRT), which was developed by legal scholars, has been particularly instructive in this practice, as it works to examine how racism contributed to the formation of, and is thus upheld by, America's social systems and power structures, including the legal system. CRT "questions the very foundations of the liberal order, including equality theory, legal reasoning, Enlightenment rationalism, and neutral principles of constitutional law."[20] Such analysis is easily extended to Canada given our foundational history of colonization, genocide, and slavery, and ongoing systemic problems of violence, inequity, and marginalization rooted in colonialism, racism and white supremacy. While the legal contexts of free speech and hate speech vary between the US and Canada, applications of Canada's hate speech regulations have been extremely limited, and as we saw in our historical examples, the legal bar for hate speech is quite high. There has been much work done within CRT on

---

18   Emily J. M. Knox, "Remarks from ALA Midwinter 2018 President's Program," *Emily J.M. Knox, PhD, MSLIS* (blog), n.d., https://emilyknox.net/media/remarks-ala-midwinter-2018-presidents-program/.

19   Julian Walker, "Hate Speech and Freedom of Expression: Legal Boundaries in Canada," Parliament of Canada, June 29, 2018, https://lop.parl.ca/sites/PublicWebsite/default/en_CA/ResearchPublications/201825E.

20   Richard Delgado and Jean Stefancic, *Critical Race Theory: An Introduction*, 3rd ed. (New York: New York University Press, 2017), 3.

freedom of speech, hate speech, and problems with their legal definitions, interpretations, and the principles informing them, which can be applied to critique libraries' commitment to intellectual freedom and freedom of expression as the primary values taking precedence over other library values.

Libraries claim neutrality through intellectual freedom and freedom of expression typically by allowing all kinds of opinions into their collections and their spaces as long as no laws are broken. As we saw in many library event protest examples, a widely accepted public idea that supports this approach is that if controversial, unpopular, or harmful views are not allowed to be shared publicly, but rather are forced underground, then they will never be appropriately challenged and subsequently conquered by logic and evidence, and so will gain power and spread. This idea also holds significant weight within the library professional discourse.[21] Writing when I am, in the time of QAnon and mass anti-vaccination campaigns during a global pandemic, I find this argument unconvincing, as I can see that logic and evidence do not necessarily triumph over harmful misinformation, and it ignores social inequities that influence knowledge creation and information dissemination. CRT has identified why and how this argument– that "the cure for bad speech is more speech," which is tied to a liberal notion of the marketplace of ideas- fails. Delgado and Stefancic argue that "[t]he idea that one can use words to undo the meanings that others attach to these very same words is to commit the empathic fallacy–the belief that one can change a narrative by merely offering another, better one–that the reader's or listener's empathy will quickly and reliably take over."[22] They suggest that as a society we are lacking in empathy because we do not encounter enough people and perspectives outside of our own cultures or social stations, so we are less open to accepting new narratives that challenge what we already think we know.[23]

Another element of failure they find in this approach is that while free speech might help resolve some types of problems, it has not proven

---

[21] American Library Association, "The Freedom to Read Statement." Issues & Advocacy. Last modified June 30, 2004. http://www.ala.org/advocacy/intfreedom/freedomreadstatement.

[22] Delgado and Stefancic, *Critical Race Theory*, 33–34.

[23] Delgado and Stefancic, *Critical Race Theory*, 34–35. They were writing this in the early 1990s, long before the days of social media echo chambers, so we might imagine that this problem has only intensified.

effective in dealing with "systemic social ills, such as racism or sexism, that are widespread and deeply woven into the fabric of society," because we have demonstrated throughout history that we, as a society, do not identify these social ills at the time, but only after the fact when the damage has been done.[24] Delgado and Stefancic also argue that power imbalances can limit one's ability to speak or challenge and respond to another's speech, as certain voices have less power, meaning fewer opportunities to speak or be heard or taken seriously, and in discussing hate speech, they note that talking back can often be physically dangerous because "much hate speech is uttered in several-on-one situations."[25] Sam Popowich's examination of problems with intellectual freedom in the Canadian public library context aligns with many of these CRT points, as he critiques the liberal assumption of equality in intellectual freedom:

> "interlocutors are not in equally good faith; many people are not searching for the truth; many arguments are in the service of power. The inequality of people *making* the arguments and the power dynamics between interlocutors is a problem for intellectual freedom. Based on an assumption of equality, democratic participation, and a common search for truth, IF [intellectual freedom] finds it impossible to deal with different social relationships and contexts, such as capital-worker relationships, relationships of cisheteronormativity, or relationships between settlers and Indigenous people. In other words, perhaps paradoxically, IF cannot deal with contemporary situations of diversity and difference." (emphasis in original)[26]

So maybe our existing philosophical and legal approach is inappropriate and ineffective for dealing with hate and discrimination. But because the majority who hold the power and make the decisions do not feel the negative impacts, and because their power comes from the existing system, the status quo, they are unwilling to change it.

---

24 Richard Delgado and Jean Stefancic, "Images of the Outsider in American Law and Culture," in *Critical Race Theory: The Cutting Edge*, 3rd ed., ed. Richard Delgado and Jean Stefancic (Philadelphia: Temple University Press, 2013), 323–24.

25 Delgado and Stefancic, *Critical Race Theory*, 33. They also discuss power imbalances on a larger scale regarding the First Amendment, but I haven't included those points because of our Canadian focus.

26 Sam Popowich, "Canadian Librarianship and the Politics of Recognition," *Partnership: The Canadian Journal of Library and Information Practice and Research* 16, no. 1 (2021): 8–9, https://doi.org/10.21083/partnership.v16i1.6126.

These CRT arguments align with those raised by many groups and individuals in our history of controversial library events, especially the 18 events involving concerns about hate speech and promotion of discrimination.[27] Contrary to the notion that bringing bad ideas into public would allow them to be discredited, those who opposed the events felt that allowing them to be expressed in the public library would give them an air of legitimacy and social power. They also raised the issue of safety, arguing that to be in a space where the invited speakers are speaking in opposition to your rights and identity, and the majority of the audience is likely there because they agree, could be physically, as well as psychologically and emotionally, dangerous.[28] So not only are they unlikely to attend the event in order to speak out in opposition, they are unlikely to even go into the library when these events are happening, and sometimes they never go back because they no longer feel safe in the library. When we look at these particular 18 contentious events, the controversial speakers were all white and cisgender speaking about the rights of more marginalized people, like racialized immigrants, Jewish and Muslim people, and transgender women, people whose concerns about their rights, identities, safety, and access were eclipsed by the supposedly neutral principles of intellectual freedom and freedom of expression. These events were not sites of some theoretical version of public debate where all are equal and welcome to share diverse opinions toward the opening of minds. They were mostly groups of like-minded people gathered to disseminate their ideologies of discrimination. As Fobazi M. Ettarh wrote about the 2019 Meghan Murphy event at TPL:

> "TPL cannot purport to be a safe space for LGBTQ people and also invite someone who *does not believe in their humanity and personhood*. There is no such thing as 'civil discourse' between someone who doesn't believe in your very existence and someone who does. Not only does the onus then fall on the marginalized group to 'prove they should exist,' but – as hatred and bigotry are based on

---

27 For an examination of the library as a marketplace of ideas, racial capitalism, and ALA's approach to meeting rooms and hate speech in an American library context, see Maura Seale and Rafia Mirza, "Speech and Silence: Race, Neoliberalism, and Intellectual Freedom," *Journal of Radical Librarianship* 5 (2019): 41–60, https://journal.radicallibrarianship.org/index.php/journal/article/view/34.

28 At this point, I will draw your attention to Sara Ahmed's *Feminist Killjoys* blog post which addresses a number of related issues of power, speech, silence, and violence: Sara Ahmed, "You are oppressing us!" *Feministkilljoys* (blog), February 15, 2015, https://feministkilljoys.com/2015/02/15/you-are-oppressing-us/.

ideology and not facts – there's no way for the marginalized to 'win' in what, is again, a hypothetical 'dialogue' TPL claims it must 'champion.' (emphasis in original)[29]

In those 18 event examples, the rights of intellectual freedom and freedom of expression were deemed most important and worth protecting, but this privileging of intellectual freedom and freedom of expression over other library values has been questioned by many within the arena of critical librarianship.[30] Joseph Good argues: "It is the perception that an idea must be given public hearing at all costs, regardless of its intrinsic worth. In such a case, the idea becomes secondary to the imperative to communicate the idea. The idea thereby loses any relevance in cultural or intellectual discourse."[31] He goes on to say:

> "What are the consequences of this practice? Simply, that any idea can be validated once attention is deflected from its claims and attached instead to some general truth or value that can be sanctimoniously affirmed. One is left not with an argument for an idea, but merely the quasi-religious certainty that the idea must be advocated for the public good."[32]

Ann Sparanese also argues that "[i]ntellectual freedom is not the only ethic of the profession of librarianship and it is not a purist value, separated from other democratic principles and human rights."[33] Similarly, Sandy Iverson builds from M. NourbeSe Philip's argument that although the ideologies of individual freedom and of racism were equally foundational to Western democracies, concern about censorship has been privileged while racism has been overlooked, to make

---

29 Fobazi M. Ettarh, "A Chronic Lack of Nuance & a Love of the Hypothetical: a Library Story," *WTF is a Radical Librarian, Anyway?* (blog), October 27, 2019, https://fobaziettarh.com/2019/10/27/a-chronic-lack-of-nuance-a-love-of-the-hypothetical-a-library-story/.

30 For a concise overview of this tension, see Kyle Shockey, "Intellectual Freedom Is Not Social Justice: The Symbolic Capital of Intellectual Freedom in ALA Accreditation and LIS Curricula," *Progressive Librarian* 44 (2016): 101–10.

31 Joseph Good, "The Hottest Place in Hell: The Crisis of Neutrality in Contemporary Librarianship," in *Questioning Library Neutrality Essays From Progressive Librarian*, ed. Alison M. Lewis (Duluth, MN: Library Juice Press, 2008), 143.

32 Good, "The Hottest Place in Hell," 144.

33 Ann Sparanese, "Activist Librarianship: Heritage or Heresy?" in *Questioning Library Neutrality Essays From Progressive Librarian*, ed. Alison M. Lewis (Duluth, MN: Library Juice Press, 2008), 77.

the point that "[w]hile librarians have been avidly anti-censorship, they have not been avidly anti-racist. In fact, they do not acknowledge the inherent racism that is active within the discourse of anti-censorship."[34] These points connect back to CRT, as Delgado and Stefancic discuss the harmful impacts of the liberal prioritization of principles over protection of marginalized groups, as we have seen playing out in public libraries:

> "Words, then, can wound. But the fine thing about the current situation is that one gets to enjoy a superior position and feel virtuous at the same time. By supporting the system of free expression no matter what the cost, one is upholding principle. One can belong to impeccably liberal organizations and believe one is doing the right thing even while taking actions that are demonstrably injurious to the least privileged, most defenseless segments of our society."[35]

Alvin M. Schrader defends librarianship's prioritization of the principles of intellectual freedom and freedom of expression. Informed by his work in the struggle for 2SLGBTQIA+ rights and representation in librarianship, Schrader argues that these principles support social justice: "Social justice triumphed through the supremacy of expressive rights, not in spite of them."[36] With appreciation that he and his colleagues were able to achieve their social justice goals through that approach, we have also seen that this is not always the case for all marginalized communities. Different goals require different strategies. Schrader is deeply invested in the liberal democratic and legal order, citing John Stuart Mill and legal decisions about hate speech, and he suggests that the arguments from those who criticize the library for controversial events advocate for censorship and reveal "an incomplete grasp not only of core values and library missions but also of the Charter and Criminal Code frameworks within which these institutions are statutorily governed and free speech is regulated."[37] He asserts that "[w]hat the library profession needs is better informed

---

34 Sandy Iverson, "Librarianship and Resistance," in *Questioning Library Neutrality Essays From Progressive Librarian*, ed. Alison M. Lewis (Duluth, MN: Library Juice Press, 2008), 27.

35 Delgado and Stefancic, "Images of the Outsider in American Law and Culture," 329.

36 Schrader, "Can Public Libraries Maintain Their Commitment to Intellectual Freedom in the Face of Outrage over Unpopular Speakers?"

37 Schrader.

critics and advocates about the core values of intellectual freedom and social responsibility and their interconnectedness."[38]

However, it is not that such critics do not understand these things, but that we seek to challenge them in their current formations, interpretations, and applications. We know that censorship serves existing oppressive power structures,[39] but so does the traditional neutral approach to intellectual freedom. It's a double bind. Popowich takes issue with the idea that critiques of library neutrality and intellectual freedom promote censorship and are based on ignorance and inexperience. In discussing the 2022 OLA Superconference Spotlight on Intellectual Freedom panel, he points out inconsistencies within the traditional intellectual freedom approach to demonstrate that, even among its defenders, intellectual freedom "is not and can never be some pure and static concept, … but has to be flexible and adapt to changing contexts."[40] He goes on to assert that:

> "Critics of the dominant view of IF are not advocates for censorship. We are advocates for abandoning the all-or-nothing, one-size-fits-all liberal 'tolerance' of Intellectual Freedom which is so easily co-opted to oppressive ends antagonistic and antipathetic to social justice."[41]

In his argument, Schrader affirms the authority of library professional associations to define and enforce these principles through mechanisms such as the relatively new Canadian Federation of Library Associations (CFLA) and its "Statement on Intellectual Freedom and Libraries" and "Position on Third Party Use of Publicly Funded Library Meeting Rooms and Facilities."[42] But not all librarians accept that au-

---

38 Schrader.

39 Alessandra Seiter, "Libraries, Power, and Justice: Toward a Sociohistorically Informed Intellectual Freedom," *Progressive Librarian* 47, (2019–2020): 112, http://www.progressivelibrariansguild.org/PL/PL47/107seiter.pdf.

40 Sam Popowich, "Who Misunderstands Intellectual Freedom?" *spopowich.ca* (blog), February 4, 2022, https://www.spopowich.ca/blog/who-misunderstands-intellectual-freedom.

41 Popowich, "Who Misunderstands Intellectual Freedom?"

42 "Statement on Intellectual Freedom and Libraries"; "Position on Third Party Use of Publicly Funded Library Meeting Rooms and Facilities," Canadian Federation of Library Associations, March 2019, http://cfla-fcab.ca/wp-content/uploads/2019/03/CFLA-FCAB_statement_meeting_rooms.pdf.

thority uncritically,⁴³ especially in consideration of the normativity of whiteness in the library profession, which upholds and is upheld by the neutrality that protects the status quo. Adkins and Hussey make the point that these policies from library professional associations:

> "still reinforce cultural hegemony as they are primarily written in the language of those in power. For example, statements on professional ethics are put together by professional organizations, the overwhelming majority of whose members are white. Intellectual freedom is influenced by the discursive formations of those who write and enforce these policies."⁴⁴

I also take issue with Schrader's dismissal of safety concerns regarding some controversial library events. In reference to psychological and emotional safety he suggests that people should not have an expectation of safety from feeling threatened in a library, and he asserts that "[s]afe space is not conceptually synonymous with social justice and social responsibility."⁴⁵ If so, that not only begs the question of what libraries mean when they declare themselves to be safe spaces,⁴⁶ it also ignores the fact that library workers are entitled to safety in their workplaces, and we heard arguments in historical examples that called for safety as an important element of social justice. Schrader also dismisses the issue of physical safety in the library as a matter of

---

43 A large number of librarians signed an open letter to the CFLA Board on Intellectual Freedom in August 2021 to speak out against three position statements by CFLA Intellectual Freedom Committee that are harmful to trans people: MacCallum et al. to the Canadian Federation of Library Associations, August 23, 2021, https://cfla-fcab.ca/wp-content/uploads/2021/09/Open-Letter-to-the-CFLA-Board-On-Intellectual-Freedom.pdf; Here is the CFLA response: Canadian Federation of Library Associations, 2021, https://cfla-fcab.ca/wp-content/uploads/2021/09/response-to-open-letter-re-IFC-brief.pdf.

44 Denice Adkins and Lisa Hussey, "The Library in the Lives of Latino College Students," *The Library Quarterly* 76, no. 4 (2006): 460, https://doi.org/10.1086/513862.

45 Schrader, "Can Public Libraries Maintain Their Commitment to Intellectual Freedom in the Face of Outrage over Unpopular Speakers?"

46 For example: "VPL Joins VPD's Safe Place Program Supporting LGBTQ Community," Vancouver Public Library, February 24, 2017, https://www.vpl.ca/library/news/2017/vpl-joins-vpd%E2%80%99s-safe-place-program-supporting-lgbtq-community; "Mayor Tory Announces Expansion to Enhanced Youth Spaces and Youth Hubs at Community Centres and Toronto Public Library Locations Across Toronto," City of Toronto, July 26, 2021, https://www.toronto.ca/news/mayor-tory-announces-expansion-to-enhanced-youth-spaces-and-youth-hubs-at-community-centres-and-toronto-public-library-locations-across-toronto/; "Community Guidelines," Halifax Public Libraries, accessed May 4, 2022, https://www.halifaxpubliclibraries.ca/library-spaces/use-of-space/community-guidelines/; "Robert Tegler Trust Outreach Services," Edmonton Public Library, Accessed May 4, 2022. https://www.epl.ca/milner-library/outreach/.

police responsibility,[47] which fails to acknowledge the harm that police can cause to marginalized communities, and it minimizes the fear of and real potential for physical violence some of these events present to marginalized communities. Moreover, given how closely psychological and physical safety are linked when issues of rights and identity are concerned, I think it is appropriate to consider them together. But even if we treat psychological and emotional safety separately, we have an example from 2012 of the Belleville Public Library cancelling a book talk about local murders in response to public outcry that it would be too upsetting for the community. The library said this did not constitute censorship because the book was still available in the library, and in my research I found no evidence of professional outcry over this decision. I am not suggesting that this particular decision of prioritizing psychological and emotional safety was an act of social justice, as there were no groups being marginalized based on their identities and there were no rights at stake; rather, it is an interesting case because its outcome was so different from most others that did involve marginalized groups where safety and rights were among their concerns. Did it really not compromise intellectual freedom and freedom of expression, as the library asserted? What made community feelings and safety more important to the library in this case than in the others?

Other librarians who have written about the issues surrounding controversial library events, many prompted by the 2019 TPL controversy, also advocate for safety in library spaces as part of libraries' social responsibility. In conversation with the work of Rachel Wexelbaum and Sarah Hasehmi Scott on the topic of libraries as safe spaces, Kris Joseph suggests that the discourse of libraries as valuable community spaces must involve "a discussion of inclusion, safety, and social justice (or, the principle of equity for all)," and Joseph references Jessamyn West's argument about the importance of safety in achieving inclusion and diversity.[48] However, Joseph also notes that this per-

---

47 Unfortunately, police forces do not protect the safety of all citizens equally or equitably, and in fact they represent a safety threat to many marginalized communities, so when libraries have extra police or security presence at events, that can put these community members at greater risk. For discussion of a recent example of harmful securitization in a Canadian public library, see: Brianne Selman and Joe Curnow, "Winnipeg's Millennium Library Needs Solidarity, Not Security," *Partnership: The Canadian Journal of Library and Information Practice and Research* 14, no. 2 (2019): 1–9, ProQuest.

48 Joseph, "The Curious Case of Free-Speech-Loving Librarians Who Don't Think the Toronto Public Library Should Provide Space for Meghan Murphy: Part Two."

spective is not as pervasive across librarianship as some might like, and that those who tend to resist it are library leaders who are holding on to "previously established patterns" and are resistant to shifts in library values because they "feel that their values are under threat."[49] Regarding the 2019 TPL controversy, Joseph discusses the context of the 2SLGBTQIA+ community in Toronto at the time, including a recent serial killer targeting queer men of colour, and argues that community context matters, despite TPL's unwillingness to consider it, and underlines the importance of safe spaces like public libraries for marginalized communities.[50] As Fobazi Ettarh argues:

> "upholding 'neutrality' goes directly against the 'safe and welcome spaces' that libraries purport themselves to be. Because the only people who can be safe in a space with Nazis (or in this case TERFs) are those who are either or both: comfortable with the ideology [or] privileged enough to not be harmed by those with said ideology. That's it. No one else."[51]

As we have seen in many examples, the values of safety, inclusion, and diversity are regularly trumped by the values of intellectual freedom and freedom of expression in libraries. In his critique of the 2019 TPL controversy, Sam Popowich argues that TPL's, as well as VPL's, "insistence on maximalist intellectual freedom" has revealed a "problem with conflicting values" in which proclaimed commitments to marginalized communities are overridden by liberal bourgeois principles.[52] He questions the sincerity and significance of the library's support for 2SLGBTQIA+ people and other library values that are compromised in favour of intellectual freedom and says: "when library values are abandoned at the first obstacle, then they are meaningless."[53] Shelley Gullikson echoes that point stating: "If they really were supporters of the LGBTQ2S+ community, they would be supporting the LGBTQ2S+

---

49   Joseph, "The Curious Case of Free-Speech-Loving Librarians Who Don't Think the Toronto Public Library Should Provide Space for Meghan Murphy: Part Two."

50   Joseph, "The Curious Case of Free-Speech-Loving Librarians Who Don't Think the Toronto Public Library Should Provide Space for Meghan Murphy: Part Two."

51   Ettarh, "A Chronic Lack of Nuance & a Love of the Hypothetical."

52   Sam Popowich, "Community, Value, and Worth," *redlibrarian.github.io* (blog), October 13, 2019, https://redlibrarian.github.io/article/2019/10/13/commmunity-value-worth.html.

53   Popowich, "Community, Value, and Worth."

community."[54] Kris Joseph also discusses competing library values and advocates for "considerations of impact and consequence," as well as context, when such values conflicts arise.[55] Joseph argues that in the 2019 TPL example, the choices made to prioritize certain library values over others resulted in harm done to communities, individuals, and relationships that outweighed the protection of intellectual freedom.[56] I think this argument could easily apply to other historical examples, especially where repeated incidents allowed the harm to continue, such as with GVPL in the late 1990s.

On the topic of competing values and harm, Gullikson points out that "[i]t is not incompatible with upholding intellectual freedom to also acknowledge that it's doing harm" and argues that the library could have put more energy and effort into community outreach and communication to work on ways of mitigating the harm caused.[57] Regarding TPL, she offered:

> "It's not as good as cancelling the event entirely, but at least it would show that TPL has been listening to its community. It would show that they have thought through the consequences of choosing values over people. It would show that they are not just 'aware' of 'anger and concern' but they *understand* the fears, risks, and harm their actions are causing... To not just say 'we uphold intellectual freedom,' but to acknowledge exactly what that means in this particular case." (emphasis in original)[58]

This approach goes beyond a neutral stance and would require honesty and transparency about the complicated values conflicts that the library is facing with these kinds of controversial events, which could facilitate accountability.

---

54 Gullikson, "The TPL Debacle."

55 Joseph, "The Curious Case of Free-Speech-Loving Librarians Who Don't Think the Toronto Public Library Should Provide Space for Meghan Murphy: Part One."

56 Joseph, "The Curious Case of Free-Speech-Loving Librarians Who Don't Think the Toronto Public Library Should Provide Space for Meghan Murphy: Part One"; Joseph, "The Curious Case of Free-Speech-Loving Librarians Who Don't Think the Toronto Public Library Should Provide Space for Meghan Murphy: Part Two."

57 Gullikson, "The TPL Debacle."

58 Gullikson, "The TPL Debacle."

In response to white nationalist groups targeting libraries, an American organization that works to combat white nationalism, Western States Center, partnered with a group of librarians to develop *Confronting White Nationalism in Libraries: A Toolkit*, which can be applied to deal with myriad bigoted, hateful groups. Regarding free speech, the authors note that these groups have politicized speech in libraries as a strategy to build their credibility, which is something we saw pointed out in historical examples, and they assert that "Our efforts to provide accurate, reliable information to the community are, understandably, undermined when white nationalists demand library platforms from which to spread ideas deeply anchored in falsehoods."[59] The toolkit recommends that library workers "can and should use our own free speech, along with creative actions, to support our values" when tactics like deplatforming are not possible, and it "define[s] success as taking action to increase community strength and safety, while minimizing the opportunities for white nationalists to undermine libraries and their values."[60] In addition to proactive measures like strengthening community relationships, incorporating restorative justice models into incident responses, and reviewing policies through a racial justice lens,[61] the toolkit also offers suggestions for how to respond to incidents, including when white nationalist groups book library meeting rooms and when they protest at library events that promote diversity and inclusion, such as drag storytimes. One suggestion is to counter-organize to make the library less hospitable to hate and discrimination in a number of ways: making displays and/or handing out educational resources that challenge the messages of the groups, which we saw that Grand Prairie public library did to counter an anti-vaccination film in 2020; supporting events that elevate and celebrate marginalized groups; and library workers and administrators using their free speech to speak out publicly against hate groups.[62] All of these ideas maintain intellectual freedom and free speech for the groups while allowing the library to actively promote social justice instead of remaining neutral.

---

59   Western States Center, *Confronting White Nationalism in Libraries: A Toolkit*, (Portland, OR, 2022), 7.

60   Western States Center, *Confronting White Nationalism in Libraries*, 5.

61   Western States Center, 9.

62   Western States Center, *Confronting White Nationalism in Libraries*, 22, 23.

In so many of the library statements we have seen, the unrelenting focus on neutrality and the principle of intellectual freedom is used as an excuse for library inaction, and it conceals the conflicts and politics behind the decision-making, while also conveying a lack of empathy, care, and consideration for the harm caused. The library is neutral, therefore it does not practice care for any community. That is the lowest common denominator of equality, and it certainly is not equity. But as Popowich notes: "In order for public libraries to be worth anything to their communities, they have to demonstrate that their communities are worth something to them."[63] So what can be done about this problematic neutral approach to intellectual freedom? Let's look at how queer, trans, and feminist theories can inform a way forward.

Conclusion: Toward a Queer, Trans, Feminist Future for Intellectual Freedom

Like the term queer, which Judith Butler asserts can be a "site of collective contestation" that must be "never fully owned, but always and only redeployed, twisted, queered from a prior usage and in the direction of urgent and expanding political purposes,"[64] queer theory encompasses a variety of meanings and resists traditional academic conceptual boundaries. And similar to CRT's questioning of the liberal order, queer theory can be understood as a "thoroughly revolutionary alternative to the established paradigm" that "avoids binary and hierarchical reasoning in general, and in connection with gender, sex, and sexuality in particular," involving queering as "the process of complicating something."[65] I also want to bring in Dean Spade's description of critical trans politics as a practice seeking "to transform current logics of state, civil society security, and social equality" while "resisting hierarchies of truth and reality and instead naming and refusing state violence."[66] Spade's work explicitly draws on CRT to exam-

---

63   Popowich, "Community, Value, and Worth."

64   Judith Butler, *Bodies That Matter: on the Discursive Limits of "Sex"* (New York: Routledge, 2014), 73, https://doi.org/10.4324/9780203760079.

65   Mimi Marinucci, *Feminism Is Queer: the Intimate Connection Between Queer and Feminist Theory*, 2nd ed. (London: Zed Books, 2016), xxii, 43.

66   Dean Spade, *Normal Life: Administrative Violence, Critical Trans Politics, and the Limits of Law* (Brooklyn, NY: South End Press, 2015), 1.

ine how administrative governance produces and distributes power.[67] I want to use these critical lenses to help us reimagine how libraries can approach intellectual freedom and freedom of expression.

Libraries have a power problem, in that they actively ignore how power functions within libraries by relying on the concept of neutrality, which has been normalized over time to prioritize the principles of intellectual freedom and freedom of expression above other library values or community needs. Spade's critique of supposedly neutral administrative systems as sites of power through which norms are established and life chances are distributed, proposes interrogating "processes of normalization by analyzing their impacts and revising [...] resistance strategies."[68] We have seen over time that libraries, like many other liberal institutions, have expanded their missions to incorporate ideas of equity, diversity, and inclusion, however those shifts have not been accompanied by substantial restructuring of power or priorities.[69] Those ideas have failed to have a meaningful impact of resistance against neutrality; rather, they have been normalized through administrative tools, such as policy statements, to function as an extension of liberal power in order to quell criticism and defend against public accusations of discrimination.[70] As Popowich argues, "Canadian librarianship stops short at recognition, allowing libraries to view themselves as defenders of human rights while resisting any actual redistribution of social justice or egalitarian democratic participation."[71] And we have seen through historical examples and critiques above that when libraries declare themselves to be diverse and inclusive spaces, that is not necessarily reflected in their

---

67   Spade, *Normal Life*, 11.

68   Spade, 4–7.

69   Baharak Yousefi, "On the Disparity Between What We Say and What We Do in Libraries," in *Feminists Among Us: Resistance and Advocacy in Library*, ed. Baharak Yousefi and Shirley Lew, (Sacramento, CA: Library Juice Press, 2017), 92; David James Hudson, "On 'Diversity' as Anti-Racism in Library and Information Studies: A Critique," *Journal of Critical Library and Information Studies* 1, no. 1 (2017) https://doi.org/10.24242/jclis.v1i1.6. For a broader examination of the disruption and negotiation that comes with institutional diversity I recommend reading *Space Invaders: Race, Gender and Bodies Out of Place* by Nirmal Puwar.

70   Sara Ahmed's *On Being Included: Racism and Diversity in Institutional Life* (Durham, NC: Duke University Press, 2012) examines how the focus on writing diversity policies can preclude real action and change. I'm sure there are other works out there about how these liberal strategies were designed for reinforcement rather than resistance or transformation, but I haven't read them yet.

71   Popowich, "Canadian Librarianship and the Politics of Recognition," 11.

actions or in the lived experiences of marginalized people in libraries. In considering the disparities between what libraries say and what they do, Baharak Yousefi posits that this progressive self-declaration by libraries and library workers as "being on the right side" helps us "to dissociate ourselves personally from our collective actions and responsibilities."[72] The diversity and inclusion strategy has resulted in institutional and professional complacency.

So we need a new strategy of resistance. Spade's critical trans politics says to look at what systems actually do, "rather than what they say about what they do," in order to "shape resistance strategies that have a better chance at actually addressing the conditions that concern us."[73] Seeing many examples of libraries failing to respond to the needs and demands of marginalized community members demonstrates that what libraries actually do for diversity and inclusion does not sufficiently challenge discrimination or work to make libraries anti-oppressive spaces. We need to push libraries beyond the progressive symbolism and virtue signalling of equity, diversity, and inclusion policies, which Spade might describe as "the window-dressing of neoliberal violence,"[74] because they function in ways that actively undermine efforts toward equity.

Queer theory can help us revise our resistance strategy by challenging the hierarchical, competitive, binary nature of the current library values. What if intellectual freedom was not prioritized above other library values? What if intellectual freedom and social justice were not in competition? What if we queered the current conception and application of intellectual freedom to expand and transform it into a value that incorporates and advances social justice? What would that look like and how would that work? Is that possible, considering its roots in liberal individualism? What are the positive parts of intellectual freedom to hold onto in queering it? Popowich notes that in the dominant library approach to intellectual freedom and freedom of expression, "the 'possessor' of the right of free expression is the isolated individual without social relationships and who owes and receives nothing

---

72   Yousefi, "On the disparity," 94–95.

73   Spade, *Normal Life*, 10.

74   Spade, 12.

from society,"[75] which he repudiates elsewhere as, "an IF that seeks to be 'neutral' and sees no connection between IF and the maintenance and reproduction of oppressive structures."[76] So he offers the proposition that treating intellectual freedom and social responsibility separately "obscures the real interrelationships of the social world of which libraries are a part," but considering them as one could advance a new approach to intellectual freedom as part of social justice, allowing libraries to participate in more positive social change.[77] This approach necessarily rejects claims to neutrality:

> "there is no objective place from which to stand in order to uphold either IF or social responsibility. Libraries and library workers are part of the social world, they are in it, they are of it, and the material forces and relations of the world determine our roles, positions, and perspectives on that world."[78]

And this approach necessarily requires recognizing and responding to social realities and community needs and concerns. Similarly, in her October 2019 deputation to the TPL board, Jane Schmidt suggested that we refocus our energies on "widening our understanding of intellectual freedom and social responsibility" to think about "an interpretation of intellectual freedom with an anti-oppressive and trauma-informed lense (sic)."[79] Alessandra Seiter also calls for "a justice-based, sociohistorically informed IF" that can break down societal barriers and engage with communities "to work in their interests instead of against them," especially "when those communities are in crisis."[80]

To reconceptualize a socially just intellectual freedom from a feminist perspective requires centring the voices, knowledge, and experiences

---

[75] Sam Popowich, "The Trouble with Intellectual Freedom, part one," *spopowich.ca* (blog), October 6, 2021, https://www.spopowich.ca/blog/the-trouble-with-intellectual-freedom-part-one.

[76] Sam Popowich, "Dialectics and Social Responsibility," *redlibrarian.github.io* (blog), October 15, 2019, https://redlibrarian.github.io/article/2019/10/15/dialectics-and-social-responsibility.html.

[77] Popowich, "Dialectics and Social Responsibility."

[78] Popowich, "Dialectics and Social Responsibility."

[79] Schmidt, "My Remarks to the TPL Board."

[80] Seiter, "Libraries, Power, and Justice," 112.

of marginalized communities.[81] In order to be equitable, anti-oppressive spaces, libraries need to listen to and understand the ways that they are participating in oppression, and learn how to do better, rather than relying on the so-called neutrality of intellectual freedom to absolve them of the harm they do. And an important part of that process is practising care. The work of practising care and all of its complexities has been much examined and pursued in Black and abolitionist feminisms. In an essay entitled "On Care," Chalay Chalermkraivuth synthesizes and builds on these examinations to emphasize the hard work of care work: "I want to make clear that care work is not easy, simple, or uncomplicatedly good. It is as much produced by our harsh world as it is an escape route from it. It can be violent. And it must be rigorous."[82] They argue that to be liberatory, care work "must strive to dismantle social hierarchies, not exist within or reproduce them," and they ask important questions that we should be asking ourselves in practising care in libraries: "How do we turn care toward revolution? How do we make a revolution *of* care?" (emphasis in original)[83]

It is complicated to talk about care in librarianship since the profession has long been feminized and associated with gendered ideas of service and empathy, but there is work about the feminist ethic of care in libraries that can help to inform a transformed, socially responsible intellectual freedom.[84] The feminist ethic of care is "a method that considers context rather than universal rules and values preservation of relationships over preservation of principle."[85] Tronto's work on the ethic of care recognizes the difficulties in applying it institutionally, but Fox and Olson identify a number of practical ways to incorporate

---

81 Shana Higgins, "Embracing the Feminization of Librarianship," in *Feminists Among Us: Resistance and Advocacy in Library*, ed. Baharak Yousefi and Shirley Lew, (Sacramento, CA: Library Juice Press, 2017), 78.

82 Chalay Chalermkraivuth, "On Care." https://crossingwalls.sandbox.library.columbia.edu/on-care/.

83 Chalermkraivuth, "On Care."

84 Although Carol Gilligan's original conception of the femin*ine* ethic of care was criticized for gendered essentialism, it has shifted through the work of Joan Tronto and others to be reoriented as a femin*ist* ethic of care grounded in social experience. Melodie J. Fox and Hope A. Olsen, "Essentialism and Care in a Female Intensive Profession," in *Feminist and Queer Information Studies Reader*, ed. Patrick Keilty and Rebecca Dean (Sacramento, CA: Litwin Books, 2013), 56–58, http://ebookcentral.proquest.com/lib/utoronto/detail.action?docID=3328252.

85 Fox and Olson, "Essentialism and Care in a Female Intensive Profession," 56.

it into libraries.[86] To build strong relationships and provide meaningful services and spaces for communities, libraries should be practising care in working *with* communities. And that practice, that ethic, is important in a social justice approach to intellectual freedom that, as Popowich says, "would allow us to make different choices in different contexts."[87] Then he goes on to offer that, "When defenders of traditional IF ask the disingenuous question 'who decides?' the answer has to be, not 'me' or 'you' or 'them', but *us. We* decide, but only as part of a community or set of communities." (emphasis original)[88] I would argue that a feminist ethic of care-infused approach to the question of neutrality and intellectual freedom was applied in Belleville in 2012, when the library made a decision informed by the local context of trauma to prioritize the feelings of the people in the community. In contrast, some of the critiques of TPL's 2019 decision accused the library of valuing principles over people, and that they ignored the local context of a serial killer in the gay village that made the city's 2SLGBTQIA+ communities feel vulnerable in spaces they would have previously considered safe. So we can see how employing an ethic of care in libraries can prevent harm, while an absence of it can cause harm. As an antidote to the dissociation Yousefi identified, Higgins offers that "a feminist ethic of care may enable us to center the collaborative, communal, and politically engaged-ness of library work."[89] As long as we are careful that our care work resists cooptation by staying centred on community relationships and grounded in social justice for collective liberation.

There is no easy fix, but as Higgins suggests, "care seems to hold possibilities as a means toward equitable, inclusive, anti-neoliberal futures,"[90] and those are the futures that I want to build. From my abolitionist commitments, to living through a pandemic and learning more than I ever thought I would about public health, what I know for sure is that we keep each other safe. Community, relationships, and protecting those who are most vulnerable are the values I prioritize personally, and I look forward to continuing the work of applying

---

86 Fox and Olson, 58–59.

87 Popowich, "Who Misunderstands Intellectual Freedom?"

88 Popowich, "Who Misunderstands Intellectual Freedom?"

89 Higgins, "Embracing the Feminization of Librarianship," 83.

90 Higgins, 73.

them professionally, collectively. To that end, I look forward to further political analysis and ideas for radical and transformative solutions. And if we find that libraries are inextricably liberal institutions that we cannot transform, but instead need to build something new, I am happy to have those conversations too. I'll close with the wise words of Mariame Kaba:

> "None of us has all of the answers, or we would have ended oppression already. But if we keep building the world we want, trying new things, and learning from our mistakes, new possibilities emerge."[91]

---

91 Mariame Kaba, *We Do This 'Til We Free* (Chicago: Haymarket Books, 2021), 4.

Afterword

In the time between when I started working on this book and when it is being published, a lot of pandemic time passed with varying degrees of lockdowns across Canada and elsewhere. The community-minded yet materially hollow slogan of being "all in this together" faded while anti-lockdown, anti-mask, and anti-vax movements formed into convoys, and now things have gone back to so-called normal. As scary as 2020 was in a lot of ways, there were also moments that felt full of potential to infuse more care into our social systems. Unfortunately, that potential went unrealized, and at the same time, hate was on the rise. According to Statistics Canada, the number of hate crimes reported by police in Canada rose from 2,646 in 2020 to 3,360 in 2021, a 27% increase, following a 36% increase in 2020; and higher numbers of hate crimes targeting a given religion (+67%; 884 incidents), sexual orientation (+64%; 423 incidents), and race or ethnicity (+6%; 1,723 incidents) accounted for most of those incidents.[1] Since events have resumed at public libraries, there has been no shortage of controversies, as far-right homophobes and transphobes have made it their mission to target drag storytimes as one strategy in their current campaign of hate.

As we saw in the Kelowna example, where the library and its board supported the drag storytimes despite the CEO's attempt to suppress

---

1 Statistics Canada, "The Daily — Police-reported Hate Crime, 2021," March 22, 2023, https://www150.statcan.gc.ca/n1/daily-quotidien/230322/dq230322a-eng.htm?utm_source=The+519%27s+Email+List&utm_campaign=0e29974485-EMAIL_CAMPAIGN_2019_01_31_03_25_COPY_01&utm_medium=email&utm_term=0_a22f669ecd-0e29974485-407384113&mc_cid=0e29974485&mc_eid=dd15bca702&fbclid=PAAaYEfL5yNz51x2kBYkNJ0WLvNOLyo8ZAGup-qDq7cf98WlglfdQgi-V-Pow. And these are just the incidents that are reported and classified as such, so the real numbers are undoubtedly higher. For discussion on the challenges and complexities of tracking hate in Canada see David Weisz and Janice Saji, "Advocacy, Community Groups Track Hate in Canada When Law Enforcement Fails Us," *National Observer*, March 10, 2023, https://www.nationalobserver.com/2023/03/10/investigations/tracking-hate-crime-incidents-canada.

them, libraries in Edmonton,[2] Calgary,[3] Toronto,[4] and likely elsewhere have continued to host these very popular events despite protests. And most, if not all, of the time, the far-right, anti-2SLGBTQIA+ protestors are outnumbered by counter-protestors who show up to support the events and to help protect attendees. We are also seeing strong support for these events from some politicians,[5] community organizations,[6] and professional library associations.[7] The firm stance being taken by the library profession on this kind of controversial event is important, but it is also to be expected, given that defending drag storytimes conveniently aligns the library's favourite value of intellectual freedom with other values of diversity and inclusion. But the problem remains when those values do not align. In the current climate of rising hate we need libraries to maintain and enhance this defence and support for 2SLGBTQIA+ people, as well as other marginalized communities, because neutrality does not suffice when the hate is happening inside the rooms of the library. The reality is that libraries need to actively resist hate to prevent harm.

---

2   Ashley Joannou, "'Focus on The Love': Drag Artist Leads Story Time at Downtown Edmonton Library," *Edmonton Journal*, August 7, 2022. https://edmontonjournal.com/news/local-news/focus-on-the-love-drag-artist-leads-story-time-at-downtown-edmonton-library.

3   Silvia Naranjo and Alejandro Melgar, "Calgary Library Drag Event Interrupted Sparks Concerns," *CityNews Calgary*, February 28, 2023, https://calgary.citynews.ca/2023/02/28/calgary-library-drag-event/.

4   Santiago Arias Orozco, "Protesters Showed up to One of This Drag Queen's Recent Storytime Performances. Here's Why She Won't Stop Reading," *Toronto Star*, June 11, 2023, https://www.thestar.com/life/together/2023/06/11/protesters-showed-up-to-one-of-this-drag-queens-recent-storytime-performances-heres-why-she-wont-stop-reading.html.

5   Kristyn Wong-Tam, "Protect 2SLGBTQI+ Communities & Drag Artists," accessed April 5, 2023, https://www.kristynwongtam.ca/protect-drag. And in response to the Feb 2023 at a public library drag storytime, Calgary City Council voted 10-5 in favour of amending a safety bylaw to prohibit protests within 100 m of an entrance to a recreation facility or library. "Calgary city council passes safety bylaws after protests at library drag events," *CBC News*, March 14, 2023, https://www.cbc.ca/news/canada/calgary/calgary-city-council-safety-bylaw-homophobic-protests-1.6779105.

6   The 519, "Army of Lovers," accessed May 2, 2023, https://www.the519.org/armyoflovers/?fbclid=PAAaaX0hZhZ31XmUV05K_z8mBOwqffKbJCYFZ0-2nsMMnRMm8oDZKHFlMq7L0.

7   The Partnership, "In Defence of Drag Storytime: A Statement of Support from Canada's Library Associations," June 27, 2023, https://librarianship.ca/news/in-defence-of-drag-storytime/.

Bibliography

"A Look Back in Anger–A Debate on Free Speech Evokes Painful." *Times Colonist,* November 10, 1996. ProQuest.

Adkins, Denice and Lisa Hussey. "The Library in the Lives of Latino College Students." *The Library Quarterly* 76, no. 4 (2006). https://doi.org/10.1086/513862.

Agahi, Emad. "Vancouver Cuts Funding to Rape Crisis Centre Over Policy Excluding Transgender Women." *CTV News,* March 16, 2019. https://bc.ctvnews.ca/vancouver-cuts-funding-to-rape-crisis-centre-over-policy-excluding-transgender-women-1.4339524.

Ahearn, Victoria. "City of Edmonton Scraps Joseph Boyden's Speaking Slot At Culture Event." *CBC,* January 19, 2017. https://www.cbc.ca/news/canada/edmonton/joseph-boyden-edmonton-1.3943534.

Ahmed, Sara. *On Being Included: Racism and Diversity in Institutional Life.* Durham, NC: Duke University Press, 2012.

Ahmed, Sara. "You Are Oppressing Us!" *Feministkilljoys* (blog). February 15, 2015. https://feministkilljoys.com/2015/02/15/you-are-oppressing-us/.

"ALC Libraries More Than Ever." In *Alberta Library Conference.* Jasper: ALC, 2017. https://www.laa.ca/alc2017/documents/ALC2017SaturdayFinal.PDF.

Allen, Mercedes. "Memorial Draws Controversy Over Invitation of Speaker Janice Raymond." Rabble. November 29, 2013. https://rabble.ca/feminism/memorial-draws-controversy-over-invitation-speaker-janice-raymond/.

American Library Association. "The Freedom to Read Statement." Issues & Advocacy. Last modified June 30, 2004. http://www.ala.org/advocacy/intfreedom/freedomreadstatement.

Andrews, Phil, ed. "Library Can Learn Lesson From Protest Debate." *Guelph Mercury,* April 22, 2013. https://www.neighbourhoodgroup.com/downloads/local-food-has-great-legs.pdf.

"Anti-Mosque Lawyer Speaks in Ottawa Despite Protests." *CBC,* February 4, 2013. https://www.cbc.ca/news/canada/ottawa/anti-mosque-lawyer-speaks-in-ottawa-despite-protests-1.1300508.

"Artificial Intelligence and Intellectual Freedom, Key Policy Concerns for Canadian Libraries." Canadian Federation of Library Associations / Fédération canadienne des associations de bibliothèques. May 2, 2018. http://cfla-fcab.ca/wp-content/uploads/2018/07/CFLA-FCAB-2018-National-Forum-Paper-final.pdf.

Balkissoon, Denise. "The Targeting of Other Women Shows Meghan Murphy Is No Feminist." *The Globe and Mail,* October 28, 2019. https://www.theglobeandmail.com/opinion/article-the-targeting-of-other-women-shows-meghan-murphy-is-no-feminist/.

"Banning controversial groups from public spaces." *The Democratic Commitment*, June, 2000. https://bccla.org/wp-content/uploads/2012/08/2000_Summer_Newsletter_Democratic_Commitment.pdf.

Barrera, Jorge. "Author Joseph Boyden's Shape-Shifting Indigenous Identity." *APTN News*, December 23, 2016. https://www.aptnnews.ca/national-news/author-joseph-boydens-shape-shifting-indigenous-identity/.

Baltic, A. Letter to the editor. *The London Free Press*. August 15, 1960.

"B.C. Group Decries Ban on Suicide Seminar." *National Post,* September 22, 2009. ProQuest.

"BCLA Announces Recipients of 2020 Awards." Librarianship. July 2, 2020. https://librarianship.ca/news/bcla-2020-awards/.

Beattie, Samantha. "Board Bars Hate Groups from Renting Library Space: Monday's Unanimous Decision Lets Staff Deny Or Cancel Bookings." *Toronto Star,* December 12, 2017. https://www.thestar.com/news/city_hall/2017/12/11/toronto-library-looks-at-barring-hate-groups-from-renting-space.html.

Beattie, Samantha. "Toronto Library Bars Hate Groups From Renting Space." *Toronto Star*, December 11, 2017. ProQuest.

Beaussart, Mary. Letter to the editor. *The Province*, October 28, 2009. ProQuest.

Bellett, Gerry. "Library Bans Assisted-Suicide Workshop." *Vancouver Sun,* September 22, 2009. ProQuest.

Bergen, Carin. "Article Stirred Memories." *Leader Post,* May 18, 2000. ProQuest.

Beth, "Greg Felton at VPL." *The (Unofficial) BCLA Intellectual Freedom Committee Blog* (blog). February 26, 2008. https://bclaifc.wordpress.com/2008/02/26/greg-felton-at-vpl/.

Bermingham, John. "Church Hosts Right-to-Die Doctor; Library Rejects Assisted-Suicide Advocate on Advice from Lawyers." *The Province*, October 25, 2009. ProQuest.

Bernham, Valerie. "Support for Toronto Public Library." Change.org. Accessed February 21, 2022. https://www.change.org/p/toronto-public-library-support-for-toronto-public-library?signed=true.

Bivens-Tatum, Wayne. *Libraries and The Enlightenment*. Los Angeles, CA: Library Juice Press, 2012.

Blair, Elgin. "City Survives Showing of Gay Film." *The Body Politic* 42. April, 1978. https://archive.org/details/bodypolitic42toro/page/6/mode/2up.

Blair, Elgin. "Crisp Controversy Spreads to Oakville." *The Body Politic* 43. May, 1978. https://archive.org/details/bodypolitic43toro/page/6/mode/2up.

Boothby, Lauren. "Edmonton Library Trustee Says She Was Forced to Resign in Dispute Over Free Speech, Tweets." *Edmonton Journal*, February 12, 2020. https://edmontonjournal.com/news/local-news/edmonton-library-trustee-says-she-was-forced-to-resign-in-dispute-over-free-speech-tweets.

Bourg, Chris, and Bess Sadler. "Feminism and the Future of Library Discovery." *Code4Lib*, no. 28 (April 15, 2015). https://doi.org/https://journal.code4lib.org/articles/10425.

Bourg, Chris. "Debating Y/Our Humanity, or Are Libraries Neutral?" *Feral Librarian* (blog). February 11, 2018. https://chrisbourg.wordpress.com/2018/02/11/debating-y-our-humanity-or-are-libraries-neutral/.

Bowles, Vickery to Chris Murray. Toronto, ON. January 6, 2021. In *Attachment 1: Toronto Public Library Response to MM 11.14*. https://www.toronto.ca/legdocs/mmis/2021/cc/bgrd/backgroundfile-164697.pdf.

Bowles, Vickery. *Letter to City of Toronto 2SLGBTQ Advisory Committee*. May 19, 2022. https://www.toronto.ca/legdocs/mmis/2022/qs/bgrd/backgroundfile-225883.pdf.

Braun, Liz. "Don't Blame the Library; Beleaguered Facility Not at Fault for Hate Gathering." *Toronto Sun*, July 14, 2017. ProQuest.

Brean, Joseph. "Fringe-Right Champion Victorious in Death, Too; Memorial for Controversial Lawyer to Proceed Unabated." *National Post*, July 13, 2017. ProQuest.

Brean, Joseph. "Meghan Murphy, the Woman Behind Trans Wars Breaking Out at the Public Library." *National Post*, October 28, 2019. https://nationalpost.com/news/meghan-murphy-the-woman-behind-trans-wars-breaking-out-at-the-public-library.

British Columbia Teachers' Federation (@BCTF). "We need to ensure that public institutions in BC are not used to promote hate in any way", Twitter, November 29, 2018, 8:31 p.m., https://twitter.com/bctf/status/1068316546408210432.

Brook, Paula. "Limits on Free Speech a Double-Edged Sword: Impediments to Free Speech Aimed at the Political Far Right Cast our Society in the Uneasy Role of Censor." *Vancouver Sun*, October 6, 1999. ProQuest.

Brook, Paula. "Pass the Milquetoast: Library Puts Tepid Spin on a Stark Issue: Instead of a Colourful Poster Dealing with Censorship and Freedom, the VPL Employs the 'a' Word (Appropriate)." *Vancouver Sun*, February 9, 2000. ProQuest.

Brown, Dave. Letter to the editor. *The Province*, July 31, 2019. ProQuest.

Bundy, Mary Lee, and Frederick J. Stielow. *Activism in American Librarianship: 1962–1973*. New York: Greenwood Press, 1987.

Burman, Dilshad. "Fay and Fluffy's Storytime Ends Toronto Public Library Affiliation Over Meghan Murphy Talk." *City News*, October 29, 2019. https://toronto.citynews.ca/2019/10/29/fay-and-fluffys-library-storytime-cancelled-meghan-murphy-event/.

Butler, Judith. *Bodies That Matter: on the Discursive Limits of "Sex"*. New York: Routledge, 2014. https://doi.org/10.4324/9780203760079.

"Calgary City Council Passes Safety Bylaws after Protests at Library Drag Events." *CBC News*, March 14, 2023. https://www.cbc.ca/news/canada/calgary/calgary-city-council-safety-bylaw-homophobic-protests-1.6779105.

Calleja, Frank. "Teacher Fired for Alleged Link to Racists Board Warned Paul Fromm in '92 about His Activities." *Toronto Star*, February 27, 1997. ProQuest

Canadian Federation of Library Associations. *Letter*. 2021. https://cfla-fcab.ca/wp-content/uploads/2021/09/response-to-open-letter-re-IFC-brief.pdf,

Canadian Parents of Trans and Gender Diverse Kids (@CPoTGDK). "Our statement on @torontolibrary renting space." Twitter, October 22, 2019, 9:39 a.m. https://twitter.com/CPoTGDK/status/1186638263118958593.

Carmichael, James V. *Daring to Find Our Names: The Search for Lesbigay Library History*. Westport, CT: Greenwood Press, 1998.

Casey, Liam. "Hundreds Protest Controversial Toronto Library Event Featuring Meghan Murphy." *Global News*, October 29, 2019. https://globalnews.ca/news/6098974/toronto-public-library-meghan-murphy-event/.

Chalermkraivuth, Chalay. "On Care." https://crossingwalls.sandbox.library.columbia.edu/on-care/.

Chan, Josh. "Beyond Tokenism: The Importance of Staff Diversity in Libraries." *BCLA Connect Perspectives Newsletter* 12, no. 1 (November 2020). https://bclaconnect.ca/perspectives/2020/11/30/beyond-tokenism-the-importance-of-staff-diversity-in-libraries.

Charbonneau, David. "When Life is Intolerable, Why Not a Graceful Exit?" *Kamloops Daily News*, October 22, 2009. ProQuest.

City Manager and Chief People Officer, People & Equity. *Reviewing City of Toronto Policies Governing the Use of Libraries and City Facilities by Individuals and Groups Promoting Intolerance or Discrimination*. Toronto, ON: City of Toronto, 2021. https://www.toronto.ca/legdocs/mmis/2021/cc/bgrd/backgroundfile-164696.pdf.

"City Librarian Statement on Upcoming Third-Party Room Rental Event." Toronto Public Library. October 15, 2019. https://torontopubliclibrary.typepad.com/news_releases/2019/10/city-librarian-statement-on-upcoming-third-party-room-rental-event-.html.

City of Toronto. *City Council Consideration on March 10, 2021*. Toronto, ON: City of Toronto, 2021. http://app.toronto.ca/tmmis/viewAgendaItemHistory.do?item=2021.CC30.2.

City of Toronto. *City Council Consideration on October 1, 2021*. Toronto, ON: City of Toronto, 2021. https://secure.toronto.ca/council/agenda-item.do?item=2021.EX26.14.

City of Toronto. *Two-Spirit, Lesbian, Gay, Bisexual, Transgender and Queer Advisory Committee Meeting Agenda*. June 22, 2021, Toronto. https://secure.toronto.ca/council/report.do?meeting=2021.QS2&type=agenda.

City of Toronto. *Two-Spirit, Lesbian, Gay, Bisexual, Transgender and Queer Advisory Committee Meeting*. June 22, 2021. Toronto, https://www.youtube.com/live/dDpzKOkYkgM.

City of Toronto. *Two-Spirit, Lesbian, Gay, Bisexual, Transgender and Queer Advisory Committee–Decision Letter*. June 22, 2021, Toronto. https://www.toronto.ca/legdocs/mmis/2021/ex/bgrd/backgroundfile-170677.pdf.

Collins, Doug. "Neither Skinheads nor Marilyn Manson." *Vancouver Sun*, July 30, 1999. ProQuest.

"Community and Event Space Rental." Toronto Public Library. January 1, 2018. https://www.torontopubliclibrary.ca/terms-of-use/library-policies/community-and-event-space.jsp.

"Community Groups Stage Protest in Support of Trans Lives." *Canada NewsWire*, October 28, 2019. ProQuest.

"Community Guidelines." Halifax Public Libraries. Accessed May 4, 2022. https://www.halifaxpubliclibraries.ca/library-spaces/use-of-space/community-guidelines/.

Contenta, Sandro and Chown Oved Marco. "Students Rally in Protest of Gilmour's Reading Lists: Others Defend Academic Freedom as Fallout Continues from Professor's Remarks." *Toronto Star*, September 28, 2013. ProQuest.

"Controversial Russian Film On Show Monday Night." *The London Free Press*, August 13, 1960.

Copsey, John. "Meghan Murphy's Gender Identity Talk at Vancouver Public Library Not Cancelled." *Global News*, December 2, 2018. https://globalnews.ca/news/4720183/controversial-feminist-speaker-meghan-murphy-cancels-vancouver-public-library-appearance/

"Council Puts Lid on Film on Gays," *Mississauga Times*, March 1, 1978, Image 370, https://pub.canadiana.ca/view/omcn.MississaugaTimes_18/370.

Crawford, Blair. "Court Upholds Public Library's Decision to Cancel Screening of Controversial Film." *Ottawa Citizen*, September 19, 2019. https://ottawacitizen.com/news/local-news/court-upholds-librarys-decision-to-cancel-screening-of-controversial-film.

Crawford, Blair. "Ottawa Library Cancels Planned Screening of Controversial 'Killing Europe' Doc." *Ottawa Citizen*, November 24, 2017. https://ottawacitizen.com/news/local-news/ottawa-library-cancels-planned-screening-of-controversial-hate-speech-film.

Crawford, Blair. "Protesters Disrupt Lecture by UOttawa 'Anti-Feminist' at Ottawa Public Library." *Ottawa Citizen*, March 27, 2018. https://ottawacitizen.com/news/local-news/protesters-disrupt-lecture-by-uottawa-anti-feminist-at-ottawa-public-library.

Cruickshank, Ainslie. "Memorial Goes Ahead at Toronto Library for Lawyer Who Represented Far-Right Extremists." *Toronto Star*, July 12, 2017.

Curlew, Abigail. "Transgender Hate Crimes Are on the Rise Even in Canada." The Conversation. August 20, 2020. https://theconversation.com/transgender-hate-crimes-are-on-the-rise-even-in-canada-121541.

Curtis, Bruce. "'Littery Merrit,' 'Useful Knowledge,' and the Organization of Township Libraries in Canada West, 1840–1860." Ontario History 78 (1986): 284–312.

Curtis, Malcolm. "100 Protest Christie's WCC Immigration Meeting: RCMP Officers Kept Busy but no Arrests made." *Times Colonist,* September 11, 1999. ProQuest.

Curtis, Malcolm. "Free Speech Supporters Jeered." *Times Colonist,* June 20, 1998. ProQuest.

Curtis, Malcolm. "Libraries Uphold Policy of Open Access to Meeting Rooms." *Times Colonist,* May 27, 1998. ProQuest.

Cuttler, Gerry, and Romy Rittler. "Call to Action by the Canadian Jewish Congress, Pacific Region." Librarians for Fairness. February 23, 2008. http://librariansforfairness.org/news_post.asp?NPI=248.

D'Amore, Rachael. "'Canadians Aren't Seeing the Whole Picture': The Meghan Murphy Event and Trans Rights." *Global News,* October 30, 2019. https://globalnews.ca/news/6102791/toronto-library-meghan-murphy-trans-community/.

Danard, Susan. "Library Honored for Allowing Controversial Christie Meeting." *Times Colonist,* April 25, 1997. ProQuest.

Danard, Susan. "No Dissenting Voices Greet Christie Group." *Times Colonist,* March 2, 1997. ProQuest.

"David Irving: Propagandists' Poster Boy." Anti-Defamation League. 2005. https://web.archive.org/web/20070405134246/http://www.adl.org/holocaust/irving.asp.

Davis, Donald F. Letter to the editor. *Vancouver Sun,* February 14, 2008. ProQuest.

Delgado, Richard, and Jean Stefancic. *Critical Race Theory: An Introduction.* 3rd ed. New York: New York University Press, 2017.

Delgado, Richard, and Jean Stefancic. "Images of the Outsider in American Law and Culture." In *Critical Race Theory: The Cutting Edge* 3rd ed., edited by Richard Delgado and Jean Stefancic. Philadelphia: Temple University Press, 2013.

Denton, William and Art Redding to Sue Graham-Nutter and Vickery Bowles. Toronto, ON. November 8, 2019. https://krisjosephca.files.wordpress.com/2019/11/yufa-letter-room-booking-20191108.pdf.

Devet, Robert. "Radical Imagination Series Back at the Halifax Central Library Where It Belongs." *Nova Scotia Advocate,* July 5, 2019. https://nsadvocate.org/2019/07/05/radical-imagination-series-back-at-the-halifax-central-library-where-it-belongs/.

Dickson, Louise. "Activists Rally to Protest Christie Meeting." *Times Colonist,* October 17, 1999. ProQuest.

Dickson, Louise. "Police Failed in Library Clash: Internal Review Criticizes Lack of Planning for Collins Dinner in Saanich." *Times Colonist*, July 24, 1999. ProQuest.

Donato, Al, Allie Graham, Robyn Matuto, and Jenny Ferguson. "Toronto Public Library Collaborators Condemn TPL's Decision On Meghan Murphy Talk." Change.org. Accessed February 21, 2022. https://www.change.org/p/toronto-public-library-toronto-public-library-collaborators-condemn-tpl-s-decision-on-meghan-murphy-talk.

Dowding, Martin. "Canadian Library Association Checks Reality in Victoria." *American Libraries* 29, no. 7 (August 1998). https://link.gale.com/apps/doc/A21043829/CIC?u=utoronto_main&sid=bookmark-CIC&xid=f76c558f.

Drabinski, Emily. "Are Libraries Neutral?" *Emilydrabinski.com* (blog). February 12, 2018. http://www.emilydrabinski.com/are-libraries-neutral/.

Drabinski, Emily. "Queering the Catalog: Queer Theory and the Politics of Correction." *The Library Quarterly* 83, no. 2 (April 2013): 94–111. https://doi.org/10.1086/669547.

"Drag Queen Storytime Is 'Controversial' and 'Potentially Divisive,' Says Okanagan Library CEO." *CBC*, September 20, 2019. https://www.cbc.ca/news/canada/british-columbia/kelowna-drag-queen-story-time-1.5292257.

Edwards, Samantha. "Pride to Hold Trans Rally on the Night of Meghan Murphy Event." *NOW Magazine*, October 23, 2019. https://nowtoronto.com/culture/books-culture/pride-trans-rally-toronto-public-library-meghan-murphy.

El Feministo. "Janice Raymond at Vancouver Public Library Montreal Massacre Memorial." Rabble. November 19, 2013. https://babble.rabble.ca/babble/feminism/janice-raymond-vancouver-public-library-montreal-massacre-memorial.

Elliott, Alicia (@WordsandGuitar). "This is a difficult decision to make." Twitter, October 15, 2019, 10:01 a.m. https://twitter.com/WordsandGuitar/status/1184107074009075713.

Elliot, Alicia, Catherine Hernandez, and Carrianne Leung. "Stop Hate Speech from Being Spread at the Toronto Public Library." Change.org. Accessed February 20, 2022. https://www.change.org/p/toronto-public-library-request-for-tpl-to-cancel-rental-booking-for-transphobic-event-at-palmerston-library.

"Emeriti Faculty." University of Massachusetts Amherst. n.d. https://www.umass.edu/wgss/emeriti-faculty-wgss.

Ettarh, Fobazi M. "A Chronic Lack of Nuance & a Love of the Hypothetical: a Library Story." *WTF is a Radical Librarian, Anyway?* (blog). October 27, 2019. https://fobaziettarh.com/2019/10/27/a-chronic-lack-of-nuance-a-love-of-the-hypothetical-a-library-story/.

"Equity Statement." Toronto Public Library. December 5, 2022. https://www.torontopubliclibrary.ca/terms-of-use/library-policies/equity-statement.jsp.

Exit International. "Toronto Public Library Censors Euthanasia Meeting." August 22, 2010. https://exitinternational.net/media/MRCanada810.pdf.

Farber, Bernie. "Library no Longer Haven; Neo-Nazis should have been Barred." *Toronto Sun,* July 16, 2017. ProQuest.

Fiamengo, Janice. "Gavin Boby Not Misguided." *Ottawa Citizen,* February 4, 2013. ProQuest.

"Film Protest Boomerangs in Ontario." *The Gazette,* August 10, 1960. ProQuest.

Fong, Petti. "Library Won't Ban Collins Speech: It Remains Resolute Against Critics Who Want the Controversial Writer's Talk Cancelled." *Vancouver Sun,* September 30, 1999. ProQuest.

"Forward Thinking Speaker Series: A Conversation About Reconciliation." Global News, February 28, 2017. https://globalnews.ca/event/3220011/forward-thinking-speaker-series-a-conversation-about-reconciliation/.

Fox, Melodie J., and Hope A. Olsen. "Essentialism and Care in a Female Intensive Profession." In *Feminist and Queer Information Studies Reader*, edited by Patrick Keilty and Rebecca Dean. Sacramento: Litwin Books, 2013.

Francine, Kopun. "'This Has Been a Valuable Debate': Toronto Librarian Says Some Good Has Come From Meghan Murphy Controversy." *Toronto Star*, October 29, 2019. ProQuest.

Fraser, Nancy. "Rethinking the Public Sphere: A Contribution to the Critique of Actually Existing Democracy." In *Public Space Reader*, edited by Miodrag Mitrasinovic and Vikas Mehta, pp. 34–41. New York: Routledge, 2021. https://doi.org/10.4324/9781351202558-6.

"Free Speech Too Important to Be Left to Politicians." *Toronto Sun*, November 3, 2019. ProQuest.

"Free Expression Doesn't Condone Discrimination." *Times Colonist,* June 16, 1998. ProQuest.

Fromm, Paul. Letter to the editor. *Times Colonist,* May 12, 1997. ProQuest.

Fumano, Dan. "'Pride Is Political'–Despite Progress, Vancouver Pride Still Fighting." *Vancouver Sun*, July 29, 2019. https://vancouversun.com/news/local-news/dan-fumano-pride-is-political-despite-progress-vancouver-pride-still-fighting.

Gallant, Jacques. "Setting the Record Straight on Freedom of Speech: Cultural Debates Reveal Common Misconceptions about Legal Rights and their Limits, Experts Say." *Toronto Star,* November 24, 2019. ProQuest.

Galvan, Angela. "Soliciting Performance, Hiding Bias: Whiteness and Librarianship." *In the Library With The Lead Pipe.* June 3, 2015. https://www.inthelibrarywiththeleadpipe.org/2015/soliciting-performance-hiding-bias-whiteness-and-librarianship/.

Gee, Marcus. "Banning Ideas from Public Spaces is Not the Way to Dispute them." *The Globe and Mail,* July 14, 2017. ProQuest.

GEM Journal, March 1978. Archives of Sexuality and Gender, Gale Online.

Ghent-Fuller, Jennifer. Letter to the editor. *Waterloo Region Record*, October 7, 2013. ProQuest.

Gillespie, Curtis. "Warning." *Edify*, January 30, 2018. https://edifyedmonton.com/urban/community/warning/.

"Gilmour Should Have Spoken Here." *Waterloo Region Record*. October 1, 2013. ProQuest.

Girvan, Robert. "Lend an Ear." *The Globe and Mail*, October 31, 2019. ProQuest.

Glavin, Terry. "Does Our Library Know There's Another Word For Anti-Semitism." *The Vancouver Sun*, February 12, 2008.

Glavin, Terry. "Freedom-To-Be-Antisemitic Week In Vancouver: The City Librarian Explains Why." *Terry Glavin Chronicles & Dissent* (blog). February 13, 2008. https://transmontanus.blogspot.com/2008/02/freedom-to-be-antisemitic-week-in.html.

Glavin, Terry. "Some Free Speech is Less Worthy of Defence." *Ottawa Citizen*, February 29, 2008. ProQuest.

Goldschmid, Robert M. "Library Cop-Out Provides Room to Grow for Message of Hate." *Times Colonist*, June 9, 1998. ProQuest.

Goldstein, Lorrie. "City Librarian Vickery Bowles Defends Free Speech." *The Toronto Sun*, October 17, 2019. ProQuest.

Good, Joseph. "The Hottest Place in Hell: The Crisis of Neutrality in Contemporary Librarianship." In *Questioning Library Neutrality Essays from Progressive Librarian*, edited by Alison M. Lewis, 141–146. Duluth, MN: Library Juice Press, 2008.

Goodyear, Sheena. "'I'm Not Going to Reconsider': Toronto's Top Librarian Refuses to Bar Speaker Critical of Transgender Rights." *CBC*, October 17, 2019. https://www.cbc.ca/radio/asithappens/as-it-happens-thursday-edition-1.5324424/i-m-not-going-to-reconsider-toronto-s-top-librarian-refuses-to-bar-speaker-critical-of-transgender-rights-1.5324431.

Grauer, Perrin. "Cancellation of Event at Vancouver Public Library Featuring Controversial Speaker Was Faked, Speaker Says." *Toronto Star*, December 2, 2018. https://www.thestar.com/vancouver/2018/12/02/cancellation-of-event-at-vancouver-public-library-featuring-controversial-speaker-was-faked-speaker-says.html.

"Guelph Library to be Site of 'Apply-a-Thon'." *Guelph Mercury*, April 17, 2013. ProQuest.

Glad Day Bookshop (@GDBooks). "Glad Day's statement on the @torontolibrary's failure." Twitter, October 29, 2019, 3:37 p.m. https://twitter.com/GDBooks/status/1189265035278929921.

Gullikson, Shelley. "The TPL Debacle: Values vs People." *shelleygullikson.wordpress.com* (blog). October 28, 2019. https://shelleygullikson.wordpress.com/2019/10/28/the-tpl-debacle-values-vs-people/.

Gunter, Lorne. "Meghan Murphy Saga Shows How Extreme Political Correctness Has Become." *Toronto Sun*, November 2, 2019. ProQuest.

Harnett, Cindy E. "Tempers Fly at Library: Anti-Racists, Free Speech Supporters Clash at Collins Fund-Raiser." *Times Colonist*, June 6, 1999. ProQuest.

Harris, Kenneth. Letter to the editor. *The London Free Press*, August 13, 1960.

Hathcock, April. "White Librarianship in Blackface: Diversity Initiatives in LIS." In *the Library With The Lead Pipe*. October 7, 2015. https://www.inthelibrary-withtheleadpipe.org/2015/lis-diversity/.

Helm, Denise. "Library Open to all Groups–Board Votes to." *Times Colonist*, November 29, 1996. ProQuest.

"Heralding Free Speech," *Vancouver Sun*, May 14, 1997, A14. ProQuest.

Herman, Jack. Letter to the editor. *Vancouver Sun*, August 3, 2019. ProQuest.

Higgins, Shana. "Embracing the Feminization of Librarianship." In *Feminists Among Us: Resistance and Advocacy in Library Leadership*, edited by Baharak Yousefi and Shirley Lew, 67–89. Sacramento, CA: Library Juice Press, 2017.

Hoard, KC. "Hundreds Protest Controversial Toronto Public Library Event Featuring Meghan Murphy." *Globe and Mail*, October 29, 2019. ProQuest.

"Homosexual Film Dumped by Library," *Mississauga Times*, February 1, 1978, Image 203, https://pub.canadiana.ca/view/omcn.MississaugaTimes_18/203.

Honma, Todd. "Trippin' over the Color Line: The Invisibility of Race in Library and Information Studies." *InterActions: UCLA Journal of Education and Information Studies* 1, no. 2 (2005). https://doi.org/10.5070/d412000540.

Honn, Josh. "Never Neutral: Critical Approaches to Digital Tools & Culture in the Humanities." Paper presented at the University of Western Ontario's Digital Humanities Speaker Series, London, ON, October 16, 2013. https://doi.org/https://doi.org/10.21985/N2SV08.

Horrocks, Norman. "CLA Ponders Library's Role." *Library Journal* 123, no. 13 (1998). https://link.gale.com/apps/doc/A21071926/CIC?u=utoronto_main&sid=bookmark-CIC&xid=b44980b5.

Hudson, David James. "On 'Diversity' as Anti-Racism in Library and Information Studies: A Critique." *Journal of Critical Library and Information Studies* 1, no. 1 (2017). https://doi.org/10.24242/jclis.v1i1.6.

Hughes, Meagan. "Misleading Public Health Propaganda Must Be Stopped." *The Manitoban*, February 24, 2020. https://web.archive.org/web/20201202210842/http://www.themanitoban.com/2020/02/misleading-public-health-propaganda-must-be-stopped/39151/.

Hum, Peter. "Library Cancels Right-Wing Lecture." *Ottawa Citizen*, November 21, 1990. ProQuest.

"Intellectual Freedom is Essential to Society's Health," *Mississauga Times*, April 5, 1978, Image 605, https://pub.canadiana.ca/view/omcn.MississaugaTimes_18/605.

"Intellectual Freedom Statement." Toronto Public Library. December 5, 2022. https://www.torontopubliclibrary.ca/terms-of-use/library-policies/intellectual-freedom-statement.jsp.

"Iron Curtain Film Brought on Request." *The London Free Press*, August 12, 1960.

Itkonen, Saara. "Libraries Aren't Neutral." *Creston Valley Advance*, November 14, 2019. https://www.crestonvalleyadvance.ca/news/libraries-arent-neutral/.

Iverson, Sandy. "Librarianship and Resistance." In *Questioning Library Neutrality Essays from Progressive Librarian*, edited by Alison M. Lewis, 25–32. Duluth, MN: Library Juice Press, 2008.

jjackunrau. "On Janice Raymond and the Value of More Speech." *The (Unofficial) BCLA Intellectual Freedom Committee Blog* (blog). November 29, 2008. https://bclaifc.wordpress.com/2013/11/29/on-janice-raymond-and-the-value-of-more-speech/.

J. J. Letter to the editor. *The London Free Press*. August 22, 1960.

Jimenez, Marina. "Libraries used to Push Hate, Group Says: `Hate Groups' Masquerading as Free-Speech Advocates are Renting Library Facilities for Racist Propaganda Purposes, B'Nai Brith Says." *Vancouver Sun*, February 5, 1998. ProQuest.

Joannou, Ashley. "'Focus on the love': Drag artist leads story time at Downtown Edmonton library." *Edmonton Journal*, August 7, 2022. https://edmontonjournal.com/news/local-news/focus-on-the-love-drag-artist-leads-story-time-at-downtown-edmonton-library.

Joaquin, Arvin, Cameron Perrier, and Erica Lenti. "Meghan Murphy, the Toronto Public Library and Fighting Transphobia: an Explainer." *Xtra Magazine*, October 30, 2019. https://xtramagazine.com/power/meghan-murphy-toronto-library-transphobia-163924.

Johal, Rumneek. "Anti-Vaccine Documentary Being Screened in Alberta Theatres, Libraries." *Daily Hive*, January 28, 2020. https://dailyhive.com/edmonton/anti-vaccine-documentary-alberta-theatres-libraries.

Johnson, Natalie. "Council Calls for Review of Toronto Facility Permits in Wake of Controversial Speech at Library." *CTV News*, October 30, 2019. https://toronto.ctvnews.ca/council-calls-for-review-of-toronto-facility-permits-in-wake-of-controversial-speech-at-library-1.4662934.

Jones, Allison, Hazel Jane Plante, Leah Tottenham, Shelby, and Syr. "Not Cis in LIS: A Roundtable Discussion About Being Trans in Libraries." British Columbia Library Association, September 5, 2019. https://bclaconnect.ca/perspectives/2019/09/05/not-cis-in-lis-a-roundtable-discussion-about-being-trans-in-libraries/.

Jones, Ziya (@ZiyaJonesA). "Hey@torontolibrary." Twitter, October 11, 2019, 5:43 p.m. https://twitter.com/ZiyaJonesA/status/1182773784492871680?s=20.

Joseph, Kris. "The Curious Case of Free-Speech-Loving Librarians Who Don't Think the Toronto Public Library Should Provide Space for Meghan Murphy: Part One." *Kris Joseph* (blog). October 23, 2019. https://krisjoseph.ca/2019/10/tpl-mm-part-one/.

Joseph, Kris. "The Curious Case of Free-Speech-Loving Librarians Who Don't Think the Toronto Public Library Should Provide Space for Meghan Murphy: Part Two." *Kris Joseph* (blog). October 28, 2019. https://krisjoseph.ca/2019/10/tpl-mm-part-two/.

Josey, E. J. *The Black Librarian in America Revisited*. Metuchen: Scarecrow Press, 1994.

Joyce, Steven. "A Few Gates Redux: An Examination of the Social Responsibility Debate in the Early 1970s and 1990s." In *Questioning Library Neutrality Essays from Progressive Librarian*, edited by Alison M. Lewis, 33–66. Duluth, MN: Library Juice Press, 2008.

Kaba, Mariame. *We Do This 'Til We Free*. Chicago: Haymarket Books, 2021.

Kahnert, Paul. Letter to the editor. Toronto Star, November 4, 2019. ProQuest.

Kay, Barbara. "How Feminist Meghan Murphy Fell Victim to Progressives' Double Standards." *National Post*, October 24, 2019. ProQuest.

Kay, Jonathan, and Mercedes Allen. "Speaking of Gender: A National Post Debate About Gender Identity and Free Speech." *National Post*, December 2, 2019. ProQuest.

Keeler, Emily M. Interview with David Gilmour. *Shelf Esteem*. Hazlitt. September 25, 2013. https://hazlitt.net/blog/gilmour-transcript.

Keller, Emily. "Anti-Vaccination Film Screenings Cause Controversy." *Everything GP*, January 29, 2020. https://everythinggp.com/2020/01/29/anti-vaccination-film-screenings-cause-controversy/.

Keller, James. "Vancouver Library Bars Assisted-Suicide Group's How-To Workshop." *The Canadian Press*, September 21, 2009. ProQuest.

Kenner, Lionel. "Limits of Free Speech." *The Globe and Mail*, July 17, 1998. ProQuest.

Kester, Norman G. *Liberating Minds: The Stories and Professional Lives of Gay, Lesbian, and Bisexual Librarians and Their Advocates*. Jefferson, N.C: McFarland, 1997.

KGS. "Op-Ed in Ottawa Citizen on CAIR-CAN Opposition to Gavin Boby: Smacks of Intimidation." *The Tundra Tabloids* (blog). February 5, 2013. https://tundratabloids.com/2013/02/05/op-ed-in-ottawa-citizen-on-cair-can-opposition-to-gavin-boby-smacks-of-intimidation/.

Khasnabish, Alex. "Library's Insistence That Police Be Invited to Speak Spells End of Popular Film and Discussion Series." *The Nova Scotia Advocate*, June 27, 2019. https://nsadvocate.org/2019/06/27/librarys-insistence-that-police-be-invited-to-speak-spells-end-of-popular-film-and-discussion-series/.

Khasnabish, Alex. "Policing the Radical Imagination." *Halifax Examiner*, July 1, 2019. https://www.halifaxexaminer.ca/featured/policing-the-radical-imagination/.

King, Lee. "Controversial Group to Meet in Colwood." *Times Colonist*, May 9, 1998. ProQuest.

Knope, Julia. "Tory 'Disappointed' in Toronto Public Library for Hosting Speaker Accused of Transphobia." *CBC*, October 17, 2019. https://www.cbc.ca/news/canada/toronto/toronto-public-library-tory-speaker-transphobia-1.5324218.

Knowles, Em Claire. "Can Libraries Be Neutral." *Simmons SLIS Blogs* (blog). March 26, 2018. https://slis.simmons.edu/blogs/emclaireknowles-publications/2018/03/26/can-libraries-be-neutral-should-they-strive-to-be-neutral/.

Knox, Emily J. M. "Remarks from ALA Midwinter 2018 President's Program." *Emily J.M. Knox, PhD, MSLIS* (blog). n.d. https://emilyknox.net/media/remarks-ala-midwinter-2018-presidents-program/.

Knox, Jules. "Despite Controversy, Kelowna Library's Drag Queen Story Time Grows in Popularity." *Global News*, November 16, 2019. https://globalnews.ca/news/6179257/kelowna-library-drag-queen-story-time-popularity/.

Kopun, Francine. "After Trans Rights Protest at Controversial Event, Toronto Votes to Review Community Space Policies." *Toronto Star*, October 30, 2019. https://www.thestar.com/news/city_hall/2019/10/30/after-trans-rights-protest-at-library-toronto-votes-to-review-community-space-policies.html.

Kopun, Francine. "Authors Warn They'll Boycott Toronto Public Library Over Speaker Accused of Being Anti-Transgender." *Toronto Star*, October 16, 2019. ProQuest.

Kotyk, Alyse, and Regan Hasegawa. "Vancouver Public Library Changes Booking Policies for Events." *CTV News*, September 30, 2019. https://bc.ctvnews.ca/vancouver-public-library-changes-booking-policies-for-events-1.4617675.

Kushner, Howard. *The Right to Know: A Complaint about the Greater Victoria Public Library Meeting Room Policy*. Victoria, BC: Office of the Ombudsman, 2003. https://bcombudsperson.ca/assets/media/Special-Report-No-23-Greater-Victoria-Public-Library-Meeting-Room-Policy.pdf.

"LAA Statement on Toronto Public Library." Library Association of Alberta. November 12, 2019. https://www.laa.ca/page/news/ezlist_item_ef11602c-54e4-48ad-8771-e4b9ecc04210.aspx.

Lakritz, Naomi. "Booking Space to Help People Check Out Not a Right." *Calgary Herald*, September 23, 2009. ProQuest.

Lankes, R. David. "My Remarks on Library Neutrality for the ALA MidWinter President's Panel." *R. David Lankes* (blog). February 11, 2018. https://davidlankes.org/my-remarks-on-library-neutrality-for-the-ala-midwinter-presidents-panel/.

LaRue, Jamesie. "Are Libraries Neutral?" *James LaRrue–MyLiBlog* (blog). February 11, 2018. https://jaslarue.blogspot.com/2018/02/are-libraries-neutral.html.

Lavoie, Judy. "Anti-Racism Fighters Braced for Onslaught as Easterners Move." *Times Colonist*, February 6, 1998. ProQuest.

"Letters–More Parks? What About Housing?" *Times Colonist*, November 9, 1996. ProQuest.

Levitz, Stephanie. "Saskatoon Library Refuses to Let MP Brad Trost Hold Anti-Abortion Meeting." CBC. January 26, 2017. https://www.cbc.ca/news/politics/saskatoon-library-brad-trost-anti-abortion-meeting-1.3954098.

Levy, Sue-Ann. "Council's Thought Police Jump on Meghan Murphy Issue." *Toronto Sun*, October 31, 2019. ProQuest.

Levy, Sue-Ann. "Sad State of Free Speech; Intolerant Radicals and their Meghan Murphy Circus." *Toronto Sun,* October 30, 2019. ProQuest.

Lew, Shirley. Letter to Alix-Rae Stefanko. April 1, 2019. https://bclaconnect.ca/wp-uploads/2019/10/Letter-to-CFLA-President-and-Board.pdf.

Lewis, Alison M., ed. *Questioning Library Neutrality: Essays from Progressive Librarian*. Duluth, MN: Library Juice Press, 2008.

"Library Again Shows It's Out of Touch." *The Intelligencer,* October 13, 2012. ProQuest.

"Library Cancels Anti-Islam Film Screening." *CBC*, November 25, 2017. https://www.cbc.ca/news/canada/ottawa/ottawa-public-library-central-branch-islam-islamophobia-public-protest-film-1.4418229.

"Library Faces Court Challenge Over Cancellation of Controversial Film." *Ottawa Citizen*, June 13, 2018. ProQuest.

"Library Hails Rights Ruling on Speeches." *Times Colonist*, October 14, 1999. ProQuest.

"Library Sickness," *Mississauga Times*, April 5, 1978, Image 605, https://pub.canadiana.ca/view/omcn.MississaugaTimes_18/605.

"Library Talk Stirs Free-Speech Debate." Letter to the editor. *Toronto Star*, October 30, 2019. ProQuest.

"Library Under Fire for Free Speech Rally–Meeting Space Provided." *Times Colonist*, October 30, 1996. ProQuest.

Little, Simon. "Event Featuring Controversial Speaker Meghan Murphy to Go Ahead at Vancouver Library." *Global News*, January 27, 2020. https://globalnews.ca/news/6469847/controversial-event-megan-murphy-vancouver-library/.

Little, Simon. "VPL Revises Room Booking Policy After Controversial Speaker Draws Protests." *Global News*, September 27, 2019. https://globalnews.ca/news/5961345/vpl-revises-room-booking-policy-meghan-murphy-protests/.

Litwin, Fred and Salim Mansur. "Mistaking Islamism for Islam; Too Many Who Oppose Fanaticism End Up Supporting the Islamist View that Muslims Cannot be Moderate." *Ottawa Citizen,* January 29, 2013. ProQuest.

"Loud Minority." *St. Thomas Times-Journal*. August 19, 1960.

MacCallum et al. "Open Letter to the CFLA Board On Intellectual Freedom." *Letter*. August 23, 2021. https://cfla-fcab.ca/wp-content/uploads/2021/09/Open-Letter-to-the-CFLA-Board-On-Intellectual-Freedom.pdf.

Mahboob, Tahiat. "How a B.C. Library's Drag Queen Story Hour Turned into a Nationwide Fight for Intellectual Freedom." *CBC*, November 7, 2020. https://www.cbc.ca/radio/docproject/how-a-b-c-library-s-drag-queen-story-hour-turned-into-a-nationwide-fight-for-intellectual-freedom-1.5786657.

Mallick, Heather. "The Best People of 2019." *Toronto Star*, December 23, 2019. https://www.thestar.com/opinion/star-columnists/2019/12/23/the-best-people-of-2019.html.

Manek, Haseena. "When Hate Goes Public." *Our Times*, August 17, 2017. https://ourtimes.ca/article/when-hate-goes-public.

Marinucci, Mimi. *Feminism Is Queer: The Intimate Connection Between Queer and Feminist Theory*. 2nd ed. London: Zed Books, 2016.

Martinez, Pilar. "EPL and Freedom of Expression." *Edmonton Public Library* (blog). November 1, 2019. https://www.epl.ca/blogs/post/epl-and-freedom-of-expression/.

May-Anderson, Glenn. "Who Decides What's Best for Us?" *The Intelligencer*, October 13, 2012. ProQuest.

"Mayor Tory Announces Expansion to Enhanced Youth Spaces and Youth Hubs at Community Centres and Toronto Public Library Locations Across Toronto." City of Toronto. July 26, 2021. https://www.toronto.ca/news/mayor-tory-announces-expansion-to-enhanced-youth-spaces-and-youth-hubs-at-community-centres-and-toronto-public-library-locations-across-toronto/.

McCune, Shane. "Collins-Christie Session Draws Protesters, Cops to Vancouver Library." *The Province*, October 1, 1999. ProQuest.

McGregor, Glen. "Muslim Group Wants Lawyer's Speech Nixed; Controversial British 'Mosquebuster' Slated to Talk at Library." *Ottawa Citizen*, February 4, 2013. ProQuest.

McLintock, Barbara. "Library Backed on Room-Rental Policy." *The Province*, October 14, 1999. ProQuest.

McVicar, W. Brice. "Author's Library Visit Called Off." *The Intelligencer*, October 19, 2012. ProQuest.

McVicar, W. Brice. "Library Appearance May Get Rough Review." *The Intelligencer*, October 12, 2012. ProQuest.

"Meeting Room Booking Policy." Ottawa Public Library, n.d. https://biblioottawalibrary.ca/en/meeting-room-booking-policy.

"Meghan Murphy: Canadian Feminist's Trans Talk Sparks Uproar." *BBC*, October 30, 2019. https://www.bbc.com/news/world-us-canada-50214341.

"Megan Murphy Transgender Controversy Raises Questions About the Limits of Free Speech." Letter to the editor. *Toronto Star*, November 2, 2019. ProQuest.

"Mindless Ruling," *Mississauga Times*, April 5, 1978, Image 605, https://pub.canadiana.ca/view/omcn.MississaugaTimes_18/605.

Minutes of the Regular Meeting of Council Held in the Council Chamber. July 26, 1999. City of North Vancouver. https://cnvapps.cnv.org/Minutes/1999_07_26_Council_Minutes.pdf.

Minvielle, Paul. "Editorial–Free Speech Isn't just for the Politically Correct." *Times Colonist,* October 30, 1996. ProQuest.

Minvielle, Paul. "Opinion–Truth and Falsehood Should be Allowed to Grapple Freely." *Times Colonist,* November 1, 1996. ProQuest.

"Mississauga Rejects Plea: Homosexuals Argue Film's Merit." *The Globe and Mail,* February 28, 1978. ProQuest.

Monteiro, Liz. "Gilmour Cancels Waterloo Event: Move Follows Outcry Over Hot-Button Remarks." *Waterloo Region Record,* September 28, 2013. ProQuest.

"Montreal Massacre Memorial 2013–Program." Vancouver Rape Relief & Women's Shelter. November 30, 2013. https://web.archive.org/web/20171021153903/http://www.rapereliefshelter.bc.ca/learn/resources/montreal-massacre-memorial-2013-program.

Morales, Myrna, Em Claire Knowles, and Chris Bourg. "Diversity, Social Justice, and the Future of Libraries." *Portal: Libraries and the Academy* 14, no. 3 (2014): 439–51. doi:10.1353/pla.2014.0017.

Moscovitch, Philip. "Diminishing Dissent." *Halifax Examiner,* July 2, 2019. https://www.halifaxexaminer.ca/featured/diminishing-dissent/.

Mosleh, Omar. "Edmonton Writer in Residence Calls Out Library CEO for Supporting Space Rental to Meghan Murphy." *Toronto Star,* November 2, 2019. ProQuest.

Mosleh, Omar. "The Toronto Library Hosted Meghan Murphy. Now an Edmonton Library Trustee Says She's Paying a Price for Speaking Out." *Toronto Star,* February 11, 2020. https://www.thestar.com/edmonton/2020/02/11/the-toronto-library-hosted-meghan-murphy-now-an-edmonton-library-trustee-says-shes-paying-a-price-for-speaking-out.html.

Munro, Nicole. "Man Refuses to Let Police Officer Speak, Loses Program Partnership With Halifax Public Libraries." *The Chronicle Herald,* July 2, 2019. https://www.saltwire.com/nova-scotia/news/man-refuses-to-let-police-officer-speak-loses-program-partnership-with-halifax-public-libraries-328251/.

Munro, Nicole. "Series Back at Halifax Library; Films on Racial Profiling to be shown with 'no Strings Attached'." *The Chronicle Herald,* July 8, 2019. ProQuest.

Naranjo, Silvia, and Alejandro Melgar. "Calgary Library Drag Event Interrupted Sparks Concerns." *CityNews Calgary,* February 28, 2023. https://calgary.citynews.ca/2023/02/28/calgary-library-drag-event/.

"NDP Culture Critic Responds to Toronto Public Library's Refusal to Cancel Event Featuring Meghan Murphy." Ontario NDP. October 17, 2019. https://www.ontariondp.ca/news/ndp-culture-critic-responds-toronto-public-library-s-refusal-cancel-event-featuring-meghan.

Neigel, Christina. "Library Meetings Rooms & Librarianship's Existential Crisis?" *Resistant Librarian* (blog). October 26, 2019. https://resistantlibrarian.home.blog/2019/10/26/library-meetings-rooms-librarianships-existential-crisis/.

nina de jesus. "Locating the Library in Institutional Oppression." *In the Library with the Lead Pipe*. September 14, 2014. https://www.inthelibrarywiththe-leadpipe.org/2014/locating-the-library-in-institutional-oppression/.

"No Cheers, No Boos As Controversy Ends." *The London Free Press*, August 14, 1960.

"No Protests As Brad Trost Meets With Anti-Abortion Supporters." CBC. January 28, 2017. https://www.cbc.ca/news/canada/saskatoon/brad-trost-anti-abortion-no-protest-1.3957044.

O'Connor, Kevin. "Controversy Continues: Panelists Say They're Proud of Gay Film Festival." *Leader Post*, May 15, 2000. ProQuest.

Oder, Norman. "Vancouver Library Under Fire for Hosting Controversial Author Called Anti-Semitic." *Library Journal*, February 15, 2008. https://www.libraryjournal.com/story/vancouver-library-under-fire-for-hosting-controversial-authorcalled-anti-semitic.

Ogden, Russel. Letter to the editor. *Vancouver Sun*, September 29, 2009. ProQuest.

Okanagan Regional Library. *Notice of Meeting*. Okanagan, BC: Okanagan Regional Library, 2019. https://orl.bc.ca/docs/default-source/library_board/meeting_agendas/bod-agd_18sep19.pdf?sfvrsn=0.

Olson, Hope A. "The Power to Name: Representation in Library Catalogs." *Signs: Journal of Women in Culture and Society* 26, no. 3 (2001): 639–68. https://doi.org/https://doi.org/10.1086/495624.

Omstead, Jordan. "Alberta Health Advocates Alarmed by Anti-Vaxx Documentary Screened in Theatres, Libraries." *CBC*, January 28, 2020. https://www.cbc.ca/news/canada/edmonton/anti-vaxx-documentary-misinformation-alberta-1.5442573.

"ORL Discussing Changes to Policy to Prevent Drag Queen Story Time." Kelowna Pride. September 17, 2019. https://www.kelownapride.com/post/orl-discussing-changes-to-policy-to-prevent-drag-queen-story-time.

Orozco, Santiago Arias. "Protesters Showed up to One of This Drag Queen's Recent Storytime Performances. Here's Why She Won't Stop Reading." *Toronto Star*, June 11, 2023. https://www.thestar.com/life/together/2023/06/11/protesters-showed-up-to-one-of-this-drag-queens-recent-storytime-performances-heres-why-she-wont-stop-reading.html.

"Ottawa Public Library Sued for Cancelling Controversial Documentary." Justice Centre for Constitutional Freedoms. June 13, 2018. https://www.jccf.ca/ottawa-public-library-sued-for-cancelling-controversial-documentary/.

Ouston, Rick. "Controversial Columnist Launches Free-Speech 'Battle'." *The Vancouver Sun*, May 12, 1997. ProQuest.

Pablo, Carlito. "Proposed Vancouver Public Library Rental Policy Affirms Commitment to Intellectual Freedom." *The Georgia Straight*, September 23, 2019. https://www.straight.com/news/1305711/proposed-vancouver-public-library-rental-policy-affirms-commitment-intellectual-freedom.

Pacholik, Barb. "Films Appal Sask. Party MLAs." *Leader Post*, May 12, 2000. ProQuest.

Pacholik, Barb. "Protesters Greet First Day of Gay Film Festival." *Leader Post,* May 9, 2000. ProQuest.

Paradkar, Shree. "Shree Paradkar: Cancel Culture Accompanied By an Eye Roll Is Usually an Excuse to Duck Accountability." *Toronto Star*, November 5, 2019. ProQuest.

Parker, James. "Experts Said Festival has Merit: Official." *Leader Post,* May 3, 2000. ProQuest.

Parker, James. "Films Approved for Queer City Cinema." *Leader Post,* May 10, 2000. ProQuest.

Parker, James. "Sask. Party Keeps Up Heat on Graphic Films." *Leader Post,* May 4, 2000. ProQuest.

Paterson, Jody. "The New Islander–Joe Easingwood." *Times Colonist,* June 28, 1998. ProQuest.

Peet, Lisa. "Meeting Room Policy Protests in Toronto, Vancouver." Library Journal. December 5, 2019. https://www.libraryjournal.com/story/Meeting-Room-Policy-Protests-in-Toronto-Vancouver.

Perreaux, Les. "Ad Campaign for Assisted Suicide Banned from Canadian Airwaves." *The Globe and Mail,* September 27, 2010, A6, ProQuest.

Petrychyn, Jonathan. "Networks of Feelings: Affective Economies of Queer and Feminist Film Festivals on the Canadian Prairies." PhD diss., York University, 2019. https://yorkspace.library.yorku.ca/xmlui/bitstream/handle/10315/36773/Petrychyn_Jonathan_R_2019_PhD.pdf?sequence=2&isAllowed=y.

Pilieci, Vito. "Muslim Missionaries Protest Boby's Speech; Lawyer's Criticisms Provocative, Clerics Say." *Ottawa Citizen,* February 25, 2013. ProQuest.

"Pipeline Protest Planned for Guelph Library Spurs Criticism." *Guelph Mercury*, April 17, 2013. https://www.guelphmercury.com/news-story/2785883-pipeline-protest-planned-for-guelph-library-spurs-criticism/.

Pitt, Bob. "Gavin Boby Addresses Small Meeting at Ottawa Public Library." *Islamophobia Watch* (blog). February 5, 2013. http://islamophobiawatch.co.uk/gavin-boby-addresses-small-meeting-at-ottawa-public-library/.

"Policy 1.8, Responsibilities and Conduct of Library Users." Greater Victoria Public Library. January 2016. https://www.gvpl.ca/board-policies/1-8-responsibilities-users/.

"Policy 0.7–Meeting Rooms." Greater Victoria Public Library. June 24, 2008. https://gvpl.ent.sirsidynix.net/client/en_US/default/?rm=POLICY+0.7+-+M0%7C%7C%7C1%7C%7C%7C0%7C%7C%7Ctrue&dt=list.

Policy for Community Events in Parks and Public Open Spaces, Public Policy C57C, City of North Vancouver (2014), https://www.cnv.org/-/media/city-of-north-vancouver/documents/parks-and-environment/regulations/policy-for-community-events-in-parks-and-public-open-spaces.ashx?la=en.

Popowich, Sam. "Canadian Librarianship and the Politics of Recognition," *Partnership: The Canadian Journal of Library and Information Practice and Research* 16, no. 1 (April 2021): 1–23, https://doi.org/10.21083/partnership.v16i1.6126.

Popowich, Sam. "Community, Value, and Worth." *redlibrarian.github.io* (blog). October 13, 2019. https://redlibrarian.github.io/article/2019/10/13/community-value-worth.html.

Popowich, Sam. *Confronting the Democratic Discourse of Librarianship: a Marxist Approach*. Sacramento, CA: Library Juice Press, 2019. https://litwinbooks.com/books/confronting-the-democratic-discourse-of-librarianship/.

Popowich, Sam. "Dialectics and Social Responsibility." *redlibrarian.github.io* (blog). October 15, 2019. https://redlibrarian.github.io/article/2019/10/15/dialectics-and-social-responsibility.html.

Popowich, Sam. "The Trouble with Intellectual Freedom, part one." *spopowich.ca* (blog). October 6, 2021. https://www.spopowich.ca/blog/the-trouble-with-intellectual-freedom-part-one.

Popowich, Sam. "Who Misunderstands Intellectual Freedom?" *spopowich.ca* (blog). February 4, 2022. https://www.spopowich.ca/blog/who-misunderstands-intellectual-freedom.

"Porn Panel at Regina Film Festival Comes Under Fire: Queer City Festival Director Defends Nature of Gay and Lesbian Pornography." *Star Phoenix,* April 29, 2000. ProQuest.

"Position on Third Party Use of Publicly Funded Library Meeting Rooms and Facilities." Canadian Federation of Library Associations. March 2019. http://cfla-fcab.ca/wp-content/uploads/2019/03/CFLA-FCAB_statement_meeting_rooms.pdf.

Prentiss, Mairin. "Library Won't Partner with Group Planning to Screen Films About Police Brutality." *CBC*, June 29, 2019. https://www.cbc.ca/news/canada/nova-scotia/halifax-library-rejects-police-film-screenings-1.5195260.

Pride Toronto (@PrideToronto). "Pride Toronto's Board of Directors public statement." Twitter, October 18, 2019, 12:40 p.m. https://twitter.com/PrideToronto/status/1185234099998543874.

Pride Toronto (@PrideToronto). "What amazing turn out tonight to declare no to hate." Twitter, October 29, 2019, 6:33 p.m. https://twitter.com/PrideToronto/status/1189309293629267969.

"Protesters Try to Disrupt 'Free Speech' Meeting." *Canadian Press NewsWire*, October 1, 1999. ProQuest.

"Protests Force London Showing of Soviet Film." *The Globe and Mail*, August 10, 1960. ProQuest.

"Public Libraries and Freedom of Expression." PEN Canada. October 28, 2019. https://pencanada.ca/news/public-libraries-and-freedom-of-expression/.

"Public Meeting Rooms & Facilities Use Policy Discussion Draft." Vancouver Public Library. May 27, 2019. https://www.vpl.ca/sites/vpl/public/DiscussionDraftPublicMeetingRoomsFacilitiesUsePolicy2019-05-27.pdf.

"Public Meeting Rooms & Facilities Use." Vancouver Public Library. September 25, 2019. https://www.vpl.ca/policy/public-meeting-rooms-facilities-use.

Puwar, Nirmal. *Space Invaders: Race, Gender and Bodies Out of Place*. Oxford: Berg, 2004.

"Queer City Fest Opens to More Controversy." *CBC*, May 9, 2000. https://www.cbc.ca/news/canada/queer-city-fest-opens-to-more-controversy-1.197824.

Rancic, Michael. "After Protesting the Library, Trans Activists Host a Teach-In." *NOW Magazine*, January 23, 2020. https://nowtoronto.com/culture/books-culture/trans-teach-in-kai-cheng-thom-library.

Rayn, Dorian. Letter to the editor. *Vancouver Sun*, February 16, 2008. ProQuest.

"Regional Roundup: North Vancouver: Neo-Nazis Spark Move to Ban Hate Groups from Public Space: Councillor Darrell Mussatto Raises the Alarm After City Library Staff Complained of Feeling `intimidated and Uncomfortable' Amid 100 Skinheads Attending Seminars at the Public Library." *Vancouver Sun*, July 28, 1999. ProQuest

Renkema, Taylor. "Library Cancels Williams' Book Author's Appearance." QNet News. October 18, 2012. http://www.qnetnews.ca/?p=28502.

Revised Member Motion MM11.14. October 29, 2019. City of Toronto. https://www.toronto.ca/legdocs/mmis/2019/mm/bgrd/backgroundfile-139260.pdf.

"RFU statement on Meghan Murphy event at Toronto Public Library," *Dead Wild Roses* (blog). October 24, 2019, https://deadwildroses.com/2019/10/24/rfu-statement-on-meghan-murphy-event-at-toronto-public-library/.

Rider, David. "John Tory 'Disappointed' Toronto Library Allowing Event with Writer Accused of Being Anti-Transgender." Toronto Star, October 17, 2019. https://www.thestar.com/news/city_hall/2019/10/17/john-tory-disappointed-toronto-library-allowing-event-with-writer-accused-of-being-anti-transgender.html.

"Robert Tegler Trust Outreach Services." Edmonton Public Library. Accessed May 4, 2022. https://www.epl.ca/milner-library/outreach/.

Robertson, A. Letter to the editor. *The London Free Press*, August 11, 1960.

Robertson, Becky. "Local Authors Are Now Boycotting the Toronto Public Library." *blogTO*. October 15, 2019. https://www.blogto.com/arts/2019/10/local-authors-boycotting-toronto-public-library/.

Rosenblum, Simon. Letter to the editor. *Toronto Star,* November 4, 2019. ProQuest.

Rosenzweig, Mark. "Politics and Anti-Politics in Librarianship." In *Questioning Library Neutrality Essays from Progressive Librarian*, edited by Alison M. Lewis, 5–8. Duluth, MN: Library Juice Press, 2008.

Rowlands, Bob. "Anti-Race Foes Angry–by Susan Danard–Times Colonist Staff." *Times Colonist*, October 27, 1996. ProQuest.

Rowlands, Bob. "Municipal Elections–City Bars Likely Hatemongers from Publicity." *Times Colonist,* November 8, 1996. ProQuest.

Rupp, Shannon. "Transsexual Loses Latest Bid to Counsel Victims of Rape." *Globe and Mail*, December 8, 2005. https://www.theglobeandmail.com/news/national/transsexual-loses-latest-bid-to-counsel-victims-of-rape/article990772/.

"Russian Film Controversy 'Ridiculous' Says Librarian." *The London Free Press*, August 10, 1960.

Samek, Toni. *Intellectual Freedom and Social Responsibility in American Librarianship, 1967–1974*. Jefferson: McFarland, 2001.

Sanborn, Earle. Letter to the editor. *The London Free Press.* August 15, 1960.

"Saskatoon Library Defends Cancelling Brad Trost's Anti-Abortion Meeting." *CBC*, January 27, 2017. https://www.cbc.ca/news/canada/saskatoon/mp-brad-trost-saskatoon-library-cancelling-1.3955605.

"Saskatoon Library Didn't Violate Brad Trost's Freedom of Speech, Says U of S Prof." *CBC*, January 30, 2017. https://www.cbc.ca/news/canada/saskatoon/brad-trost-freedom-of-speech-1.3958652.

"Saskatoon Public Library Responds to Cancellation of Brad Trost Campaign Event." 650 CKOM. January 27, 2017. https://www.ckom.com/2017/01/27/saskatoon-public-library-responds-to-cancellation-of-brad-trost-campaign-event/.

Schlesselman-Tarango, Gina, ed. *Topographies of Whiteness: Mapping Whiteness in Library and Information Science.* Sacramento, CA: Library Juice Press, 2017, ProQuest.

Schmidt, Jane. "My Remarks to the TPL Board." The Incidental Academic Librarian. October 22, 2019. https://incidentalacademic.wordpress.com/2019/10/22/my-remarks-to-the-tpl-board/.

Schrader, Alvin M. "Can Public Libraries Maintain Their Commitment to Intellectual Freedom in the Face of Outrage over Unpopular Speakers?" *Centre for Free Expression* (blog). August 15, 2019. https://cfe.ryerson.ca/blog/2019/08/can-public-libraries-maintain-their-commitment-intellectual-freedom-face-outrage-over.

Schrader, Alvin M. "Community Pressures to Censor Gay and Lesbian Materials in Public Libraries of Canada." In *Liberating Minds: The Stories and Professional Lives of Gay, Lesbian, and Bisexual Librarians and Their Advocates*, ed. Norman G. Kester. Jefferson, N.C: McFarland, 1997.

Schrader, Alvin M. "Prairies News." ELAN: The Ex Libris Association Newsletter. Fall, 2017. https://www.exlibris.ca/lib/exe/fetch.php?media=newsletters:elan_issue_62_fall_2017.pdf.

Schrader, Alvin M. "Prairies News." ELAN: The Ex Libris Association Newsletter. Spring, 2018. https://www.exlibris.ca/lib/exe/fetch.php?media=newsletters:elan_issue_63_spring_2018.pdf.

Seale, Maura, and Rafia Mirza. "Speech and Silence: Race, Neoliberalism, and Intellectual Freedom." *Journal of Radical Librarianship* 5 (2019): 41–60. https://journal.radicallibrarianship.org/index.php/journal/article/view/34.

"Second Film Ruling Sought," *Mississauga Times*, March 22, 1978, Image 517, https://pub.canadiana.ca/view/omcn.MississaugaTimes_18/517.

Seiter, Alessandra. "Libraries, Power, and Justice: Toward a Sociohistorically Informed Intellectual Freedom." *Progressive Librarian* 47, (2019–2020): 107–17. http://www.progressivelibrariansguild.org/PL/PL47/107seiter.pdf.

Selley, Chris. "Attack on Public Libraries for Letting Meghan Murphy Speak Is a Nauseating Spectacle." *National Post*, October 30, 2019. ProQuest.

Selley, Chris. "Libraries Are No Enemy of Pride, but They Are the Original Free Speech 'Safe Spaces'." *National Post*, July 25, 2019. https://nationalpost.com/opinion/chris-selley-libraries-are-no-enemy-of-pride-but-they-are-the-original-free-speech-safe-spaces.

Selley, Chris. "Toronto's Public Libraries Make an Imperfect but Brave Stand for Free Speech." *National Post*, December 15, 2017. https://nationalpost.com/opinion/chris-selley-torontos-public-libraries-make-an-imperfect-but-brave-stand-for-free-speech.

Selman, Brianne and Joe Curnow. "Winnipeg's Millennium Library Needs Solidarity, Not Security." *Partnership: The Canadian Journal of Library and Information Practice and Research* 14, no. 2 (2019): 1–9. ProQuest.

Seucharan, Cherise. "Trans Advocates Criticize Vancouver Public Library for Welcoming Controversial Speaker." *Toronto Star*, November 28, 2018. https://www.thestar.com/vancouver/2018/11/28/trans-advocates-criticize-vancouver-public-library-for-welcoming-controversial-speaker.html.

Shakeri, Sima. "Christian Website Accuses Toronto Drag Queen Storytime Of Trying To 'Indoctrinate Kids.'" *Huffington Post Canada*, July 21, 2018. https://www.huffpost.com/archive/ca/entry/drag-queen-storytime-at-toronto-public-library-tries-to-indoctrinate-kids-lifesitenews_ca_5cd55bb1e4b07b-c729775a95.

Shockey, Kyle. "Intellectual Freedom Is Not Social Justice: The Symbolic Capital of Intellectual Freedom in ALA Accreditation and LIS Curricula." *Progressive Librarian* no. 44 (2016): 101–10.

Shore, Randy. "Right-to-Die Group Fails to Convince Vancouver Library Board to Rent Space; Seminar to Discuss Suicide may Contravene Canadian Laws, Legal Advisers Tell VPL." *Vancouver Sun,* October 21, 2009. ProQuest.

"Should Not Condemn Without Prior Knowledge." *The London Free Press*, August 11, 1960.

Simons, Paula. "If Takei is Allowed to Speak, He should have to Say Something." *Edmonton Journal,* November 16, 2017. ProQuest.

Simpson, Stacy H. "Why Have a Comprehensive & Representative Collection?: GLBT Material Selection and Service in the Public Library." *Progressive Librarian*, no. 27 (2006): 44–51. https://doi.org/http://www.progressivelibrariansguild.org/PL_Jnl/contents27.shtml.

Singer, Zev. "Anti-Mosque Talk Causes No Fuss; British Lawyer Gavin Boby Draws Small Crowd." *Ottawa Citizen*, February 5, 2013. ProQuest.

Smith, Hazel. Letter to the editor. *The London Free Press*. August 12, 1960.

Smith, S. J. Letter to the editor. *The London Free Press*. August 11, 1960.

Snowdon, Wallis. "Amid Ancestry Controversy, Edmonton Library Defends Joseph Boyden Event." *CBC*, January 20, 2017. https://www.cbc.ca/news/canada/edmonton/amid-ancestry-controversy-edmonton-library-defends-joseph-boyden-event-1.3944855.

Sokoloff, Heather. "Board Upholds Teacher's Firing for Racist Views: Peel Educator 'Consorted with Known Racists'." *National Post*, March 13, 2002. ProQuest.

Soloway, David. "Confronting the Borg." SAFS Newsletter. April, 2018. https://www.safs.ca/newsletters/issues/nl79.pdf.

Spade, Dean. *Normal Life: Administrative Violence, Critical Trans Politics, and the Limits of Law*. Brooklyn, NY: South End Press, 2015.

Sparanese, Ann. "Activist Librarianship: Heritage or Heresy?" In *Questioning Library Neutrality Essays from Progressive Librarian*, edited by Alison M. Lewis, 67–82. Duluth, MN: Library Juice Press, 2008.

Star Editorial Board. "Toronto City Council Falls Short on Free Speech." *Toronto Star*, October 31, 2019. https://www.thestar.com/opinion/editorials/2019/10/31/toronto-city-council-falls-short-on-free-speech.html.

"Statement from City Librarian on Room Rental Event." Toronto Public Library. October 12, 2019. https://torontopubliclibrary.typepad.com/news_releases/2019/10/statement-from-city-librarian-on-room-rental-event.html.

"Statement from City Librarian Vickery Bowles on Last Evening's Event at Richview Library." Cision Canada. July 13, 2017. https://www.newswire.ca/news-releases/statement-from-city-librarian-vickery-bowles-on-last-evenings-event-at-richview-library-634362023.html.

"Statement from VPL's Chief Librarian Regarding March 21 GIDYVR Event." Vancouver Public Library. January 27, 2020. https://www.vpl.ca/statement-on-gidyvr-event.

"Statement on Intellectual Freedom and Libraries." Canadian Federation of Library Associations. April 12, 2019. https://cfla-fcab.ca/en/guidelines-and-position-papers/statement-on-intellectual-freedom-and-libraries/.

"Statement Regarding Dr. Janice Raymond Speak at the Montreal Massacre Memorial." Vancouver Rape Relief & Women's Shelter. November 22, 2013. https://rapereliefshelter.bc.ca/statement-regarding-dr-janice-raymond-speak-at-the-montreal-massacre-memorial/.

"Statement Regarding Library Safe Use." Saskatchewan Public Library. January 27, 2017. https://web.archive.org/web/20190606070923/https://saskatoon-library.ca/sites/default/files/Statement%20on%20Library%20Safe%20Use%20January%2027.pdf.

Statistics Canada. "The Daily — Police-reported hate crime, 2021." March 22, 2023, https://www150.statcan.gc.ca/n1/daily-quotidien/230322/dq230322a-eng.htm?utm_source=The+519%27s+Email+List&utm_campaign=0e29974485-EMAIL_CAMPAIGN_2019_01_31_03_25_COPY_01&utm_medium=email&utm_term=0_a22f669ecd-0e29974485-407384113&mc_cid=0e29974485&mc_eid=dd15bca702&fbclid=PAAaYEfL5yNz51x2kBYkN-J0WLvNOLyo8ZAGup-qDq7cf98WlglfdQgi-V-Pow.

Stefanko, Alix-Rae. Letter to Christina De Castell. "RE: Feminist Current Event at VPL." Canadian Federation of Library Associations. January 15, 2019. http://cfla-fcab.ca/wp-content/uploads/2019/01/VPL-Letter-of-Support-190115.pdf.

Stonebanks, Roger. "Racism Foes Out in Force Tonight." *Times Colonist,* June 19, 1998. ProQuest.

Strand, Karla J. "Disrupting Whiteness in Libraries and Librarianship: A Reading List." The Office of the Gender and Women's Studies Librarian. 2019. https://www.library.wisc.edu/gwslibrarian/bibliographies/disrupting-whiteness-in-libraries/.

Sundaram, Chantal. "Ottawa Shuts Down Far-Right 'ACT! for Canada.'" Socialist. November 26, 2017. http://www.socialist.ca/node/3489.

Takeuchi, Craig. "LGBT Activists and Organizations Concerned About Vancouver Public Library Event Featuring Controversial Speaker." The Georgia Straight. November 29, 2018. https://www.straight.com/life/1171981/lgbt-activists-and-organizations-concerned-about-vancouver-public-library-event.

Taylor, Greg. "Statement from CUPE Local 391." CUPE BC. February 19, 2020. https://www.cupe.bc.ca/statement_from_cupe_local_391.

"Terms and Conditions." Ottawa Public Library, n.d. https://biblioottawalibrary.ca/en/terms-and-conditions-0.

The 519, "Army of Lovers," accessed May 2, 2023, https://www.the519.org/armyoflovers/?fbclid=PAAaaX0hZhZ31XmUV05K_z8mBOwqffKbJCYFZ0-2nsMMn-RMm8oDZKHFlMq7L0.

The Partnership, "In Defence of Drag Storytime: A Statement of Support from Canada's Library Associations," June 27, 2023, https://librarianship.ca/news/in-defence-of-drag-storytime/.

The Minutes of the Regular Meeting of the Belleville Public Library Board. October 16, 2012. Belleville, ON. https://www.bellevillelibrary.ca/photos/custom/Lib%20Documents/Minutes%20Regular%20Committee%2016%20Oct%202012.pdf.

"The Pro-Death Lobby." *Ottawa Citizen,* September 23, 2009. ProQuest.

Thomas, Deborah A. "Intellectual Freedom and Inclusivity: Opposites or Partners?" *Journal of Intellectual Freedom and Privacy* 4, no. 3 (2019). https://doi.org/https://doi.org/10.5860/jifp.v4i3.7129.

"Times Telescope," *Mississauga Times*, April 26, 1978, Image 789, https://pub.canadiana.ca/view/omcn.MississaugaTimes_18/789.

Todd, Douglass. "Use of Library for Collins' Rally Sparks Outcry." *Vancouver Sun*, May 10, 1997, B1. ProQuest.

"Toronto Library Defends Allowing Controversial Memorial Service to Go Ahead." *CBC*, July 13, 2017. https://www.cbc.ca/news/canada/toronto/toronto-library-controversial-memorial-1.4202658.

"Toronto Library Staff Can Now Refuse Event Bookings 'Likely' to Promote Hate." *CBC*, December 11, 2017. https://www.cbc.ca/news/canada/toronto/toronto-library-board-hate-room-booking-1.4443914.

Toronto Comic Arts Festival (@TorontoComics). "While we also support the ideals of free speech." Twitter, October 16, 2019, 3:42 p.m. https://twitter.com/TorontoComics/status/1184555231503364097.

Toronto Public Library Board Meeting. Toronto, ON: Toronto Public Library, October 22, 2019. https://www.torontopubliclibrary.ca/content/about-the-library/pdfs/board/meetings/2019/oct22/09-communications-combined.pdf.

Toronto Public Library. *2SLGBTQ+ Advisory Committee Report-Back: Toronto Public Library Update*. Toronto, ON: Toronto Public Library, May 19, 2022. https://www.toronto.ca/legdocs/mmis/2022/qs/bgrd/backgroundfile-225831.pdf.

Toronto Public Library. *Community Space Rental at Palmerston*. Toronto, ON: Toronto Public Library, 2019. https://www.torontopubliclibrary.ca/content/about-the-library/pdfs/board/meetings/2019/oct22/10a-community-space-rental-at.Palmerston.pdf.

Toronto Public Library. *Toronto Public Library Board Meeting No. 10*. Toronto, ON: Toronto Public Library, 2017. https://www.torontopubliclibrary.ca/content/about-the-library/pdfs/board/meetings/2017/dec11/B20171211-full-agenda-revised.pdf.

Toronto Public Library. *Toronto Public Library Board Meeting*. Toronto, ON: Toronto Public Library, 2017. https://www.torontopubliclibrary.ca/content/about-the-library/pdfs/board/meetings/2017/sep25/09-communications-combined.pdf.

Tory, John (@JohnTory). "My statement on tonight's meeting at the Richview Library." Twitter, July 12, 2017, 5:28 p.m. https://twitter.com/JohnTory/status/885249533302759424.

Turcato, Megan. "Okanagan library board won't intervene in Kelowna's Drag Queen Story Time." *Global News*, November 20, 2019. https://globalnews.ca/news/6195547/okanagan-library-board-drag-queen-story-time/.

"Trans Advocates Rally Against Controversial Feminist Speaker Meghan Murphy." *CTV News*, January 11, 2019. https://bc.ctvnews.ca/trans-advocates-rally-against-controversial-feminist-speaker-meghan-murphy-1.4249890.

Vancouver Public Library (@VPL). "Statement regarding Feminist Current Event." Twitter, November 28, 2018, 5:58 p.m. https://twitter.com/VPL/status/1067915660401885185.

"Vancouver Public Library Banned from Pride Parade After Allowing Controversial Speaker." *The News*, July 23, 2019. ProQuest.

"Vancouver Public Library's 'Freedom to Read' Week Controversy; February 25, 2008: 7.30 P.m." CUPE 391. February 25, 2008. https://cupe391.ca/2008/02/25/vancouver-public-librarys-freedom-to-read-week-controversy-february-25-2008-7-30-p-m/.

"Vickery Bowles Wins Ola's Les Fowlie Intellectual Freedom Award." Freedom to Read. February 3, 2018. https://www.freedomtoread.ca/2018/02/vickery-bowles-wins-olas-les-fowlie-intellectual-freedom-award/.

"Victoria Bans Hate." *Star Phoenix*, November 16, 1996. ProQuest.

Vonn, Micheal. "The Toronto Public Library's New Community Room Booking Policy." British Columbia Library Association. March 5, 2018. https://bclaconnect.ca/perspectives/2018/03/05/the-toronto-public-librarys-new-community-room-booking-policy/.

Vosdingh, William. Letter to the editor. *The London Free Press*, August 13, 1960.

VPL Board Regular Meeting Minutes. April 24, 2019, Vancouver, BC. https://www.vpl.ca/sites/vpl/public/BrdMinutes2019-04-24.pdf.

"VPL Joins VPD's Safe Place Program Supporting LGBTQ Community." Vancouver Public Library. February 24, 2017. https://www.vpl.ca/library/news/2017/vpl-joins-vpd%E2%80%99s-safe-place-program-supporting-lgbtq-community.

"VPS Statement on VPLS Entry in the 2019 Pride Parade." Vancouver Pride. May 26, 2020. https://vancouverpride.ca/news/vps-statement-on-vpls-entry-in-the-2019-pride-parade/.

"VPL Statement Regarding Speaker Janice Raymond at Vancouver Rape Relief Event at the Central Library." Vancouver Public Library. November 22, 2013. https://web.archive.org/web/20170421094531/https://www.vpl.ca/news/details/vpl_statement_regarding_speaker_janice_raymond_at_vancouver_rape_relief_eve.

Walker, Julian. "Hate Speech and Freedom of Expression: Legal Boundaries in Canada." Parliament of Canada. June 29, 2018. https://lop.parl.ca/sites/PublicWebsite/default/en_CA/ResearchPublications/201825E.

"Weld V. Ottawa Public Library." Justice Centre for Constitutional Freedoms. October 10, 2019. https://www.jccf.ca/court_cases/weld-v-ottawa-public-library/.

Weichel, Andrew. "Meghan Murphy Threatens Legal Action If Vancouver Library Rejects March Event." *CTV News*, January 28, 2020. https://bc.ctvnews.ca/meghan-murphy-threatens-legal-action-if-vancouver-library-rejects-march-event-1.4759505.

Westad, Kim. "Free Speech Group Sues Sihota." *Times Colonist*, August 7, 1998. ProQuest

Western States Center. *Confronting White Nationalism in Libraries: A Toolkit*. Portland, OR, 2022, 1–35.

Whatcott, Bill. "Misinformation Claim Disputed." *Leader Post*, June 16, 2000. ProQuest.

Whatcott, Bill. "Statements Challenged." *Leader Post*, May 17, 2000. ProQuest.

"What Is C-Far?" CFAR. n.d. https://wayback.archive-it.org/227/20100803161133/http://www.populist.org/what_is_cfar.html. This information was sourced from the Wayback Archive and captured on 16:11:33 Aug 03, 2010.

"What's that doing in my library? Intellectual Freedom Stories and Advice." In 2009 *BCLA Conference Session Summary*. Burnaby: BCLA, 2009. https://core.ac.uk/reader/290480280.

"What We Do and Who We Serve." Vancouver Rape Relief & Women's Shelter. n.d. https://rapereliefshelter.bc.ca/who-we-serve-and-what-we-do/.

Whitney, Paul. Letter to the editor. *Vancouver Sun*, February 13, 2008. ProQuest.

Wiegand, Wayne, and Shirley Wiegand. *The Desegregation of Public Libraries in The Jim Crow South: Civil Rights and Local Activism*. Baton Rouge: Louisiana State University Press, 2018.

Willcocks, Paul. "Their Views are Vile, but Rent them a Room the Victoria Library has Taken a Commendable Stand for Free Speech." *The Globe and Mail*, July 13, 1998. ProQuest.

Wirth, Christopher and Sakshi Chadha. "Court Rules That Termination of Rental Agreement by Public Library Is Not Subject to Judicial Review." The Canadian Bar Association. November 29, 2019. https://www.cba.org/Sections/Administrative-Law/Articles/2019/Court-rules.

Wong-Tam, Kristyn. "Protect 2SLGBTQI+ Communities & Drag Artists." Accessed April 5, 2023, https://www.kristynwongtam.ca/protect-drag.

Yousefi, Baharak. "On the Disparity Between What We Say and What We Do in Libraries." In *Feminists Among Us: Resistance and Advocacy in Library Leadership*, edited by Baharak Yousefi and Shirley Lew, 91–105. Sacramento, CA: Library Juice Press, 2017.

Zwibel, Cara, and Joan Moriarity. "Should Meghan Murphy Have Been Allowed to Speak at the Toronto Public Library?" *Toronto Star*, November 5, 2019. ProQuest.

Index

2SLGBTQIA+. *See* Two-Spirit, Lesbian, Gay, Bisexual, Transgender, Queer and/or Questioning, Intersex, Asexual+

Abrams, Harry, 17-18, 21-23
academic librarians. *See* librarians, academic
academic libraries. *See* libraries, academic
accessibility, 4
ACT! For Canada, 47-49, 69, 71, 74, 114
Acton, Laura, 20
Ainslie, Paul, 98
ALA. *See* American Library Association
American Library Association, 117, 119-121
Anderson, Sandra, 17, 20, 22, 24, 28
Andrew, Jill, 93
Another Story Bookshop, 107
anti-abortion, 57-59
anti-racism, 4, 27, 32
antisemitism, 14, 15, 20, 22, 27, 37, 39
Appleby, Timothy, 44-46
Australian League of Rights, 14

B'nai Brith Canada, 15, 17, 21-23
BC Civil Liberties Association. *See* British Columbia Civil Liberties Association
BC Government and Service Employees Union. *See* British Columbia Government and Services Employees Union
BC Human Rights Commission. *See* British Columbia Human Rights Commission
BC Human Rights Tribunal. *See* British Columbia Human Rights Tribunal
BC WCC. *See* British Columbia Western Canada Concept Party
BCCLA. *See* British Columbia Civil Liberties Association
BCLA. *See* British Columbia Library Association
Beatty, John, 13-14
Bedassie, Elijah, 73-74
Belaire, Alexandra, 71
Belleville Public Library, 44-49, 58
Benaway, Gwen, 97, 102, 107
Birtwistle, David, 50

Bivens-Tatum, Wayne, 118
Blair, Elgin, 10
Boby, Gavin, 47, 69, 70
Bodis, John, 11, 13
Body Politic, 13
Bowles, Vickery, 65-66, 68-69, 89-91, 95, 101, 103, 104, 108
Boyce, Egerton, 45
Boyden, Joseph, 60-62
British Columbia Civil Liberties Association, 22, 34, 42, 43, 56-57, 69
British Columbia Government and Services Employees Union, 25
British Columbia Human Rights Code, 54, 55
British Columbia Human Rights Commission, 28
British Columbia Human Rights Tribunal, 30, 31, 53
British Columbia Library Association, 21-22, 69, 77, 82, 88-89
British Columbia Western Canada Concept Party, 15-16
Brook, Paula, 33
Butler, Erica, 14
Butler, Judith, 133
Butt, Terry, 11

CAERS. *See* Canadian Anti-Racism Education and Research Society
CAIR-CAN. *See* Canadian Council on American-Islamic Relations
Calgary Herald, 43
Calvin, Phyllis, 14-15
Campbell, John, 64
Campaign Life Coalition of Saskatchewan, 57, 59
Canada-Israel Committee, 39
Canadian Anti-Racism Education and Research Society, 17, 21, 31
Canadian Charter of Rights and Freedoms, 17, 20, 55, 58, 65, 109, 110
Canadian Citizens for Charter Rights and Freedoms, 71
Canadian Civil Liberties Association, 15, 92, 96

Canadian Council on American-Islamic Relations, 47-49
Canadian Criminal Code, 67, 70, 73, 80, 109
Canadian Federation of Library Associations, 77, 96, 127
Canadian Film Institute, 8
Canadian Free Speech League, 15-17, 19-20, 22, 24-27, 30-34, 39, 43
Canadian Jewish Congress, 14, 32, 39, 64
Canadian League of Rights, 14
Canadian Library Association, 12, 17
Canadian Parents of Trans, Two-Spirit & Gender Diverse Kids, 94
Canadian Rights and Civil Liberties Federation, 15
Canadian Union of Public Employees, 23-24, 26, 40, 64-65, 77, 93, 103, 112
Canadian Urban Libraries Council, 96
Canadians for Vaccine Choice, 109
Capital Region Race Relations Association, 17, 21, 25
Carroll, Sidney, 16
CATA. *See* Coalition Against Trans Antagonism
Caudle, Katrina, 56
Caulfield, Timothy, 110
CCLA. *See* Canadian Civil Liberties Association
censorship, 7-11, 13, 17, 23, 31
Centre for Free Expression, 68, 96
Centre for Israel and Jewish Affairs, 67, 68
CFLA. *See* Canadian Federation of Library Associations
CFSL. *See* Canadian Free Speech League
Chalermkraivuth, Chalay, 137
Choy, Carolina, 25
Christian Truth Activists, 36
Christie, Doug, 15-16, 19-20, 21, 28
Citizens for Foreign Aid Reform, 14-15
CJC. *See* Canadian Jewish Congress
CLA. *See* Canadian Library Association
Coalition Against Trans Antagonism, 78-80
Collins, Doug, 16, 23, 27, 30-33, 39
communism, 7-8
Cook, Tyson, 86
Cooley, Carol, 58-59
Cossman, Brenda, 102
Council of Women, 7-8
COVID-19 pandemic, 3, 112, 140
Cressy, Joe, 105
Criminal Code of Canada, 23, 28, 30, 34, 41, 47, 55, 121

Crisp, Quentin, 9
critical librarianship. *See* librarianship, critical
critical race theory, 2, 121-124, 126, 133-134
Cross, Bob, 19-20
Crouch, Richard E., 8
CRRRA. *See* Capital Region Race Relations Association
CRT. *See* critical race theory
Cryderman, Deb, 109-110
Cullen, Alex, 15
cultural appropriation, 60
CUPE. *See* Canadian Union of Public Employees

Dahl, Karen, 84-85
Dandelion Books, 37
De Castell, Christina, 76, 111
Democracy Street, 33
Désormeaux, Monique, 74
diversity, 4
Donato, Al, 99
Douglas, Janice, 37
Drag Queen Storytime, 86-89
Draude, June, 34-35
Dutton, Alan, 21

East Enders Against Racism, 68
Eby, David, 42, 44
École Polytechnique Massacre of 1989, 53
Edeie, Ann, 10
Edmonton Community Foundation, 62
Edmonton Journal, 62
Edmonton Public Library, 60-63, 105
El Feministo, 54-55
Elliott, Alicia, 91
Epperson, Steven, 43
Ethier, Val, 27
Ettarh, Fobazi, 124-125, 130
Exit International, 41-44
Extraordinary, 51

Farber, Bernie, 14, 64, 66-67
Felton, Greg, 36-41
Feminist Current, 75, 111
feminist ethic of care, 4, 137-138
feminist theory, 2, 133
Feser, Ken, 109
Fiamengo, Janice, 47, 73-74
Films for Thinkers, 9, 12
Findlay, Ian, 50
Fletcher, Victor, 68

Forrester, Monica, 107
Forward Thinking Speaker Series, 60, 62
Fowler, Bill, 25
Frappier, Gilles, 14
Fraser, Nancy, 118
Free Thinking Film Society, 48-49
freedom of expression, 6, 18, 20, 27, 30, 50, 125-127, 132, 134-135
Freedom to Read Week, 36-41
French, Max, 65
Friedland, Bob, 19, 28
Fromm, Paul, 15-16, 21, 23, 63-65, 67-68

Gallant, Chanelle, 107
GAP. *See* Guelph Anti-Pipeline Action Group
Gardee, Ishan, 47-48
Gardner, Jack, 19-20
Gaucher, Monica, 88
Gay Equality Mississauga, 9-12
gay oppression, 9
GEM. *See* Gay Equality Mississauga
gender identity, 1
Gender Identity YVR, 111
Georgia Strait, 78
Gilmour, David, 51-53
Glad Day Bookshop, 98-99
Glavin, Terry, 37-38, 41
Global News, 101-102
Globe and Mail, 44, 66, 92
Goldman, Nisson, 32
Goldschmid, Robert, 24-25
Good, Joseph, 125
Gore, Tom, 18
Gostick, Ron, 14
Grand Prairie Public Library, 109-110
Greater Victoria Public Libraries, 15-30
Green Party of Canada, 28
Guelph Anti-Pipeline Action Group, 49-51
Guelph Mercury, 49-51
Guelph Public Library, 49-51, 112-113
Gullikson, Sheldon, 130-131
GVPL. *See* Greater Victoria Public Libraries

Haley, Brendan, 93-94
Halifax Examiner, 83, 85
Halifax Public Library, 82-85
Harrison, Sybil, 22-23
Hashim, Mohammed, 67
hate speech, 3, 15-16, 23, 30, 49, 121
Haycock, Ken, 12
Heppner, Ben, 35
Hernandez, Catherine, 91

Higgins, Shana, 138-139
Holocaust deniers, 14, 15, 20
Holyday, Stephen, 104-105
homophobia, 10, 11
Hooper, Fred, 11
HPL. *See* Halifax Public Library
Hughes, Bob, 36
Human Rights Code of Canada, 28, 65, 81
Human Rights Commission, 28-29
Human Rights Council, 16
Hurt, John, 9

intellectual freedom, 1, 6, 9-10, 15-17, 20, 22, 25, 33, 125-127, 132
Intelligencer, 45-46
International Socialists, 27, 33
Iron Curtain Lands, 7-8
Irving, David, 15
Isitt, Ben, 27-28
Islamophobia, 47-49
Itkonen, Saara, 106-107
Iverson, Sandy, 125-126

JCCF. *See* Justice Centre for Constitutional Freedoms
Jewish Federation of Victoria and Vancouver Island, 23-25, 29, 39
Johnston, J. Allan, 7-8
Joseph, Kris, 103, 129-131
Joyce, Steven, 118
Jule, Arlene, 35
Justice Centre for Constitutional Freedoms, 71-72

Kaba, Mariame, 139
Kamloops Daily News, 43
Kay, Barbara, 93
Kay, Jonathan, 92-93
Kelowna Pride Society, 87-88
Kemble, Whitney, 1-2
Kent, Dean, 8
Kerner, Hilla, 56
Khan, Fareed, 70
Khasnabish, Alex, 82-85
Killing Europe, 69
Klatt, Bernard, 23
Kulaszka, Barbara, 63-64
Kushner, Howard, 29-30

Layton, Michael, 98, 104
Leavers, Frank, 9-10
Leipciger, Nathan, 64

Lemire, Marc, 64
Les Fowlie Intellectual Freedom Award, 69
Leung, Carianne, 91
Lew, Shirley, 77
librarians, academic, 2, 82, 97, 103
librarianship, critical, 4, 125
libraries, academic, 2, 5
libraries, public
   concerns about political interference in library policy, 9, 50, 113, 141
   false narrative as neutral spaces, 117-141
   neutrality of, 1, 2, 4-5, 6, 10, 27, 29, 33, 50
   protection of intellectual freedom, 1, 113
   third-party room bookings at, 1-2, 6, 23, 29, 32
Link Magazine, 10
Litwin, Fred, 48
Lloyd, Andy, 45
Lloyd, Jessica, 45
Lokritz, Naomi, 43
London Board of Education, 7-8
London Free Press, 7, 9
London Public Library, 7-9
LPL. *See* London Public Library
Lunt, Jane, 19

Machum, Ashley, 86, 89
Mansur, Salim, 48-49
Martinez, Pillar, 105-106
Mathan, Carisisma, 102
Mathis, Heather, 44
McAleer, Tony, 16
McCallion, Hazel, 10, 11-12
McDonald, Danielle, 48, 72
McInnis, Cathy, 50
McKay, Ken, 22
McKechnie, Frank, 11
McKenney, Catherine, 70
McKenney, Sean, 71
Medicine Hat Public Library, 109-110
Member of the Legislative Assembly, 25, 34, 35
Miller, Genevieve, 11-12
Mississauga Public Library, 9-13
Mississauga Times, 10, 12-13
MLA. *See* Member of the Legislative Assembly
Mosaic Institute, 64
Moses, Richard, 13-14
Moses, Tony, 16
Mounce, Jack, 31
MPL. *See* Mississauga Public Library

Murariu, Madi, 67
Murphy, Meghan, 1, 75, 77-79, 89-93, 95, 97, 99-100, 102, 108, 111-112, 124-125
Mussatto, Darrell, 32

Naked Civil Servant, 9, 13-14
National Post, 68, 92-93
Neigel, Christina, 119
Nettleton, Don, 87, 89
New Kind of Monster, 44
Nitschke, Philip, 41-42, 44
Norman, Ken, 59
North Shore News, 27
North Vancouver Public Library, 31-32
Nuamah, Olivia, 97

O'Reilly, Maureen, 64-65
Oakville Public Library, 13-14
Off, Carol, 95
Oger, Morgane, 57, 75, 79
Okanagan Regional Library, 86-89
Ontario Court of Justice, 72
Ontario Human Rights Code, 47, 67, 70, 73
Ontario Library Association, 69
OPL. *See* Ottawa Public Library
ORL. *See* Okanagan Regional Library
Ottawa Against Fascism, 71, 73
Ottawa Citizen, 15, 42-43, 47-49, 73
Ottawa Congress Center, 15
Ottawa Labour Council, 70, 71
Ottawa Public Library, 13-15, 47-49, 69-74

Paquette, Aaron, 61
Pasternak, James, 64
Peel Board of Education, 21
Perks, Gord, 97-98
Peters, Michael, 17-18
political violence, 83
Popowich, Sam, 123, 127, 130, 135-136
populists, 14
pornography, 34-36
prejudice, 10, 11
Pride Alliance, 107
Pride Parade, 79
Pride Toronto, 94-95, 97-98
Pross, Trevor, 45-46
public libraries. *See* libraries, public
public protests. *See also* entries for individual libraries
   Belleville Public Library, Belleville, Ontario (2012), 44-49

Edmonton Public Library, Edmonton, Alberta (2017), 60-63
Grand Prairie Public Library, Grand Prairie, Alberta (2020), 109-110
Greater Victoria Public Library, Broughton Street Branch, Victoria, British Columbia, (1996), 16-21
Greater Victoria Public Library, Colwood, British Columbia (1998), 22-26
Greater Victoria Public Library, Juan de Fuca Branch, Colwood, British Columbia (1999), 27-29
Greater Victoria Public Library, Nellie McClung Branch, Saanich, British Columbia (1999), 26-27
Guelph Public Library, Guelph, Ontario (2013), 49-51, 112-113
Halifax Public Library, Central Branch, Halifax, Nova Scotia (2019), 82-85
London Public Library, London, Ontario, (1960), 7-9
Medicine Hat Public Library, Medicine Hat, Alberta (2020), 109-110
Mississauga Public Library, Central Branch, Mississauga, Ontario (1978), 9-13
North Vancouver Public Library, North Vancouver, British Columbia (1999), 31-32
Oakville Public Library, Oakville, Ontario (1978), 13-14
Okanagan Regional Library, Kelowna, British Columbia (2019), 86-89
Ottawa Public Library, Main Branch, Ottawa, Ontario (2017), 69-73
Ottawa Public Library, Ottawa, Ontario (1990), 14-15
Ottawa Public Library, Ottawa, Ontario (2013), 47-49
Ottawa Public Library, Ottawa, Ontario (2018) 73-74
Regina Public Library, Regina, Saskatchewan (2000), 34-36
Saskatoon Public Library, Alice Turner Branch, Saskatoon, Saskatchewan (2017), 57-60
Toronto Public Library, Palmerston Branch, Toronto, Ontario (2019), 1, 89-108
Toronto Public Library, Richview Branch, Toronto, Ontario (2017), 63-69
Vancouver Public Library, Vancouver, British Columbia (1999), 32-34
Vancouver Public Library, Vancouver, British Columbia (2008), 36-41
Vancouver Public Library, Vancouver, British Columbia (2009), 41-44
Vancouver Public Library, Vancouver, British Columbia (2013), 53-57
Vancouver Public Library, Vancouver, British Columbia (2019), 75-82
Vancouver Public Library, Vancouver, British Columbia (2020), 111-112
Waterloo Public Library, Vancouver, British Columbia (2013), 51-53
West Vancouver Memorial Public Library, West Vancouver, British Columbia (1997), 30-31
Public Utilities Commission, 7

Qmunity, 75-76, 78
Queer City Cinema, 34-36
queer theory, 2, 133-136

racial profiling, 83
racism, 15-16, 51
Radical Feminists Unite, 89-108
Radical Imagination Film and Discussion Series, 82-85
Ravick, Joseph, 21
Raymond, Janice, 53-56
RCMP. *See* Royal Canadian Mounted Police
Regina Public Library, 34-36
resistance strategy, 134-135
Robertson, Kaleb, 99
Robertson, Tara, 56
Robeson, Paul, 7
Robinson, Joan, 110
Rosenweig, Mark, 117-118
Royal Canadian Mounted Police, 24, 27-28, 32
Ryan, Noel, 12
Ryder, Bruce, 69

Sa'd, Caryma, 48
Safe Place program, 76
Saskatchewan Coalition Against Racism, 36
Saskatchewan Party, 35
Saskatoon Public Library, 57-60
Scheyk, Jill, 106
Schmidt, Jane, 97, 136
Schrader, Alvin M., 25, 126-129
Scott, Jim, 16-17
Scott, Sarah Hasehmi, 129
Seaman, Catherine, 72
Serby, Clay, 35
sexism, 151
Sihota, Moe, 25-26

Simpson, Jaye, 75
Singh, Sandra, 55
Smith, Eric, 33
social justice, 2, 4, 6, 115, 126, 128-129, 136, 138
Solidarity Ottawa, 71
Soloway, David, 74
Spade, Dan, 133-135
Sparanese, Ann, 125
Spence, Mary, 11
SPL. *See* Saskatoon Public Library
St. Thomas Times-Journal, 7
Starlight, Tami, 78
Statistics Canada, 119, 140
Status of Women Action Group, 28
Stefanko, Alix-Rae, 77
Stepanic, Matthew, 106
Stephenson, Chris, 86, 89
Stern, Leonard, 42-43
Stevens, Paul, 51
Stratis, Niko, 101-102
Students for Free Speech, 73
Sumner, Wayne, 42

Takei, George, 62-63
Tannis, Ernie, 48
Taylor, Larry, 10
TCAF. *See* Toronto Comic Arts Festival
The Province, 80
Thom, Kai Cheng, 107
Thomas, Deborah A., 81-82
Tierney, Tim, 70
Times Columnist, 16, 18, 24, 26
Toronto and York Regional Labour Council, 67
Toronto Comic Arts Festival, 94
Toronto Public Library, 1, 44, 63-69, 89-108
Toronto Star, 75, 96, 100, 102, 104
Toronto Street News, 68
Toronto Sun, 66, 92
Tory, John, 64, 66, 93
Tough, Don, 10-12, 93
TPL. *See* Toronto Public Library
trans politics, 133, 135
trans theory, 2, 135
transphobia, 82, 91, 95, 97, 100, 104
Trost, Brad, 57-60
Trotz, Alisa, 102
Turk, James L., 68
Two-Spirit, Lesbian, Gay, Bisexual, Transgender, Queer and/or Questioning, Intersex, Asexual+, 1, 87, 97, 104, 108-109, 126, 130-131, 141

University of Victoria Students Society, 27
Urban Libraries Council, 68, 96

Vancouver Association of Chinese Canadians, 32
Vancouver Courier, 36, 38
Vancouver Pride Society, 79
Vancouver Province, 43
Vancouver Public Library, 32-34, 36-44, 53-57, 75-82, 111-112
Vancouver Rape Relief and Women's Shelter, 53-57
Vancouver Sun, 31-32, 33, 37, 39, 43, 80
Victoria Civil Liberties Society, 18
Victoria Labour Council, 25, 28
Victoria's Committee of the Whole, 19
Vonn, Micheal, 69
VPL. *See* Vancouver Public Library
VPS. *See* Vancouver Pride Society
VRR. *See* Vancouver Rape Relief and Women's Shelter

Warman, Richard, 64, 70
Waterloo Public Library, 51-53
WCC. *See* Western Canada Concept party
Weld, Madeline, 71-72
West Vancouver Memorial Public Library, 30-31
Western Canada Concept party, 27-28
Western States Center, 132
Westwood, John, 22
Wexelbaum, Rachel, 129
Whatcott, Bill, 36
Whitney, Paul, 25, 37-38, 39, 41
Williams, Neil, 22, 24
Williams, Russell, 44-45
Winter Cities Shake-Up Conference, 60
Wong-Tam, Kristyn, 98, 104
Wooldridge, Lloyd, 89
Words Worth Books, 51, 52
workplace safety, 4, 128-129
Worsley, David, 52

York University Faculty Association, 105
Young, Geoff, 19

Zundel, Ernst, 15, 63-64
Zwibel, Cara, 92

www.ingramcontent.com/pod-product-compliance
Lightning Source LLC
Chambersburg PA
CBHW062026290426
44108CB00025B/2801